The Boomers' Eldercare Handbook

Oh $@#!, My Parents Are Old!

(INCLUDING VALUABLE INTERNET AND OTHER RESOURCES PLUS JUST ABOUT EVERYTHING THAT YOU NEED TO KNOW ABOUT SHIFTING THE COST OF LONG TERM CARE)

Copyright © 2003 by Lillian S. Kachmar, Esq.
and John F. Steele

All rights reserved. No part of this book shall be reproduced or transmitted in any form or by any means, electronic, mechanical, magnetic, photographic including photocopying, recording or by any information storage and retrieval system, without prior written permission of the publisher. No patent liability is assumed with respect to the use of the information contained herein. Although every precaution has been taken in the preparation of this book, the publisher and author assume no responsibility for errors or omissions. Neither is any liability assumed for damages resulting from the use of the information contained herein.

This work also contains public domain information as to which neither the authors nor publisher assert any rights or assume any responsibility.

ISBN 0-7414-1398-1

Published by:

519 West Lancaster Avenue
Haverford, PA 19041-1413
Info@buybooksontheweb.com
www.buybooksontheweb.com
Toll-free (877) BUY BOOK
Local Phone (610) 520-2500
Fax (610) 519-0261

Printed in the United States of America

Printed on Recycled Paper

Published February 2003

DISCLAIMER

Nothing in this book is to be considered or construed as legal or financial advice. The contents contain general information about the various topics. Everybody is strongly advised to consult with their own attorney, accountant and financial advisor with respect to the facts of their own circumstances and their individual state law requirements.

Also, even though certain information regarding government benefits is subject to change on an annual or other basis, such as dollar amounts of benefits, we will in the narrative provide current amounts in order to explain certain underlying formula or concepts.

ACKNOWLEDGEMENT

This book has been a long time in the making, and we have buried a number of wonderful souls along the way. We started our caregiving journey over twenty years ago with Aunt Mottie and Uncle Henry to whom we wish to make special tribute. We had the privilege of meeting Esther Whitfield whose love, support and guidance helped us through our darkest days with Uncle Henry. We watched Mom, Lillian Kachmar, a super caregiver, struggle with Dad's terminal condition while balancing a gazillion other demands, and then all of the changes that followed his passing. Finally with the passing of John's Mom, Nelda Steele, and Lillian's Dad, Michael Kachmar, as well as a few dear Aunts, we knew that we had to commit our experiences and the knowledge we accumulated along the way to writing.

FORWARD

We use the term "parents" in this guide generically. You are probably reading this because someone, somewhere, at some time birthed you, and nurtured you to adulthood. Through infant dependency, childhood illnesses and adolescent angst, some "one" got you through, physically, emotionally and financially.

If they raised you right, and instilled in you some sense of decency, you will feel morally obligated to support them emotionally and, perhaps, financially through their end years. We hope that this book will be of some help as the tables turn and you become the nurturer and they the nurtured.

TABLE OF CONTENTS

DISCLAIMER i

ACKNOWLEDGEMENT iii

FORWARD v

1. **DeNile is a river in Egypt.** 1

2. **Caregivers and Caregiving:**
   The Impact of Cultural Downsizing 3

   Cultural Downsizing and Outsourcing 3
   Family Caregivers 4
   Survival Tips 5
   Siblings 7
   It's the Money! 8
   Elder Abuse and Neglect 10
   Taking Care of Caregivers 12
   Long Distance Caregiving 14
   Professional Caregivers 15
   Geriatric Care Managers 17

3. **When to intervene:**
   Activities of Daily Life 19

   What are the Indicators? – ADL's and IADL's 19
   Depression 22
   Making a Move 24
   Taking Away the Driver's License
   and Car Keys 25
   Smarter Than Strangers, or Talk to Your
   Folks About Scams and Predators 27

4. **Some Living Options for the Golden Years** 31

   Retirement Apartments 31
   Adult Day Care 32
   Home Health Care 34

Home Health Care Providers 35
Congregate Housing..36
Continuing Care Retirement Communities 37
CCRC Admission Requirements............................38
Assisted Living/Personal Care Homes 41

5. Nursing Homes 43

When is a nursing home the right decision?...........43
How do I decide which nursing
home is right? 43
Codes of Conduct or Compliance Plans.................44
Long term Care Ombudsman..................................46
What is a nursing home? 46
State Licensing and Federal Certification...............47
Surveys: Assessing Quality of Care 47
Interpreting Survey Reports 48
Nursing Home Resident Rights...............................49
Specified Resident Rights 51
Resident Abuse 53
Transfers and Discharge...56
Access to Residents 57
Malnutrition and Dehydration 57
Pressure Ulcers 58
Nursing Home Documents and Buzz Words 59

6. Who is going to pay for this?
Sources of Payment for Care...............................63

Medicare v. Medicaid: Centers for
Medicare & Medicaid Services 64
What does Medicare cover and when?
Medicare Part A Coverage and Eligibility 65
Medicare Part B Coverage and Eligibility 66
What Doesn't Medicare Cover? 67
Medicare and Long Term Care 68
Medicare At Home 69
Medicare Benefits Periods 70
Medigap Insurance 71
Basic or Plan A Medigap Coverage 71
Medigap Plans B through J:

Additional Coverage 72
Medicare v. Managed Care? 73
Long Term Care Insurance 74
Hospice Care and Medicare 79
So what do I do now? 80
Medicaid Eligibility 81

7. Financial and Medicaid Planning: What You Need To Know About Shifting the Cost of Long Term Care 83

Medicaid Planning 84
Medicaid Basics:
Excluded and Available Assets 86
So what's "exempt?" 88
What about Asset Transfers before a
Medicaid application is filed?
Look Back Dates and
Look Back Periods 90
Spousal Transfers 90
Other Exempt Transfers of a
Principal Residence 92
What is fair market value? 92
So what is "valuable consideration"? 92
So what is a period of ineligibility?
The Divestment Penalty rules. 93
Multiple Transfers 95
Unmarried Nursing Home Residents 95
Community and Institutionalized Spouses:
Even More Rules 96
Assets: The Community Spouse's
Resource Allowance 96
Income: The Community Spouse's
Minimum Monthly Needs Allowance 97
Trusts and Irrevocable Trusts 98
Annuities 101
Gifts 103
"Half a Loaf" Gifting 103
Burial Funds or Trusts 104
Estate Recovery 104

8. Essential Documents ... 107

    Powers of Attorney ... 109
    Durable Powers of Attorney ... 109
    When is a DPA Effective? ... 110
    Qualifications of Agent ... 112
    Multiple Agents ... 112
    Living Wills/ Advance Directives ... 112
    What is a Living Will? ... 113
    Things to consider ... 114
    Health Care Proxies – Do's and Don'ts ... 116
    Do Not Resuscitate ... 118
    Guardianships ... 118

9. Hospitalization ... 121

    Monitoring Medical Treatment ... 121
    ICU (Intensive Care Unit) ... 121
    Heroic Measures ... 123
    Social Services ... 124

Final: No one gets out of here alive ... 125

    Terminal Illness ... 125
    Hospice ... 126
    Letting Go and Saying Goodbye ... 129
    Funerals ... 130
    Funerals and Kids ... 130
    Preneed Funeral Contracts ... 131
    Probating a Will ... 133
    Grief ... 136

Websites ... 139

    Government Resources ... 141
    Health ... 144
    Geriatric Care Managers ... 145
    Home Health Care, Caregiving, and Housing ... 145
    Hospice Care, Death and Grief ... 147
    Insurance Rating Services ... 148
    Miscellaneous ... 148

Sources 151

Appendices 153

    A: AoA Elder Abuse Factsheet 155
    B: Form of Living Will 161
    C: Durable Power of Attorney Form 167
    D: Medicare Nursing Home Checklist 183
    E: Medicare Website Information 201
    F: Medicare Plan Choices 217
    G: AoA/NIA Resource Directory for
          Older Persons 225

Chapter One

DeNile is a river in Egypt.

It is a fact of life – we are all going to either die young or get old. You can try to ignore it, deny it and pretend otherwise, but death is an inescapable fact of life.

Somewhere along the way, your parents will grow or have grown old. You might have recently noticed their graying hair, or the slowness of their gait. There are many signs of aging, and one day or another you are going to notice "the change" in your folks.

Wake up. It's time to address the inevitable.

There are health and medical decisions to be made. Living arrangements to be determined. Financial considerations to be weighed. Documents to be drafted and signed. And, ultimately, funerals to be planned, and estates to be settled. It's not pretty, but it is unavoidable.

Chapter 2

Caregivers and Caregiving:

The Impact of Cultural Downsizing

Cultural Downsizing and Outsourcing

Throughout history, sons and daughters took care of moms and dads, wives took care of husbands, and husbands took care of wives. So, there is nothing new about the young and healthy taking care of the sick and elderly. Back then, it was just part of the routine of the family. Mom stayed at home and tended to the care taking matters, and Dad went out to work. The kids, as well as Aunts, Uncles and other members of the family were also around to help. The culture of the extended family created a safety net for all of its members.

What is new is the way we live our lives. We are mobile, often establishing households very far from our parents. Or, our parents at retirement move to sunny locations, far from us and where they raised their family. Our divorce rate has skyrocketed. Single heads of household are commonplace. Many women are employed outside of the home, not for personal fulfillment but out of economic necessity. And, our kids' lives are packed so full of activities that they have little free time themselves, and virtually none to spare to help other family members.

We have been "culturally downsized" – there are less people-hours available to do what used to be the work of many. And, what we must do, we may have to do long distance. As with corporate downsizing, what this means is that we are required to outsource many functions that previously had been done "in-house". This often times includes the care of our homes, our lawns, as well as our children and our elderly.

Do not feel guilty about this. This is out of your control and my control. We are simply victims of the culture in which we live. In order to survive, you must be prepared to adapt. And adapting many times means recognizing that there are not enough hours in the day for you do to everything that needs to be done, and outsourcing the duties you simply have no time to perform.

Outsourcing care duties does not mean that you are not a good person. Or that you are inadequate, incompetent or incapable. It does not mean that you do not care about or love your family. Certain tasks need to be done and if you do not have the time to attend to them personally, you must hire others to do them for you. Outsourcing is a solution to time demands and personnel shortages, corporately and personally.

Family Caregivers

Despite the vast number of us who are the primary caregivers for the elderly loved ones in our lives, we are still a misunderstood and under supported breed. We assist those who, due to age or medical conditions, need help in the living of their lives. The net result of what we do can leave us isolated from others whose lives do not include a caregiving function, and from other caregivers who also have no spare time to commiserate with similarly situated people.

If your folks live with you, you understand the day-to-day anxiety of dealing with their problems and issues as well as those of your kids and spouse while still trying to maintain some sense of self, and probably a job as well.

Even if your folks live hundreds of miles away, you still can be a caregiver long distance and, most certainly, still feel the deep sense of anxiety about maintaining the quality of their lives now and prospectively.

Survival Tips

- ***Prioritize and delegate.*** There are only twenty-four hours in each day; you simply cannot do everything. There is never enough time to do everything that needs to be done – you "make" the time to do the important things. Do the things that you need to do to survive – things that cannot be delegated to others. Let go of the things that are not essential to your life and the lives of those with whom you share your life. As for the rest, outsource.

- ***Accept help when offered.*** Be prepared when an offer to assist comes from other family members or friends. Too often, our response is a simple "thank you" and "I'll call if there's anything you can do." Reprogram yourself to automatically say "yes". The task does not have to directly benefit the person for whom you care. It can be something that will help you as the caregiver – such as having someone pick up some items at the grocery store or dry cleaners. However small the favor, it is one less thing that you will need to do.

- ***Remember that you are not alone.*** Nor are your circumstances unique. You are not the only person in the world who has had to provide care for another. There are books devoted exclusively to this topic, support groups and websites with chat rooms for caregivers to share experiences and obtain emotional support and useful information from those similarly situated. Reach out for help, sympathy, empathy or understanding from family, friends and members of the clergy.

- ***Remember that your days of caregiving are finite.*** The person for whom you are caring will eventually die or be institutionalized. This is a bittersweet chapter of your life and the lives of your Mom and Dad. The experience can leave you stronger, wiser and more mellow and at peace, or it can drive you to the brink of insanity and leave you bitter, angry and resentful. Only you can control how the experience will affect you – for good or for bad.

- **Recognize and understand your motivations for assuming this responsibility.** If you find no joy or personal satisfaction in what you are doing, don't do it. If you have got a bad attitude, you are probably doing a lousy job as a caretaker and your Mom or Dad would probably be better off under someone else's care. There are always alternatives and options. Find the one that is right for you and your parent.

- **Remember to take care of yourself and your needs.** Don't be a martyr. Tend to your own medical needs promptly. You will be of no use to anyone if you become ill. Eat properly and get enough rest. Dragging yourself through the day, day after day, is no way to live your life. If your parent interrupts your sleep, talk to their doctor about a sleep aid for them.

- **Remember to take time each and every day to do something special for yourself**, something that makes you happy and brings you a sense of peace. Find your spiritual side and do what is necessary to nourish it. Do not give into depression. Give yourself permission, guilt free, to soak in a hot tub, page through a catalog, watch television or a movie, or listen to your favorite music while doing mundane chores.

- **Do not feel guilty.** No one should tell you how you should feel or diminish you for what you do not do or cannot do. Don't let anyone manipulate you emotionally, including especially the individual for whom you are caring. Since you may have to make decisions that affect you and the one for whom you care, and you will have to live with the consequences of those decisions, make sure those decisions are truly your decisions and not imposed on you by another. If the decision is to move Mom or Dad to a nursing home, then do it. Do it without guilt or recriminations. Do not beat yourself up for outsourcing the care function. You are still providing care and acting as the caregiver. It is just that your duties have changed.

Admitting a parent into a nursing home is not a personal failure and do not make it one. It is simply another form of outsourcing that is a function of our culture and of the times in which we live. Still feeling guilty? Get over it!

Siblings

Caregiving can kind of creep up on you. Doing a few errands leads to more errands and chores, doctors visits, and the like and before you know it, Mom or Dad "depend" on YOU to get things done, make things happen, take care of problems. If you have any brothers and sisters, they can become the biggest source of additional grief for you as a caregiver of a parent – if you let them.

In too many cases, as long as one child is carrying the ball, the others will sit back and do nothing or as little as possible to help (other than criticize). Sometimes they may use denial as an excuse (Mom is not as bad as you make her sound). Or they may try personal assaults (you've always been so bossy so you can just do it yourself). Or they may avoid active involvement in decisions that need to be made (I'm sure you will do the right thing for Dad). They may even resist the notion of a nursing home when the caregiver becomes overwhelmed (how can you even consider warehousing Dad?).

So what do you do? You can renounce your caregiving responsibilities or you can drop your expectations of your siblings to "zero". Option number 2 is probably the most realistic. If you do not change your attitude and drop your expectations, you will drive yourself crazy with anger and frustration.

You must accept the fact that you are going to do what you feel *you* need to do and you do not have the power to make someone else be responsible or dutiful. Although you can pack someone's bags for a guilt trip, you cannot make them take the journey. And, your efforts to force someone to do something you believe they should do may actually backfire on you, leaving you even more bitter, angry and resentful.

Having said that, you should still make the effort to keep everyone in the family advised of what is going on, and include them in the decision making process, when possible, even if they try to skirt any involvement in the decisions being made. When offers to assist are made, grab them and be specific (take Mom to her doctor appointment; check out this home health care agency or adult day care center). And do not criticize another sibling's efforts to help or be involved, even if you feel the efforts are inadequate or misguided, not unless you are prepared to go it alone. Keep an open mind and remain flexible.

Sometimes, family mediation with an independent third party mediator, a member of the clergy or family counselor, may help everyone focus on problems and solutions that are equitable for all involved.

At the end of the day, we all need to live with the consequences of our actions or inactions, as the case may be. Spend less time dwelling on what your brothers or sisters can, but do not, do. We are sorry to say, but you are in a no-win situation. If it is not by your choice, then look around for alternatives that do not involve sharing the burden with others. You always have the option to outsource.

It's the Money!

There's a famous (or should be famous) expression that "when they say it's not about the money, it's the money." When money is involved, perfectly normal folks seem to go a bit crazy. Even small sums can turn people's heads around and bring out their very worst natures. So, when someone tells you that it's not about the money, you can be sure that it's the money they are talking about.

This phenomenon happens all too often in families dealing with the crisis of long term care for elder family members. Children stop thinking of themselves as children and start to view themselves as "heirs". Parents cease to be parents and instead become "estates". Things can get pretty ugly when people start counting OPM (other people's money) as their money – their rightful inheritance.

We mention this in passing only so that you the reader will not be blind sided by your own dark side or that of your brothers and sisters, or other relatives. Later we will discuss Powers of Attorney (POA), and, in many cases, it is with a document such as a POA (giving a designated person control over the finances of another) that the dark side emerges. Children not designated as the agent under the POA can become resentful and suspicious of the brother or sister who has been given the control over a parent's finances. And, the designated agent can become a bit arrogant with the power of the POA and secretive about Mom or Dad's financial affairs, thereby exacerbating an already tense situation.

Another time that this can arise is when Mom or Dad move in with one of their children. If such a move requires improvements to be made to the caregiver's residence to accommodate a parent, this, more likely than not, will involve an expenditure of funds. If Mom or Dad is to be the source of those funds or are expected to reimburse the caregiver child, get the renovation budget and any other financial arrangement such as rent payments (remember, this is taxable income) worked out with them up-front and before any construction or improvements have been made. Reduce your understanding to writing. Be prepared to make a full disclosure to your brothers, sisters or other relatives who may have an interest, and be prepared to stay on budget. This is no time to be vague or secretive, or your motivations may become suspect. The bad blood that can result from a failure of the caregiver child to be open with sisters or brothers, or from a defensive or adversarial posture by the caregiver child, can outlive the parent for whom the accommodations were made. These are difficult and emotional times for families. Don't add to the stress by infighting or dredging up past sins of each other.

Do not think that this could never happen in your family. It can and does happen all of the time, with both small and large estates, with brothers and sisters (or other relatives) who always used to get along. We have no answers for this problem. We can only warn you about it. The green-eyed monster has a nasty habit of rearing its ugly head during time of crisis, so be prepared to put the "fun" in your own dysFUNctional family and deal with financial issues openly and always with the best interest of your parents at heart. Remember that your parent's money is not your money or that of any of your brothers and sisters.

Domestic Elder Abuse and Neglect

This is a difficult and unsavory topic, but, unfortunately, statistics show that incidences of domestic abuse and neglect of the elderly (as opposed to institutional abuse such as in a nursing home context) occur most frequently at the hands of family members, specifically, adult children and spouses of the care recipient. Also disturbing is the fact that incidences of domestic elder abuse and neglect continue to trend upward.

Other than young children, the elderly represent the most vulnerable segment of our society. Their frailty, dependence on their caregiver to meet their physical and emotional needs, and, in many cases, cognitive impairments, render them unable to defend themselves against the abuse and the abuser, or, in some instances, even complain about the abuse.

Abuse and neglect can assume many forms, and include the obvious such as

- physical abuse (hitting, pinching or similar uses of physical force to cause pain or injury as well as overmedication and restraints),

- neglect (failure to provide for basic physical and environmental needs of elderly care recipients, including food, clothing, housing and medical attention), and

- abandonment (desertion of the elder by the caregiver.)

Another form of abuse includes what is called "self-neglect". This occurs when someone fails to take care of themselves properly, risking their own health and safety. Failure to eat, drink or dress properly, failure to maintain hygiene or to take necessary medications – this type of behavior by an elderly person can be symptomatic of self-neglect and requires appropriate intervention.

Other recognized forms, and in many ways more insidious manifestations, of abuse include

- Emotional or psychological abuse which may consist of verbal or nonverbal acts of a caregiver designed to cause or inflict emotional distress on or anguish to the care recipient. This type of abuse can take so many forms that any attempt to list them would be inadequate. However, a few examples include the silent treatment, forced isolation, humiliation, threats, insults, and intimidation.

- Financial or material exploitation which is understood to consist of the improper or unlawful use of an elder's assets, funds or property, including diversion of funds or valuables, improper use of a power of attorney and undue influence to cause an elder to change a will or agent under a power of attorney, to name a few examples.

Many abusive actions are unlawful, even criminal, without reference to the age of the victim. Theft is theft, and assault is assault. In addition to standard law enforcement agencies, each state also has a form of Adult Protective Services agency which is charged with investigating incidences of elder abuse and neglect, and providing services and treatment for victims.

For further information, refer to the Appendix where you will find an Elder Abuse Fact Sheet reproduced from the Administration on Aging website.

Taking Care of Caregivers

Husbands that care for wives, and wives that care for husbands – these caregivers, who frequently are battling illnesses or other chronic conditions of old age themselves, need care too. As adult children, it is sometimes easy to overlook the special needs of our parents who are trapped by the medical and physical demands of becoming and being old.

On the surface, things are probably pretty much the same as they always were. Mom always took care of Dad and the kids when they were sick. But things are different now. Mom is not as young as she used to be and the stress of taking care of Dad and herself at the same time can be overwhelming. In this situation, you need to be supportive of and sympathetic to the caregiver. This can come in the form of respite services. Make the time (or hire someone) to step in and give the caregiver a break – to get out of the house, go shopping, run errands, have lunch with some friends, attend religious services – whatever may help to bring a sense of peace to the caregiver.

More importantly, if Mom has been providing other caregiving services for you and your own children, back off. Find a babysitter instead of expecting Mom to continue to take care of the grandkids while caring for a sick spouse; do your own shopping and cooking and chauffeuring of kids. It's time for you to grow up!

When you call, do not just ask about the health and condition of the ill parent. Ask how the caregiver parent is doing and feeling, and if there is anything you can do just *for them*. And then listen and hear what they are saying. Give them a chance to complain (without accusing them of whining) and to vent emotionally (without you becoming confrontational or critical). These are physically draining and emotionally exhausting times for spousal caregivers. Sometimes, they may just need a sympathetic ear or a shoulder to cry on. Be vigilant for signs of decline in the health and mental attitude of the caregiver and then make sure they receive medical attention if they become ill or show signs of depression. Too often caregivers ignore their own medical needs.

Acknowledge to them the great job they are doing. Always remember that if they were not there on the front lines, you would probably be required to provide the caregiving services they are providing.

Help in tangible and practical ways. Take the ill parent to appointments to give the caregiver a break. When you visit, bring some special food treats that the caregiver especially loves or other items like a favorite magazine or new novel or flowers. Don't act like a guest and expect to be waited on. Take a look around the house and see what you can do to help. Then, just do it. Run the vacuum. Scrub the bathroom. Dust the furniture. Wipe down the kitchen counters. Wash a load of towels. Always leave the place cleaner and more pleasant than it was before you arrived.

Sometimes, it is the reverse, where the husband is caring for the wife. That was the case with Uncle Henry and Aunt Mottie (who had the good sense to marry a man ten years her junior). When Mottie became ill, Henry did a great job for a guy who had never even boiled water. Nevertheless, meals became an ongoing issue, and both of them soon tired of TV dinners. We stepped in and brought real food we had cooked at our home and packaged for them for quick re-heating. Housekeeping was also not one of Henry's fortes, and Henry and Mottie, always quite frugal, rejected the idea of a housekeeper. So, when we visited, we worked.

Finally, when and if the time should come that the daily caregiving demands exceed your parent's abilities, do not make your Mom or Dad feel guilty about placing the ill parent in a nursing home. There may come a time when the survival of the caregiving spouse must take precedence over the desires or demands of the sick spouse.

Long Distance Caregiving

There is no substitute for personal observation and familiarity with household routines and moods. So what do you do if you are among the thousands of adult children who live far from their folks? Even if you live nearby but do not share the same house, you may still need to find other sets of eyes to help you keep tabs on your parents, on their condition, their health, and on their frames of mind and attitude.

You need information. You need to find someone logistically close to your parents, perhaps a relative or neighbor, whom you trust to report honestly and whom your parents trust enough to allow them access to their personal lives and homes. You need to be proactive.

Talk to their doctor and let them know who and where you are, find out with what hospital the doctor is affiliated, and where it is located. Always be prepared for the worst – that phone call in the dead of night when you learn that Mom or Dad is in the hospital for emergency care.

If you can, you should exchange telephone numbers with a neighbor who lives close to your folks so that they will be able to contact you if an emergency occurs. Also, if you find yourself unable to reach your parents by phone, it is very reassuring to be able to call someone locally who can investigate for you.

If and when necessary, you may wish to check into electronic home monitoring systems which are designed to alert emergency services if the senior requires assistance.

Be sure to have an attorney review the contract terms closely. You do not want to be tied into a long term obligation if the services are no longer required due to a change in circumstances.

As for making arrangements, get a telephone book from your parent's locality so you can check out local senior centers, home health providers, equipment vendors and community support and housekeeping services. There is also a wealth of information on the web that can be useful to you so please refer to the extensive list of websites that are included at the end of this book, many of which have eldercare locator databases that can help you find local resources and support services.

You can also reach the federal Administration on Aging, Eldercare Locator service at 1.800.677.1116 or at the website maintained by the AoA for information on services available in your parents' community.

All in all, whether you live with, close to, or far from your parents, your biggest enemy will be time. Everything takes time – educating yourself about your parents medical and other needs (which will change over time) and the resources available to help meet those needs, making arrangements and telephone calls, medical appointments, filling out forms – taking care of an elderly relative is a full time job.

As discussed elsewhere, you may need to outsource not just some of the care duties, but also the supervision of the delivery of the care. It is in the supervisory capacity that a Geriatric Care Manager may be a possible solution to the time crunch.

Professional Caregivers – Esther and Henry

There are professional caregivers who can make the impossible, possible and the unbearable, livable. If you are lucky enough to find the right one, they can also make an awful situation, joyful.

It was about a month after Uncle Henry moved in with us, that he was diagnosed with Alzheimer's. We made the decision that we wanted to avoid a nursing home, if possible. That left home healthcare as the only option. We struggled with nurse after nurse, kissing a lot of frogs that never turned into princes. Monitoring the nurses that paraded in and out of our home became a full time job in and of itself. Did they come when they were supposed to come? Did they do what they were supposed to do? Was it an adequate job? And, most importantly, did Henry like and cooperate with them?

After struggling for months, our persistence paid off and we found "the right one." Esther has a gift, a natural talent, for dealing with patients with Alzheimer's. She knew how to manage Henry. How to calm him down when he became agitated or violent (not uncommon with Alzheimer's). She also knew how to calm us down and take the edge off of the bizarre world of Alzheimer's that we found ourselves living in. She became Henry's companion and a member of our family – a source of strength for all of us.

When Henry would go to the hospital with recurrent bouts of congestive heart failure, Esther would continue to tend to him. When he would be in rehab following a hospital stay, she would go to the nursing home each day to make sure that he ate, and that he was behaving himself. She was his beacon in a fuzzy world. Uncle Henry (a very well mannered gentleman in his pre-Alzheimer days), was argumentative with us, his family, throwing us out of "his house" at least once a week. Esther acted as the buffer for everyone.

We learned how to handle Henry through Esther. One thing that worked for us was letting Henry "go over" to his Alzheimer reality. We stopped forcing him to remember us, or the day of the week, or who was President, or whether it was summer or winter. We joined and learned to enjoy his reality. We would always acknowledge how beautiful his Mother was (never arguing with him that we could not see her or that she had been dead for forty years). Or how beautiful Peg was (our beloved Aunt Mottie and his deceased wife). Or any of the other countless surreal things he saw. Once we let him go, much of the tension was gone. (Anyway, who are we to say he did not see what he said he saw.) The things in his world made him happy and that made an unbearable situation joyful for all of us.

Esther was with us right to the end and will always be counted as a dear member of our family. She continues to help families and to move on when a patient passes away.

Geriatric Care Managers

Every new dilemma or problem gives rise to a new breed of consultants. There are available in the marketplace "experts" in the field of elder care who call themselves Eldercare Consultants or Geriatric Care Managers (GCMs). A qualified GCM may hold a college degree in social work, nursing or counseling, and is versed in the availability of services required by the elderly in a particular locale and the costs and quality of those services.

For those who live far away from their parents or are in a time crunch due to work or other life demands, a GCM might be a solution to a number of problems. A GCM can either assist or find someone to assist with the activities and chores of daily life and routine household problems of an elderly person who wishes to live at home. They can track the needs and condition and manage the health care of the elderly client, report to the family on a regular basis, and act as a liaison for the elderly client and his family and advisors. If a higher level of care becomes necessary, they should also be able to provide assistance in relocating the elderly and monitoring the transition.

As for costs, this is like everything else – a function of market demand - where the elderly client lives in the country and how many GMC's are available to provide services in that area. A ballpark amount is about $200 to $300 for the initial assessment which requires the GCM to acquire a substantial amount of information about the elderly client, and then an hourly fee of $50+ thereafter.

To state the obvious, this is not much different than finding a babysitter for your kids in that you need to be extremely careful who you select. Ask around. Ask your parents' doctor, an elder care attorney, a hospital or nursing home social worker. Check the credentials and references of persons referred to you for this type of position. You are going to have this person intrude on your parents lives, and ask your folks to confide personal and sensitive information. You have got to do everything you can to assure yourself that this person is qualified and is the right person for you and your parents.

As far as we have been able to determine, there is no licensing requirement in order to hold yourself out as a Geriatric Care Manager, and no professional or ethical body to which they are accountable like doctors and nurses. However, many licensed social workers, psychologists and nurses have entered this field. A good place to start your investigation is with the National Association of Professional Geriatric Care Managers (**www.caremanager.org**). Also, some home health care agencies offer these types of services.

Chapter 3

When to intervene:

Activities of Daily Life

First, let me say that just because your folks are old, they have not automatically become stupid, incompetent, or unable to manage their own affairs. Aging affects different people different ways. Some people become old way before their years, unable to cope with life and its demands. And others never lose their zest for living and ability to deal with the demands of life.

Know your parents but do not stand in judgment about what is best for them unless and until you are pretty darn sure that circumstances and their health or welfare require you to take action. They are your parents and you are their child. Keep your place, show respect and help them to keep their dignity.

Having said that, let's review what you should keep an eye out for with respect to the aging of your parents. The activities or chores that made you dependent on your parents when you were young are pretty much the same indicators that need to be considered in assessing your parents' ability to continue to live alone without assistance, or to help determine the type and amount of assistance they need to continue to live independently.

What are the Indicators?
ADL's and IADL's

Activities of daily life or ADL's are the commonly accepted indicators of the ability of a person to properly care for himself.

Generally, ADL's include:

- Bathing – the ability to bath oneself and to maintain personal hygiene without assistance;

- Toileting – the ability to use the toilet without assistance;

- Eating – the ability to feed oneself without assistance;

- Dressing – the ability to dress oneself without assistance;

- Mobility – the ability to ambulate or move around a living unit without assistance, with or without assistant devices such as wheelchairs or walkers;

- Transferring – the ability to transfer to and from a bed or chair without assistance; and

- Continence.

If someone requires assistance with one or more ADL's they are considered to have an ADL deficiency or disability.

There are also instrumental activities of daily life (IADL) which are activities and skills required for a person to live independently such as

- Grocery shopping,

- Meal preparation,

- Using the telephone,

- Doing laundry,

- Housekeeping,

- Paying bills and handling finances,

- Transportation,
- Taking medications,
- And other routine daily chores related to the maintenance of a household.

Declines in the ability to perform the activities and chores of daily life are the most common reason for considering an alternate lifestyle such as a move to a relative's home or an institutionalized setting such as an assisted living facility or nursing home.

In addition to these indicators, there are a lot of other signs that may be peculiar to your Mom or Dad. Pets are a very good indicator of the self-sufficiency of an individual. We think every senior who is capable of the responsibility should have a pet, not just for companionship (studies have proven that pets are one of the best antidepressants), but also to act as the "canary in the coal mine", an early warning sign of trouble. As long as Fido the dog or Fifi the cat is being well cared for in terms of nutrition and medical attention, it is probable that their caretaker is taking care of herself as well. If the dog or cat begins to lose weight or develop medical conditions that are not being adequately addressed, you have got a pretty good clue that there is a problem in the household that needs to be addressed, pronto. (It was when we noticed Uncle Henry giving his heart medication to his dog that we knew Henry could no longer live alone. The dog and Henry survived for three years after that harrowing incident.)

Check the obvious things first. Poor vision and hearing impairments can make the performance of some of ordinary tasks within the IADL group, like writing a check or following instructions on taking medications, difficult or impossible for a senior who may otherwise be capable of self-sufficiency.

However, if mail remains unopened, bills go unpaid, collection letters start to arrive, it may be more than a temporary lapse. If the house seems to be dirtier than usual, if the lawn seems to consistently need to be mowed, if laundry remains unwashed, if the refrigerator has an abundance of items that have long since seen their "Use By" date, you may need to step in and take action. Hire a housekeeper, a lawn service, or other supplemental assistance where you have identified a deficiency, or do those chores yourself.

Be vigilant. Ask questions. You are not being nosy. Find out which doctors they are seeing, and what medications they are on, and why. You need to monitor the status and condition of your folks. You need to know when and what type of help they may need.

Depression

Loss of weight is another sign of trouble with seniors, not just because of the serious physical ramifications of malnutrition and dehydration, but because lack of appetite is a common sign of depression, and depression is a common treatable ailment of the elderly that too often remains unrecognized and untreated. Depression is *not* a normal part of the aging process, but it is often triggered by medical conditions, and psychological and emotional influences common to the elderly.

Depression may also overlap with other medical illnesses further complicating a diagnoses and treatment, and some symptoms may also be attributable to reactions to medications. In addition, depression is also a very common problem of those with Alzheimer's Disease, and may be difficult to separate from dementia.

Some typical signs of depression, other than loss of appetite and refusing to eat, include

- Apathy to or lack of interest in activities previously enjoyed;

- Decrease in physical activity not attributable to any physical condition or illness;

- Persistent fatigue or lethargy;

- Indecisiveness and inability to concentrate, and memory lapses;

- Clinginess;

- Excessive sadness, crying and feelings of worthlessness;

- Changes in sleeping patterns, oversleeping or insomnia. However, this symptom is given with the following caveat. As you age, your sleep cycle may change. Your internal clock, your day/night cycle, may shift. You still need the same amount of sleep but grow tired at an earlier or later time. Sleeping can become difficult – an additional source of frustration and anxiety for the elderly.

- Persistent or chronic aches and pains that are unresponsive to conventional treatment;

- Self-neglect and questionable personal hygiene;

- Thoughts of death and dying, suicide.

All of these symptoms are also common to grief following the loss of a loved one, including a pet. However, grief tends to subside with the passage of time, generally two to six months after a death, and depression can persist indefinitely, if left untreated.

None of these symptoms of depression will be evident if you do not take the time to visit your parents frequently enough to notice these changes, some of which can be subtle.

Making a Move

Moving is always stressful, for anyone, young or old. However, for the elderly, a move can be an emotional rabbit hole.

There are generally two kinds of moves. The first type is a move made "by" someone – Mom or Dad decides to move to smaller quarters or to a retirement community. They downsize. It is their decision and they are still in control. They may still need an enormous amount of support. Packing, dealing with movers, getting rid of stuff, changing utilities – it is exhausting, time consuming and anxiety provoking. It can also be very depressing for you and them since they may be leaving the old family homestead and years of memories. Closing chapters of our lives is always difficult and even positive changes can produce angst.

The second is the move "of" someone. This one can be much tougher for the caregiver since in this scenario, the "movee" for any one of a number of reasons is not an active participant in the move. The move is an indisputable indication that someone is no longer truly independent, and that the end for them is nearer, if, in fact, they are aware of the move.

Whether the move is into a family member's house or an assisted living facility or a nursing home, there is the element of unfamiliarity that can spin an elderly person around. If you can, you should always make sure when moving an elderly person into a new environment to move some of their favorite things – family pictures, an afghan or blanket, a chair. This should help to anchor them and alleviate the inevitable disorientation.

For someone with dementia, moving can be easier than it is for someone who has no cognitive impairment and is capable of appreciating the implications of a move. Uncle Henry was discharged from the rehab center to our home. We had time to recreate his living room and bedroom in a small apartment that was part of the main house. From day one, he was "at home" in familiar surroundings because he was surrounded by his stuff. The transition for him was seamless, and he proceeded on a regular basis, when he was in one of his Alzheimer's manias, to throw us out of "his" house.

Taking Away the Driver's License and Car Keys

There comes a time when a person is just no longer capable of driving a motor vehicle safely. This may be due to a chronic condition or a physical impairment or simply old age. Taking away someone's ability to drive is a very hard thing to do. Just like getting your license in your teens gave you a sense of enormous independence and freedom, losing your license and the ability to drive can leave you feeling depressed, dependent and confined. For many seniors, the car is the last vestige of an independent life.

Most states now require re-testing or place other limitations on driver license renewals for persons over certain ages. Some elderly are ornery enough to not care if they have lost their license and will continue to drive without it. For others, the driver's license is very significant and they will discontinue driving after they have lost this privilege. As the adult child/caretaker, you must decide which approach best suits your parents – taking away the license or the keys.

Our first clue with Uncle Henry was the first ticket he had ever received in his 60+ years of driving. He moaned and complained and argued that he was not at fault and did nothing to warrant the citation. He reluctantly paid it and shortly afterwards came "the accident". Fortunately, it was not serious and he had not harmed himself or anyone else. Unfortunately, even the car was still drive-able, and he made it clear that he intended to continue to drive. We laid down the law and told him he had to give up driving. He told us to mind our own business and that he would do whatever he wanted. That was the end of the discussion as far as he was concerned.

At the time, Henry was living alone in a small town. We were desperate and in constant fear that Henry would cause serious harm to himself or another person. Our solution was to call the local police station and talk to the officer who had issued the last citation in connection with "the accident". He was familiar with Henry and his driving habits and the potential hazard he posed to everyone in the community. As a community service, he offered to visit Henry at home and tell him (a lie) that his driver's license had been revoked. Although we hated the duplicity, we immediately agreed. It was months before Henry was scheduled to be re-tested as part of his license renewal. More than enough time for him to kill himself or someone else with his car. And we had to do something now.

Needless to say, Henry was beside himself as a result of the police officer's visit. He had never had any legal trouble, and had much respect for the law. He called us very sheepishly to tell us about the visit from the policeman and that he had decided it was time to give up driving. Although the loss of the license caused a whole new problem, making transportation arrangements for Henry, we were enormously relieved to have Henry off of the roads. We immediately contacted a local surrey service that was available to take Henry where he needed to go - to and from Church and the grocery store.

If there is a moral to this story, it is to be observant about the driving habits and abilities of your elderly loved one and, when the time comes, to find a way to get your folks out of the driver's seat of their car before they kill someone. Depending on the attitude of your elderly loved one, this can mean having a driver license revoked or not renewed, or, actually taking away the car (don't just take the car keys unless you are sure you have all of the duplicate keys as well). The right circumstances may present themselves that eliminate the problem (one friend of ours had an elderly aunt that also had a drinking problem. She fell off of the stool at her local tavern, broke her hip and never drove again). Or, like us and Uncle Henry, you may have to have a hand in developing a set of circumstances that facilitate the process.

Smarter Than Strangers, or Talk to Your Folks About Scams and Predators

When our daughter was young, she loved the Berenstein Bear stories. Each had a moral or an important lesson to be learned by the child/reader. One of her favorites was called "Smarter Than Strangers" which taught kids to be cautious with people that they did not know regardless of their appearance. Even now as an adult we still remind her from time to time to be "smarter than strangers".

Although it is a very sad commentary on the state of our society, the elderly are prime targets for con artists and financial predators. We, as adult children, need to caution our folks about being "smarter than strangers" because these tactics are unfortunately widespread. We need to talk openly about this problem, and our folks need to know that if they do make a mistake, they can talk to us about it without being made to feel like idiots. They need to be reassured that we will not add to the problem by berating them.

So why is this segment of our society targeted? Is it because the elderly are stupid? We don't think so. The elderly are victims of discrimination – they are treated differently and victimized simply because of their age.

This became very clear to us recently when Mom needed new windows. Now, let me say that Mom is a very savvy lady with years of business experience and tons of common sense to boot. She was getting estimates and her first sales call was from a national franchise window replacement company. (Here's your first rule – "Just because a company has an advertising budget and you recognize its name, does not mean that they are reputable!")

By the time I walked in at the end of the sales call, she had already signed a binding contract (the salesman said it was not binding – a patent lie). When I told him we did not need a particular window replaced, he said okay. I told the guy we wanted an estimate, not a contract. When he prepared the "estimate" it was for almost twice the amount of the "contract price". Due to "one-day only sale" he told us he could not hold the contract price. We threw him out.

After the salesman left, my normally "tough as nails" Mom was visibly shaken by the experience. Although she had not lost any money, her confidence in her judgment had been diminished. We then compared notes. She had also told the salesman we did not want to replace a particular window. He told Mom that it had to be replaced despite her protests. This was the same window that he gladly removed from the estimate at my request. After we debriefed each other, it became painfully clear that Mom had been treated very differently than I because of her age. It was not that she had failed to ask the right questions or failed to specify clearly what she wanted, we were simply given different answers to the exact same question. Because of her age, the sales guy assumed that she was gullible and an easy mark.

These predators are everywhere, selling everything from home improvements to insurance products to investment opportunities to estate planning services. All elderly should be cautioned never to sign anything without having someone else review it first. Even if they have no attorney, they should be programmed to say that they need to have their lawyer look at any contract presented to them for signature (even if it just to stall for time), or before they write a check or give someone a deposit for any extraordinary item. No one should ever allow himself or herself to be pressured or rushed into signing anything.

If you are told that you have to "act now", that should be the cue to hang up the phone, close the door or throw out in the trash the "You are a winner if..." notice. Other red flags include demands for cash payments only, warnings not to tell anyone else about the deal or opportunity, today-only offers, demands for payments in exchange for a prize, instructions to call "900" numbers, and bogus charities, to name just a few.

The elderly are prime targets for telemarketing schemes for a number of reasons: seniors, who are often lonely and isolated, are at home during the day when many of these calls are made, and they have more time to chat and to listen. The elderly must be very cautious about giving personal information by phone especially to unsolicited callers or over the internet. Identity theft is becoming commonplace and someone's social security number, bank account numbers and credit card numbers are to a large extent their identity in today's world. Urge your folks to carefully review their monthly credit card statements to verify that all charges are proper.

Senior citizens must also be on the alert to attempts by con artists to use ethnic or religious connections to establish trust, sometimes referred to as affinity fraud. Don't trust anyone who attempts to part you and your money because you belong to the same church, came from the same neighborhood, are of the same ethnic background, etc.

The elderly also need to be cautioned about letting any strangers into their homes, ever. There are no laws that say that you must open your door to anyone who knocks. In fact, no one at any age should ever open his or her door to any stranger, even if it is someone in a uniform – law enforcement or utility. Besides con artists, there are far too many incidents of home invasions where the victims are senior citizens.

Somewhere there is a fine line that needs to be drawn between healthy skepticism, and crippling fear and paranoia. Make sure your folks know that they are targets, not because they are stupid, but because of who and where we are as a society. We cannot allow our elderly to be diminished by con artists and other motherless slime who count on the fact that people who have been duped usually are too embarrassed or ashamed to tell anyone or take any corrective action.

If your elderly loved one has fallen victim to one of these schemes, report the incident to your state Attorney General

Consumer Fraud Office or Consumer Protection Agency, or other applicable local, state or federal government office. You might be able to save another consumer from financial hardship and embarrassment.

Chapter 4

Some Living Options for the Golden Years

Nursing homes are not the only option to consider when one or both of your parents are unable to live alone or in their present situation. Here are some alternatives to consider that are less restrictive and can be more cost effective, or more costly, as the case may be.

Retirement Apartments

Every community has apartment buildings or condominiums that attract senior citizens and have reputations as being senior-friendly. Many seniors will consider a move when a spouse has passed on and/or the obligations of maintaining the "family home" have become a burden. They may want or need, for medical reasons, to downsize, but for many reasons may not be prepared to move into an "old age" home.

These types of retirement apartments can be an ideal and safe environment for many seniors who are still capable of getting around and taking care of themselves, but are not financially able or emotionally prepared to make a move to an assisted living facility or retirement community. These types of apartments provide autonomy and a network of similarly situated seniors who can and do look out for each other. This network can go a long way toward extending the amount of time that Mom or Dad will be able to live life independently and provide a chapter of life that can be fulfilling and happy. People generally like to be around other people with whom they have commonality – shared historical and life experiences.

Our advice here is to ask around the community to identify this type of apartment building or complex. Certainly, a local real estate agent probably knows which apartment buildings are senior-friendly. And your folks probably already know through their friends where they can be found. A move to this type of informal retirement community can be satisfying for your parents and provide a sense of comfort to you.

Some of these types of apartments are federally funded for low-income residents who qualify. Section 202 housing is specifically designed for low-income senior citizens, and, in addition to housing, may include other supportive services such as meals. Because demand is high for government subsidized housing, you should plan ahead, and get on "the waiting list", if your parent qualifies from an income/asset point of view. Contact your local Area Agency on Aging or housing authority to find out about location, availability and qualifications for Section 202 housing.

Adult Day Care

Adult Day Care is modeled after child day care and is just what it sounds like. Generally, these centers are for adults, who may or may not be cognitively or physically impaired, and who do not need around the clock care but do need care and companionship during normal business hours when their primary caregivers are at work or need a break. Just like child day care, in making a choice, you need to assess each program and your parent's particular preferences and needs. Usually, but not always, these centers require that the adult be ambulatory.

These centers typically will provide breakfast, lunch and snacks, offer recreational and social activities and community involvement, and assistance with and supervision of prescribed medications. Many of these centers are linked with hospitals and nursing homes. Many have medical professionals on call.

Participation in a day care program can be beneficial to an elderly loved one, providing them with an opportunity to be with their peers in a controlled setting. The activities can help to keep them alert and ward off depression which many times result from feelings of alienation and isolation. Day care can also provide a much-needed respite for the caregiver.

In selecting an adult day care program, you should check out the following:

- Is it clean and odor free?
- Is it comfortable and inviting?
- Is it licensed by the state?
- Have there been any complaints about the facility to the state department of health or other licensing body?
- What are its hours and days of operation?
- How do they charge? Hourly, daily or monthly?
- What is the ratio of staff to participants?
- What types of participants do they accept in terms of physical or mental impairments?
- Are there nutritious meals and snacks available? Any extra charge?
- Do they help with medications? With eating?
- Are the staff and elderly participants cheerful?
- Do they make assessments of and treatment plans for applicants to determine their needs and the services they may require?
- Do they involve the family in the assessment?
- What type of recreational, rehabilitative, educational, counseling, and therapeutic services do they offer?
- What are the qualifications of the staff?
- What about staff turnover?

You should not be shy about shopping around as the per day costs, as well as the programs and services, vary. Some have subsidies or are available through a Medicaid waiver program that can reduce the participant's cost. Most centers do not provide transportation so that is an additional factor to consider in making a choice. Most can help you make transportation arrangements through local surrey services.

Home Health Care

Although the trend appears to be slowly changing, by and large, the government for some reason seems to think that it is more cost effective to provide care for people in institutionalized settings such as nursing homes than to subsidize care for the elderly in their own homes. Where many nursing homes accept indigent individuals, those who are Medicaid eligible for health or financial reasons, these subsidies are generally not available to someone who wants to continue to live in their own or a relative's home. What this means is that there is very little in the way of government services or financial support available to elderly who choose to stay at home.

An exception to this general rule is upon discharge from a hospital or rehabilitation facility after a hospital stay. Medicare will pick up the cost of certain rehabilitation services and equipment and home health care assistance where it has been prescribed by your attending physician after a three day hospital stay. The home health care services are available for a finite period of time.

Also, check your phone book for available services. Your county/local department of aging often makes a variety of home health services available at below market costs for qualified (lower income) applicants. Be prepared to work the phones and fill out applications if your parents are in a low-income bracket. Be prepared to pay out the nose if they are not in a low-income bracket.

Another exception to this general rule is Medicaid and Home and Community Based Services (HCBS) waivers. These are called waiver programs because the federal authorities, now known as Centers for Medicare & Medicaid Services (CMS), in response to applications from individual states or state agencies can waive portions of the Medicaid Act and allow Medicaid funds to be used for home health care benefits for qualified seniors. Also, some states are using some of the notorious Tobacco Settlement or state lottery monies to support these at-home programs.

The aging waiver is specifically designed to provide the indigent elderly with the assistance they need to continue to live independently in their own homes and communities as an alternative to long term care in a nursing home. However, these waivers are generally not a solution that is available to the elderly who are not Medicaid eligible and they can be very time consuming to obtain. However, if your elderly loved one is Medicaid eligible under the waiver standards (which differ a bit from the general Medicaid eligibility rules), then these community-based programs should definitely be investigated as a possible solution to your parent's home health care needs.

Some of the services provided under the Medicaid aging waiver program can include home health and personal care services, home support, adult day care, transportation, home modifications, specialized equipment and supplies, home delivered meals and companions. Since these waivers are creatures of Medicaid (not Medicare), you must check with your particular state's department of aging or county office of aging in order to determine the nature and scope of services available, and the specific eligibility rules for the waiver. Some states (Delaware and New Jersey) have applied for and been granted Medicaid waivers for assisted living providers thus making assisted living facilities an available option for the low income elderly in those states. One can only hope that this is the beginning of a trend.

Home Health Care Providers

There are many home health care agencies in the marketplace. When you hire an agency, they become responsible for helping to determine the type and amount of help that is needed and providing a qualified person, who is an employee of theirs, to perform those functions. You still need to monitor and evaluate the services provided, and, of course, the agency will need to be paid.

In addition to determining the costs and type of services provided, in assessing a home health care agency, you should ask if they are accredited, Medicare certified, and licensed by the applicable state. You should also ask about what type of screening they do in the process of hiring their employees (drug testing, criminal background). You should find out what type of evaluation they conduct in assessing a patient's needs and who performs the evaluation (a registered nurse or therapist or other). You need to know if and how frequently their employees are supervised during home health visits, and who you are to call with any problems or complaints.

There are typically three types of home health care providers available:

- Homemakers – provide housekeeping and cleaning services; usually they provide no personal care services

- Home Health Aides – provide personal care (bathing, shampoos,) and may assist with some household chores (change linens)

- Registered Nurses – administer treatment, monitor and evaluate care and maintain records of medications and medical progress.

If you are prepared to pay for home health care privately or through a long term care insurance policy, there are tons of independent and agency providers in the marketplace from which to choose. Like everything else, choose wisely, after getting referrals from your parents' doctor or other trusted source, and independently investigating the provider. And be persistent. It may take some time to find the right person to provide the right care for your Mom or Dad.

Congregate Housing

Congregate Housing is a generic term that includes a variety of housing and living alternatives. Two major types include Continuing Care Retirement Communities, or CCRCs, and Assisted Living or Personal Care Homes. Unlike skilled nursing home facilities, these types of housing in many states are not highly regulated, and usually are not subsidized, by the government.

Continuing Care Retirement Communities

A CCRC is a facility, sometimes called a life care community, that combines various types of senior retirement housing in one complex and provides a continuum of care for its residents, from independent living, to assisted living and ultimately, skilled nursing care. During the 1980's and 1990's, there was an enormous amount of growth in the number of CCRCs. As a result, there are now about 1,500 of these communities in the United States.

CCRCs are not cheap, catering mostly to upper and middle-income retirees. In many cases, residences in CCRCs are not purchased, but are leased to the occupant. Most require an upfront, sometimes non-refundable, entry fee, which can be quite hefty, usually in excess of $100,000. Another form of CCRC is similar to a condominium or cooperative structure. Here residents actually purchase their units or buy shares in a cooperative, and enter into management agreements with management companies to manage the daily affairs of the community and provide the required services, again for a monthly fee.

In the lease situation, a resident is required to sign a contract that spells out the entry and monthly fees payable by the resident and the recreational, housekeeping, health and related services to be provided by the CCRC as part of or, in some cases, in addition to, the monthly fee. The financial incentives often include locking in a fixed, usually below market, rate for continuing care and ultimately nursing home care.

Most CCRCs have residence options that reflect the level of care required by the occupant. In a typical case, a resident starts with an independent living unit which can be anything from an apartment, townhouse, or single-family residence. As the resident ages or becomes infirm increased level of care and assistance with living services may be provided in their unit or they may be required to relocate to the assisted living section of the facility. Finally, most CCRCs operate skilled nursing home facilities on their campuses for when intensive around the clock care is required. At this highest level of care, Medicare and Medicaid quality of care standards must be adhered to if the facility is to be able to seek reimbursement from these government programs.

Most CCRCs have a variety of recreational facilities available. Most offer housekeeping and laundry services as well as meal plans, usually in common dining rooms.

Although CCRCs offer flexibility in living arrangements that meet residents' physical needs as their health declines, some of the drawbacks include the lack of control over the decision as to when and where within the community residents will be relocated when their needs increase. These decisions are usually made by the medical director of the CCRC and should be spelled out in the admission contract.

A plus for CCRCs include the ability of a husband and wife to remain together in either the same unit or within the same community even though they may have or develop different health demands requiring different levels of care.

CCRC Admission Requirements

In addition to the payment by the prospective resident of entry fees, CCRCs may have additional admission requirements, such as

- Satisfactory completion of a physical examination to help insure that the community resources will not be unduly burdened;

- Satisfactory proof of ability to meet financial commitments associated with residence in the community;

- Proof of enrollment in Medicare, Parts A and B, and Medigap insurance, or other financial resources to pay health care costs not covered by Medicare. Prospective residents with modest financial means may also be required to purchase long term care insurance.

- Execution of Living Wills/Advance Directives and durable powers of attorney for asset management.

- Execution of an admission agreement with the CCRC which may include some the above requirements as conditions precedent to admission.

There are three different types of admission agreements that a prospective resident of a CCRC may be required to sign. These probably are binding lifetime contracts, not short term or cancelable leases, so great care must be exercised before signing. Certainly, the input of an attorney with experience in elder law issues is strongly suggested.

The major difference between the types of admission contracts is often the way by which health care costs will be paid by the resident.

First, there is the "extensive care" agreement where the CCRC offers unlimited specified health services. Under this version, regardless of the level of care required by the resident, the monthly fee will not be raised unless monthly fees are increased for all residents.

Second is what is called the "modified agreement". Here, a resident may receive a particular type or amount of long term care for his/her lifetime without any substantial increase in the monthly fee. For example, the resident may be entitled without any additional fee to a set number of days of nursing home care per year or over the life of the contract. After that maximum is met, there will be a daily rate charged.

Finally and more commonly, there is the "fee for service" contract. Here, each resident pays for his own health related services as they are provided by the facility on a fee basis that is usually below market. Under this arrangement, residents are often encouraged to buy long term care insurance to defray the potential costs.

The contract should also address a number of other issues that are significant such as the description of the unit, responsibility for maintenance and repairs, parking accommodations, housekeeping and laundry services, meal plans, payment of utilities, furnishings and equipment, pets, responsibility for personal injury and damage to personal and community property, insurance requirements, facility rules and regulations, increases in fees, transportation, and social services.

Also, and of great importance, the contract should spell out the resident's rights such as the circumstances under which a resident may be required

- to relocate due to a decline in health, who makes that decision and the resident's right to appeal that decision,

- to share a unit with another resident,

- to be evicted.

Do not forget to carefully check out the organization that owns the facility for financial stability. You're making a big investment. Especially if the up front fee is refundable, it is like making an interest free loan to the owner. You need to assure yourself that when the time comes, the owner will be in a financial position to return the money.

Finally, the Continuing Care Accreditation Commission, a private accreditation body with no governmental or regulatory authority or affiliation, has established standards and a review process for those retirement communities that wish to obtain the CCAC "seal of approval". In your search for the right retirement community, you may want to ask if communities you are considering have been accredited, as well as check out the CCAC website for more information.

Assisted Living/Personal Care Homes

There is no definition under federal law of "Assisted Living Facility", and the definition varies from state to state in the states that actually recognize and regulate this type of housing. The terms assisted living facilities and personal care homes are sometimes used interchangeably. Usually personal care homes are more like private residences where a relatively small number of unrelated persons reside together and receive additional services such as meals and personal care services.

Assisted living facilities are more institutionalized in that it is a facility that can accommodate larger numbers of residents who may have individual apartments or bedrooms or who may share bedroom space with others and who are provided support with the activities of daily life and health care services.

These types of facilities should not accept residents that require a skilled level of care only available at a nursing home. In some states, these types of facilities also need to be licensed and are subject to applicable state regulations, though commonly at a substantially reduced level of scrutiny than nursing home facilities.

Assisted living facilities and personal care homes are for individuals who due to age or other infirmity may actually, or may fear that they soon will, require some assistance with the activities of daily life but do not need the level of care provided in a nursing home. Almost all assisted living facilities and personal care homes will provide certain care or assistance within an individual's unit as well as recreational and social activities and meals in common eating areas on site. Most also offer laundry and housekeeping services.

Many assisted living facilities have nurses on duty 24 hours a day and physicians on call which make these arrangements attractive to residents and their families.

Assisted living facilities run the gamut in terms of accommodations and quality of care. Some are like five star hotels and others like economy inns. Unlike nursing homes where Medicaid under certain financial conditions can pick up the tab 100%, assisted living facilities are usually private pay. Although there are some facilities that will accept an individual's Social Security monthly allotment as payment in full, these are obviously of the economy variety. Like anything else in life, you get what you pay for.

Chapter 5

Nursing Homes

When is a nursing home the right decision?

Very few people decide that they want to move to a nursing home. Usually, the decision is made for someone by someone who is responsible for the care of the prospective nursing home resident. There may come a time when your Mom's or Dad's needs exceed your ability to provide care for her or him. When you as the caregiver have decided that you cannot provide the level of care needed, either directly or with the assistance of home health aides or others, a nursing home may be the answer and the best solution for everyone. Do not feel guilty about this. Having reached that decision, you need to find the right nursing home for your folks.

How do I decide which nursing home is right?

There are a number of things that you need to consider in evaluating a nursing home for suitability for your parent. Some of these include (presented in no particular order of importance) -

- Its reputation in the community

- Medicare and Medicaid certification

- Nature and status of state licenses of facility and professional staff

- Staffing ratios (the number of staff per resident)

- Quality of life it offers its residents (the look, feel and smell of a facility)

- Quality of care (physical appearance of residents, responsiveness of staff to resident needs, and state survey deficiencies and plans of correction)

- Nutrition and hydration (appearance and taste of food, availability of assistance with food and fluid intake, appearance of dining areas)

- Safety (handrails in hallways, grab bars in bath rooms, clutter and lighting of hallways, smoke alarms, sprinklers)

- Policies regarding physical restraints of residents, bed sores, incontinence, weight loss, behavioral problems of residents.

You will find a comprehensive nursing home questionnaire in the Appendix at the end of this book that was reproduced from the Medicare website. This questionnaire should help you with the quantitative and qualitative elements of the decision-making process. (**www.medicare.gov/nursing/ checklist.asp**)

In making the final decision, the location of the home in relation to where you and other friends and family members live is critical. Even after admittance to a home, your caregiving duties do not end, they just change. You will still need to monitor closely your parent's condition and adaptation to the new environment. Are they happy? Are they eating properly? It is important to send a message to the home that you intend to be vigilant. And, it helps if other members of the family are close enough to visit regularly.

No matter how attentive and caring the staff of a facility may be, there is simply no substitute for the familiar faces of loved ones to a nursing home resident.

Codes of Conduct or Compliance Plans

One thing not mentioned in the Medicare questionnaire discussed above, however, is that a due diligence investigation of a home should include determining if the facility is currently operating under a Corporate Integrity Agreement (more below on this subject) or has adopted and implemented a Code of Conduct or Code of Ethics for the facility and its staff members, operators and owners. Although not mandated by law, many facilities have voluntarily adopted Codes of Conduct, also called Compliance Plans, as a preemptive or defensive move should the government find fault with their operations. The federal Office of Inspector General (OIG) issued guidelines during 2000 as to the content and implementation of these plans for nursing home operations.

These plans typically are modeled after Corporate Integrity Agreements (CIA) imposed by the government in settlements of legal actions against care providers for violations of various laws, commonly in health care abuse and fraud actions for billing practices that fail to comply with Medicare/Medicaid rules and regulations (e.g., billing for services not actually rendered or insufficiently documented to be deemed to have been rendered). These compliance plans state a home's commitment to comply with all applicable laws and regulations, and set out its policies and internal procedures designed to foster compliance respecting such matters as billing practices, provision and documentation of appropriate resident care, resident rights, employee relations, employee screening and background checks, confidentiality of resident records, to name but a few.

In addition to these types of policy statements (which, in many cases, are self-serving), this type of document will also provide you with the names of and contact information for the members of the home's compliance committee and designated compliance officer to whom complaints may be directed should a care or other type of issue arise. Many plans also include anonymous hotlines that may be called to register a complaint if there is any concern over the possibility of retaliatory action against a resident or employee "whistle blower". Make sure you ask for a copy of this plan as you research your options for long term care facilities. All nursing homes, regardless of size or geographical location, should have this type of a plan in place and operating.

Long Term Care Ombudsman

The term "Ombudsman" is derived from a Swedish word that means "citizen representative". Under mandate of the federal Older Americans Act each state is required to have an Ombudsman Program which is funded on the federal level by the Department of Health and Human Services Administration on Aging. Therefore, in your search for the right nursing home, you may want to contact your state's Long Term Care Ombudsman for information about nursing homes in your state.

The role of the ombudsman is to provide information and assistance to nursing home residents and their families and to act as an advocate for them in resolving problems that may arise, including such issues as resident rights, resident care, finances and quality of life. Check the Medicare website (**www.medicare.gov**), or the Administration on Aging Resource Directory included in the Appendix for a complete list of each state's Ombudsman Office.

What is a nursing home?

A skilled nursing home facility is a state licensed and regulated institution that provides nursing care and supervision, medical, dietary, therapy, pharmacy and related services and assistance to elderly or otherwise infirm residents. A skilled care facility is required to have nursing supervision twenty-four hours a day, and an intermediate care facility is required to have such supervision for only eight hours a day. All residents must be under the care of a physician who is responsible for directing the medical care of the resident. A nursing home can only act under the orders of a physician with respect to medical treatment, medications, therapy, dietary matters and restraint.

Nursing homes may be owned by not-for-profit corporations (charitable or religious institutions), or, like any other business, they may be owned by for profit corporations, partnerships, or sole proprietorships. They may be stand-alone businesses or one of a chain of homes. They may be operated by the owner or managed by an outside management company. In looking into a nursing home, you should check out the backgrounds and history of the owners and, if applicable, the management company.

The day-to-day operations of a nursing home are overseen by an Administrator who must be licensed by the state as a nursing home administrator and may work for the owner or the management company. In addition to the Administrator, each skilled nursing home facility is required to have a Director of Nursing who is charged with responsibility for overseeing nursing care and clinical matters of the residents.

State Licensing and Federal Certification

Every nursing home is required to be licensed by the state in which they are located and regulated for purposes of the delivery of care and services to residents.

In addition to state licensing, most nursing homes are also "certified" for purposes of participating in the Medicare and Medicaid programs (that means they are eligible to receive reimbursement from the Medicare and Medicaid programs). The certification process is the means by which the federal government (the U.S. Department of Health and Human Services, Centers for Medicare & Medicaid) determines if the facility is in "substantial compliance" with the federal requirements of participation (ROP) in the Medicare and Medicaid programs.

Surveys:
Assessing Quality of Care

The federal government contracts with individual state governments to conduct onsite inspections and to monitor nursing homes for compliance with federal requirements. This is accomplished through annual or more frequent surveys conducted by trained state inspectors, including a nurse. During an inspection survey, the survey team makes observations, conducts interviews, reviews records and evaluates the facility for compliance with regulatory standards.

There are over 150 regulatory standards that nursing homes are required to meet on a continuous basis. These include a variety of matters such as quality of resident care such as dietary needs, physical or mental abuse, physical plant matters such as fire safety, and resident medical records, to name but a few. Every aspect of the facility, its operation and the care and treatment of residents is under scrutiny, from staffing ratios to meal preparation and delivery.

If, as a result of a survey, the survey team determines that a facility fails to meet a specific regulatory standard or participation requirement, a Statement of Deficiencies is issued. The facility is required to submit a Plan of Correction (POC) in response to the Statement of Deficiencies.

Part of your inquiry into any nursing home should be to review a copy of the facility's last survey report and any plan of correction submitted by the facility in connection with the deficiencies. Don't expect to see a lot of deficiency-free facilities. Bear in mind that just because the facility had findings of deficiencies in their survey does not necessarily mean that it is a bad place.

Interpreting Survey Reports

To be able to understand the survey report, you need to understand some basics about deficiencies, because not all deficiencies are created equally. Deficiencies are classified into 12 categories by (i) scope – how isolated or widespread is the deficiency, and (ii) severity – from no actual harm to immediate jeopardy to health or safety of a resident.

Deficiencies with the letters "A" through "C" equal "substantial compliance" for purposes of participation in Medicare and Medicaid.

Deficiencies "D" and "E" are not great, but not that bad either, indicating no actual harm with a potential for more than minimal harm but not immediate jeopardy; the facility might also be fined.

Starting with "F" through "L", you should be concerned about the level and quality of care at the facility as these are issued only in very severe cases.

In response to the more serious deficiencies starting with "G", the government can impose punitive measures against the facility, such as denial of Medicare and Medicaid payments for new admissions (the life blood of many facilities) and fines called Civil Money Penalties. Deficiencies "J" through "L" can result in a mandated temporary manager being appointed to operate the facility, termination of participation in the Medicare and Medicaid programs and substantial fines and loss of state license. Deficiencies "G", "H" and "I" indicate actual harm to one or more residents but not immediate jeopardy. "J", "K" and "L" indicate immediate jeopardy to resident health or safety.

The Nursing Home Compare feature of the federal Medicare website includes survey information on every nursing home that participates in the Medicare and Medicaid programs. Although this site is not updated as frequently as it should, it does provide some objective data that can be used in assessing the suitability of a home for a loved one. (See **www.medicare.gov**).

Nursing Home Resident Rights

In 1987 the federal Nursing Home Reform Law (Omnibus Budget Reconciliation Act of 1987 – OBRA 1987) was passed by Congress, and has been expanded through the adoption of subsequent amendments. Although this law does not require equality in admissions by nursing home facilities, it does prohibit Medicare and Medicaid discrimination in the admissions process.

Nursing homes -

- are not permitted to require applicants to waive their rights to Medicare or Medicaid benefits, or to provide written or verbal assurances that applicants are not eligible or will not apply for Medicare or Medicaid benefits;

- are required to prominently display at the facility and provide applicants with written information describing the application for and use of government benefits, and how to receive refunds for payments made for covered benefits;

- are prohibited from requiring a third party guaranty of payment as a condition to admission to or continued stay at a facility;

- are prohibited from charging, soliciting, accepting or receiving any gift, money, donation or other consideration as a condition to admittance or expediting the admittance or continued stay of a resident of the facility.

In addition, the federal Nursing Home Reform Law addresses standards of care by requiring facilities to deliver and provide care and services to their residents in a way that enables each resident to attain and maintain the highest practicable physical, mental and psychosocial well being. This is accomplished through regular resident assessments and individualized plans of care.

Facilities are required to conduct a comprehensive assessment of every resident's functional capacity that describes the resident's ability to perform daily life functions, and significant impairments to functional capabilities using standardized measures and identified medical problems. These assessments are required to be conducted within four days of admission to the facility and after significant changes to the resident's physical or mental condition, and, at a minimum, once every 12 months.

Using these assessments, facilities must develop a care plan for each resident, and periodically review and revise these plans. Care plans describe the medical, mental and nursing care needs of a resident and how these needs will be satisfied. They should be prepared by an interdisciplinary team consisting of a physician, registered nurse with responsibility for the resident and the resident or his family or representative, and revised at least once a year after each assessment is conducted.

Specified Resident Rights

Upon admission, each resident is required by law to be provided with a written and oral statement of specified resident rights that are to be preserved and protected by the facility, which include the following:

1. The right to receive admission, treatment and access to care on a non-discriminatory basis, regardless of the source of payment for the care.

2. The right to be free from verbal, mental or physical abuse, corporal punishment and involuntary seclusion. This includes abuse from other residents.

3. The right to be free from the inappropriate use of physical or chemical restraints not required to treat the resident's medical symptoms.

4. The right to access to his or her personal and clinical records upon request by the resident or his legal representative within 24 hours of making such request (excluding weekends and holidays) and to enjoy the privacy and confidentiality given to those records and information, including the right to privacy in their personal communications, to receive mail that is unopened, and to use a telephone in private.

5. The right to participate in his or her care and treatment, to choose a personal physician, to be fully informed in advance about care and treatment and his or her health status, including diagnosis, treatment plan, care decision dilemmas, advance directive options, organ donation and procurement, and an explanation of the risks, benefits and alternatives, and to participate in treatment decisions, including the right to refuse treatment, unless adjudged incompetent or incapacitated.

6. The right to manage his or her financial affairs or permit the facility to hold and manage personal funds, and to be assured that such personal funds are not used to pay for items or services paid for by Medicare or Medicaid. Where the resident gives the facility the right to hold, manage and account for personal funds deposited with the facility, funds over $50 must be deposited into an interest bearing account separate from any of the facility's operating accounts, and the facility must have a system to assure complete and separate accounting.

7. The right to reside and receive services with reasonable accommodation of individual needs and preferences, and to receive notice before there is a change of the resident's room or roommate.

8. The right to voice grievances regarding treatment or care provided, or lack thereof, without reprisal or discrimination for voicing such grievances, and the right to prompt efforts by the facility to resolve the issues.

9. The right to organize and participate in resident groups in the facility, and to meet with family members and families of other residents.

10. The right to examine upon reasonable request the results of the most recent survey of the facility conducted by applicable governmental entities with respect to the facility and any plan of correction submitted by the facility in response to such survey.

11.   The right to refuse a transfer to another room within the facility with a higher level of care.

12.   The right to retain and use personal possessions as space permits provided it does not infringe on the rights, health or safety of other residents

13.   The right to share a room with his or her spouse when married residents reside in the same facility and both spouses consent to the arrangement.

14.   The right to self-administer drugs provided the interdisciplinary team determines this practice to be safe.

15.   The right to refuse to perform services for the facility, or the right to perform services if the resident so chooses.

Resident Abuse

No discussion of nursing homes is complete without briefly touching on the subject of resident abuse. With the threat of the installation of "grannie-cams" in resident rooms, fortunately, this topic is being more freely discussed. However, the reality is that it happens even at the best of homes, and it is rarely a black and white issue.

In order to understand the issue, it must be remembered that there is a delicate balance between the rights and quality of life of a resident and the obligation to protect the resident, other residents and members of the nursing home staff.

Under federal law and guidelines, a nursing home resident has the right to be free from abuse which is defined as the intentional infliction of injury, unreasonable confinement, intimidation, or punishment with resulting physical harm or pain or mental anguish. Abuse includes verbal, sexual, physical and mental abuse and involuntary seclusion.

- Verbal abuse is any oral, written or gestured language that willfully includes disparaging and derogatory terms directed to, or with hearing range of, residents or their families, without regard to their age, disability or ability to understand.

- Sexual abuse includes sexual harassment, sexual coercion or sexual assault.

- Physical abuse includes hitting, slapping, pinching, kicking and corporal punishment.

- Mental abuse includes humiliation, harassment, threats of punishment and deprivation.

- Involuntary seclusion is the separation of a resident from other residents or from his room, or confinement to his room against the resident's or his representative's wishes.

When is something a violation of a resident's rights and abusive, and when is it not in violation of the resident's rights and not abuse? There is sometimes a fine line between the two. As we discussed above, a resident of a nursing home has the right to be free from the inappropriate use of physical or chemical restraints not required to treat the resident's medical symptoms. In the context of abuse, inappropriate use of chemical or physical restraints is often a function of the purpose of the imposition of the restraint – as a disciplinary measure or for the convenience of the staff. Conversely, appropriate use of restraints is not abuse – as a means of protecting the resident or other residents from harm. In fact, the failure of nursing homes to restrain residents (e.g. secure them to their bed or chair) that result in harm to the residents has been the basis of successful lawsuits against nursing homes.

Involuntary seclusion is another example of the tightrope a nursing home must walk when trying to protect residents from harm. A nursing home may separate a resident from other residents or his room for monitored and limited periods of time (less than 24 hours) as a response to an emergency situation or as a therapeutic measure to reduce agitation pending the facility's development of a plan of care to mitigate the underlying cause of the outburst that led to seclusion.

Cognitively impaired residents who reside at facilities with specialized care units designed to limit a resident's mobility within a facility are not considered to be in involuntary seclusion where they or their legal representatives have participated in the decision for placement of the resident in the special unit.

All nursing homes are required to protect residents from abuse, regardless of the source, whether from other residents or from staff members of the nursing home.

In order to protect residents from abuse by employees and staff members, nursing homes are required to develop and implement written policies and procedures that prohibit the mistreatment, neglect, and abuse of residents.

Under federal regulations, all allegations of abuse including injuries of unknown origin must be reported to the Administrator of the facility immediately and to other officials as determined by each state's particular legal requirements. The facility is required to thoroughly investigate all allegations of abuse and to prevent abuse during the investigation. The results of an investigation must be reported to the Administrator and to the applicable government officials as determined by state law, including to the state survey and certification agency, within 5 working days of the incident.

Many states have regulations or laws that require notification of state officials of serious incidents such as injuries to residents or transfers to hospitals as a result of injury or accidents within much shorter periods of time than the 5 days described under the federal Medicare and Medicaid regulations.

Transfers and Discharge

A transfer of a resident is a move to another institution or hospital, and a discharge is the release of a resident to his home.

A facility may discharge or transfer a resident under the following circumstances:

- when necessary for the resident's welfare and the welfare concerns cannot be satisfied in the facility;

- when the resident's health has improved sufficiently so that he no longer requires the services provided by the facility;

- when the safety or health of individuals at the facility is endangered;

- when the resident has failed, after reasonable and appropriate notice, to pay for his residence at and services provided by the facility; and

- when the facility ceases to operate.

A facility must provide notice to the resident and his legal representative or family, if known, of the transfer of the resident, the reason for the transfer, and the circumstances under which he would be permitted to be readmitted to the facility.

At discharge, the facility must provide the resident with a discharge summary that includes a recapitulation of his stay, a final summary of his status at the time of discharge, and a post-discharge plan of care to assist the resident in adjusting to his new living arrangements.

Access to Residents

Subject to the right of the individual to deny or withdraw consent, the facility must provide immediate access to a resident by various governmental representatives, including the Ombudsman, the resident's physician, immediate family or other family members, or any entity or individual that provides health, social, legal or other services to the resident.

Malnutrition and Dehydration

Malnutrition and dehydration are all too common problems of the elderly. It may not be fair to mention it in the context of nursing homes, since many elderly not living in nursing homes also suffer from the condition. But the problem is prominent in nursing homes, even the most expensive, because of the aged and infirm nature of their residents and the duty of the homes to provide nourishment to and a certain quality of care of their residents. In addition, nutrition has a direct impact on skin integrity, the lack of which results in pressure ulcers, and a diminished ability to fight infections, other awful problems associated with non-ambulatory persons.

There are a number of reasons why elderly people do not eat adequately, and many do not realize that they are not eating and drinking enough to sustain their health. Some common physical and emotional causes include medications with appetite suppressing side effects, poor dental health, poorly fitted dentures, difficulty with swallowing, chewing or holding a fork, forgetfulness, depression, grief, dementia, and a host of other medical and emotional problems too numerous to mention.

A nursing home is the caregiver with responsibility for the welfare of its residents, and this includes monitoring and recording their weight and taking steps to identify and deal with unexplained weight loss. Overworked and undereducated staffs are certainly a factor. However, even if you try to charm and cajole, sometimes you just cannot get an elderly person to eat for any one of a number of reasons. It is one of the last things they have absolute control over and sometimes they will refuse to eat just to be difficult.

So what do you do? You watch closely. Weight loss of 5% in 30 days, 7.5% in 90 days, or 10% ever, is considered significant. If you see signs of weight loss, if you can, talk to your Mom or Dad and find out why they are not eating. If it is the taste of the institutionalized food, you can bring food from home or request that the facility's dietician provide more appealing dishes. Talk to their doctor to determine if it is a side effect of some prescribed medication or if there is a medication to enhance their appetite. Talk to the facility's Director of Nursing or Administrator to determine what steps they are taking to monitor and mitigate the situation and their recommendations for treatment.

However, at the end of the day, the question remains, when and where do you draw the line between respecting someone's wishes and dignity and forcing nutrition into their bodies with a feeding tube?

Pressure Ulcers

Persons residing in nursing homes are at a higher risk for the development of pressure or decubitus ulcers, commonly known as bedsores, not because of where they live, but because of the underlying reason that initially required them to be admitted to a skilled nursing care facility. Similar to malnutrition, the occurrence of bedsores is a function of the underlying health of the individual, regardless of whether they reside at home or in a hospital or a skilled nursing care facility.

According to federal regulations, nursing homes must ensure that people who enter the facility without bedsores, do not develop them unless they were unavoidable due to the person's clinical condition. Also, residents with bedsores must receive treatment and services to promote healing, prevent infection and prevent new sores from developing.

There are a number of factors that place a person at risk for pressure sores – age, poor nutrition, lack of mobility, sensory deficits, presence of excessive moisture due to incontinence or perspiration, and the existence of other chronic conditions such as diabetes.

There are four stages of pressure ulcers. Stage I is the least severe with no skin loss, but the skin may be discolored and warm to the touch; Stage II is represented by an abrasion type blister or shallow crater; Stage III is a full lesion or a deep crater with tissue damage; and Stage IV is extensive skin and tissue destruction and may involve damage to muscles and bone. The risk of infection increases with the stage of the ulcer.

Having said all of this, you need to be vigilant about the skin condition of loved ones who are bedridden due to age or illness, whether they reside in nursing homes or not. In a nursing home environment, you should be able to better monitor the situation as the nursing facility must maintain applicable written records and should have protocols in place for the prevention and treatment of these types of ulcers. The real trick here is to prevent them, which in actuality is easier said than done when dealing with aged and infirm persons. Certainly, if your loved one is at risk, then his care plan at the nursing home should address these issues and the measures being implemented by the staff to avoid or mitigate this risk.

Nursing Home Documents and Buzz Words

There are some documents that are unique to the long term care industry as result of federal reimbursement and regulation. You may need to know them in connection with monitoring a loved one's condition and care while at a nursing home.

Sometimes, usually in connection with the care plan developed for a resident, you may hear the term "RUG Rates" which describes the level of care received by a nursing home resident. This is an acronym for Resource Utilization Groups and is a factor used in determining the amount of compensation a home will receive from government programs such as Medicaid for caring for a resident.

There are 44 Resource Utilization Groups that are based on clinical and other information that is collected about a resident using an assessment tool called the minimum data set (MDS). The purpose of an MDS is to produce a comprehensive, accurate, and standardized assessment of a nursing home resident's functional capacity. This process is required by federal law to be done shortly after admission to a facility and then periodically unless there is a significant change in the resident's condition requiring reassessment.

There are also "Resident Assessment Protocols" or RAPs which are used by facilities to develop care plans for specific problems, such as nutrition. These are triggered by certain findings that result from the MDS process.

On a quarterly and annual basis, federal law also requires that parts of a resident's MDS be reassessed in order to identify changes in the resident's condition. As a result of these reassessments, the facility nursing staff is able to determine if a resident's care plan needs to be revised.

If you are a nursing home operator, you care about the RUG rates and MDS's of your residents as your government reimbursement is based on these criteria.

If you are a nursing home resident on Medicare or Medicaid, how much the nursing home gets paid for the care it provides probably seems of little concern to you. On the practical side, it can directly impact the quality of care that you receive – the less money the home receives from these government programs can bear directly on the amount and quality of care that a resident receives.

If you have power of attorney and are responsible for the supervision of care of a loved one in a nursing home, you may need to request copies of these documents so that you may have an appropriate medical professional assess the care being received by your loved one.

Chapter 6

Who is going to pay for this? Sources of Payment for Care

The alternatives for payment of long term care expenses are pretty simple.

A person can anticipate personally paying for all of his potential long term care costs (which may run the gamut from home health care to skilled nursing care in a nursing home for an indeterminate period of time), and, in effect, self-insure against the financial risk. For someone who is unable to purchase long term care insurance due to health or age, and/or who has substantial financial resources over which he does not wish to lose control or which will not be severely diminished as a result of the possibility of personally paying for these types of health care costs, this is not an unreasonable plan.

In the alternative, a person can insure against the financial risk by purchasing appropriate long term care insurance coverage. Here there are two things to consider – the ability to qualify for the purchase of this type of coverage, and the annual cost of premiums. Again, with nursing home costs averaging about $6,000 per month, and the average annual premium for someone in their seventies being in the range of $6,000 to $10,000+, this option should be seriously considered by folks who can afford the insurance costs and who qualify for coverage.

If, however, you or your parents expect that the government is going to pay for their long term care needs, think again.

Medicare will pay virtually nothing toward the costs of long term care.

Medicaid will pay for everything, but the price may be a lot higher than you ever anticipated. Medicaid IS welfare, and, for a lot of hardworking folks who were never dependent on government handouts, the idea of going on welfare is more than they can handle.

Medicare v. Medicaid:
Centers for Medicare & Medicaid Services

Medicare and Medicaid are not the same.

Medicare, an entitlement program, is a federal health insurance program for all elderly and disabled Americans, administered by the Centers for Medicare & Medicaid Services (CMS), formerly known as the Health Insurance Financing Administration (HCFA). This agency has been overseeing the day-to-day administration of the Medicare and Medicaid programs since 1977. As a result of the overhaul in 2001, the agency now splits its responsibilities among three centers, two of which are new - the Center for Medicare Management (CMM) and the Center for Beneficiary Choices (CBC), and the existing Center for Medicaid & State Operations (CMSO).

Medicare does not pay for the cost of long term care in a nursing home facility, but will pay for the costs of rehabilitation in such a facility for finite periods of time after a hospital stay.

Medicaid, a welfare program, is a joint state and federal health benefits assistance and medical services program for Americans who qualify based on financial and medical need. Determinations of eligibility are made by local county assistance or aging offices. (The Administration on Aging website has a locator database to help you find your local Area Agency on Aging – there are over 650 of them in the U.S.).

The basic qualifications for Medicaid include –

- U.S citizenship or resident alien status,

- residence in the state where application for benefits is to be made,

- age 65, or disabled or blind,
- care deemed to be medically necessary, and
- countable (as opposed to excluded and not available to pay for care) financial resources of not more than $2,000 ($2,400 for those who are 65 or older), or they must be eligible to receive Supplemental Security Income, a needs based program with strict income and resource availability requirements.

If someone qualifies, Medicaid will pay for all or part of the costs of long term care in a nursing home facility based on a person's income and the medical assistance payment rate for a specific nursing home. Medicaid, however, pays nothing toward assisted living or personal care homes (except for a couple of states that have sought a waiver. This is discussed later).

What does Medicare cover and when?
Medicare Part A Coverage and Eligibility

Medicare Part A is the federal hospital insurance benefit program that pays for medically necessary care consisting of

- inpatient hospital services,
- post-hospital extended care services (skilled nursing home services);
- certain limited home health services, and
- hospice care.

Medicare is a fee for service health care plan, and unless someone chooses to join a Medicare managed care plan with a private insurance company, they will automatically be a participant in Medicare upon turning 65 years old. No premiums are paid for this coverage as long as the individual or his spouse worked and paid Medicare taxes.

For a hospital stay during each Benefit Period (see discussion below for a description of a Benefit Period), the Medicare recipient must pay a total of

- $792 for a hospital stay of 60 days;
- $198 per day co-payment for days 61-90; and
- $396 per day co-payment for days 91 through 150 (every Medicare recipient is entitled to 60 lifetime reserve days at no additional charge. It is these additional co-insurance or deductible costs that a Medigap policy is designed to help pay.)

Medicare Part B Coverage and Eligibility

Medicare Part B is a Supplemental Medical Insurance Program (and is not the same as Medigap Insurance). It is a voluntary program and eligible individuals need to enroll in order to receive the Part B services consisting of

- "medically necessary" physician services,
- outpatient hospital services,
- durable medical equipment,
- laboratory services,
- therapy services, and
- radiology services.

During the 7 month period beginning 3 months before someone turns 65 and continuing for 4 months after they turn 65, they can enroll for Part B benefits and lock in the cost of their premium. After this window of 7 months, a person can still enroll but at a higher cost. With Part B, a monthly premium of $50 (during 2001) is required to be paid. Usually, for those who enroll, this amount is deducted from their Social Security payment. By the way, you can sign up for Medicare Part B by visiting your local Social Security office or calling the Social Security Administration at 1-800-772-1213.

What Doesn't Medicare Cover?

Services *not* covered by Medicare include

- Lower levels of care (sometimes called "custodial care" such as assistance with walking, bathing, dressing, taking medications) in institutionalized settings or at home

- Private duty nursing care

- 24 hour a day care

- Home delivered meals

- Housekeeping/homemaker services including shopping, cleaning and laundry

- Most outpatient prescription drugs

- Most dental care and dentures

- Hearing aids

- Routine eye and foot care

- Eyeglasses (except after cataract surgery)

- Health care while outside of the United States (except under limited circumstances.)

Medicare and Long Term Care

Medicare covers a very small percentage, probably less than 3%, of the cost of long term care, and Medigap insurance is not designed to pick up coverage for long term care. Medicare pays $0 on account of long term "custodial" care, the kind of care that most people in nursing homes require.

In other words, you cannot check yourself into a nursing home and expect Medicare to pay for anything. However, when you have been discharged *to* a nursing home *from* a hospital after a minimum three consecutive day stay and have been determined to be in need of therapeutic or restorative services, Medicare will pay the cost of nursing home care for a limited period of time. Your physician upon discharge from a hospital must actually prescribe a stay in a skilled nursing home in order to have Medicare Part A pick up the tab.

If these conditions are met, Medicare Part A kicks in and will pay for just about everything (except television and phone) including nursing services, bed and board, therapies, drugs, and related supplies for a finite period of time, a maximum of 100 days per Benefits Period in a skilled nursing home as listed below. (See below for a discussion of a Benefits Period.)

- 100% for days 1 though 20
- 100% except for $99 per day coinsurance payment for days 21 through 100
- From day 101, Medicare pays 0%.

In other words, for a stay at a skilled nursing home (following at least 3 days in a hospital) for each Benefit Period, the **Medicare recipient must pay**

- $0 for the first 20 days (no need for a Medicare supplemental or Medigap policy at this point);

- up to $99 per day for days 21 through 100 (this co-pay is required by federal law to be covered by all Medigap policies as a Basic Benefit for those who have purchased Medigap coverage); and

- all costs beyond the 100th day of the Benefit Period.

Medicare At Home

Medicare will pay for certain home health benefits such as therapy and health aide services provided in one's home, as well as durable medical equipment (DME) such as a hospital bed, wheel chair, walker, portable toilet, again, if

- it is in conjunction with a hospital stay of at least three days, perhaps followed by a stay in a Medicare qualified nursing home, and

- prescribed by a physician, and

- the commencement of the home care services is within 14 days of discharge from the hospital or nursing home.

To qualify for these home health benefits, the Medicare beneficiary must meet the following criteria:

- Be housebound

- Have a doctor's order for the care or DME needed and a care plan

- Require at least one of either intermittent skilled nursing care or Physical Therapy or Occupational Therapy, and

- Use a home health aide or equipment provider that is a Medicare certified provider.

As for the home health aide, don't get your hopes up. This benefit is very limited. It will only pay for part time (less than 8 hours a day) and intermittent (less than 7 days a week) care for usually a few weeks at best. It is by no means a long term care solution.

For these services, the Medicare recipient pays $0 for the home health care services, and 20% of the Medicare approved amount for the durable medical equipment (which amount is required to be covered by all Medigap policies as part of basic coverage but does not include the $100 annual deductible.)

Medicare Benefits Periods

Confused? Well, there are even more rules to know. Medicare benefits are paid on the basis of what is called a Benefit Period. The beginning of a Benefit Period is the first day someone who is eligible for Medicare is admitted into a hospital and terminates when they are out of the hospital or the skilled nursing home facility for 60 consecutive days. A period of 60 days without a re-hospitalization must elapse before a new Benefits Period begins, and the 100 days discussed above begins to run again, and the deductible amount must be paid again. If someone is re-hospitalized in less than the sixty day period, their benefits entitlement from their previous hospitalization are counted towards the 100 day maximum, but there is no additional deductible to pay. There is no statutory limit on the number of Benefits Period that can occur in a year.

The majority of people entering a skilled nursing facility following a hospital stay are discharged from the nursing home or rehabilitation facility prior the expiration of the 100 day period on the basis that they have reached a maximum level of improvement. The nursing home should notify the resident or their family that the Medicare coverage is exhausted. At that point, unless the person is Medicaid eligible, financial arrangements will need to be made if the person is to continue to reside at the facility, either through private pay or benefits under a long term care insurance policy. As a general rule, if Medicare benefits have been exhausted, then the Medigap insurance is probably not paying benefits either. You're on your own dime now.

Medigap Insurance

Medigap insurance is just what it sounds like – insurance that covers the gaps in Medicare Parts A and B coverage, such as the co-insurance amounts. For someone enrolled in a Medicare Managed Care plan or HMO, a Medigap policy is unnecessary as it will pay no benefits except in conjunction with standard Medicare.

In all states except Massachusetts, Minnesota or Wisconsin, there are ten standard policies, Plans A through J, with differing combinations of benefits and costs. Obviously, the greater the number of benefits, the higher the monthly premium, starting at about $100 per month for basic Medigap Plan A.

Basic or Plan A Medigap Coverage

By federal law, all Medigap plans, that is, Plans A through J, must include the basic minimum benefits consisting of

- Medicare Part A Co-payments for
  Days 1-60 $0
  Days 61-90 $198 per day
  Days 91-150 and 60
  lifetime reserve days $396 per day
  Coverage for 365 additional lifetime days after termination of Medicare benefits

- Medicare Part B co-pay of 20% of Medicare approved expenses

- The first three pints of blood per year

In addition, all Medigap plans must

- guaranty renewability,
- eliminate waiting periods for pre-existing conditions for replacement policies, and
- cover pre-existing conditions after a maximum waiting period of 6 months.

Medigap Plans B through J - Additional Coverage

Medigap Plans B through J provide for all of the Basic Benefits described in the preceding section on Medigap Plan A coverage, and a variety of additional benefits that may include

- Medicare Part A deductible (Medigap Plans B and above)
- The skilled nursing care co-payment for days 21 through 100 in a skilled nursing facility (Medigap Plans C and above)
- Foreign travel emergency medical services, up to 80% of the costs and a lifetime maximum benefit of $50,000 (Medigap Plans C and above)
- Prescription drug discounts and discounts for vision, hearing and other medical care (Medigap Plans C and above)
- Medicare Part B deductible (Medigap Plans C, F and J)
- Home health care (certified by a doctor pursuant to a Medicare approved home treatment plan for personal care only during a recovery from illness) of up to $40 per visit for up to seven visits per week and an annual maximum (Medigap Plans D, G, I and J)

- Basic Drug Benefit pays for 50% (after $250 deductible) of basic out-patient prescription drugs up to a maximum annual benefit of $1,250 (Medigap Plans H and I) or a maximum annual benefit of $3,000 (Medigap Plan J)

- Preventive medical care (for example, flu shots, rectal exams, mammograms ordered by a physician) up to a maximum amount of $120 per year (Plans E and J).

As you can see from the above, Plan J is the top of the line policy, as it includes all of the basic and all of the additional benefits.

The Medicare website (**www.medicare.gov**) has a valuable interactive search tool called Medigap Compare that allows you to compare various plans that are pertinent to your geographic area, and can help you locate and contact insurance companies in your state that sell Medigap insurance.

Medicare v. Managed Care?
Medicare + (plus) Choice

Well, no discussion of Medicare is complete without touching on the private insurers that contract with the government to provide health insurance coverage for the Medicare eligible.

You can do nothing, and you will automatically be covered by Medicare starting at age 65. (Don't forget that you still need to make a decision about Part B Medicare coverage and enroll during a 7-month window around the 65th birthday.)

Or, you have the right to opt out of Medicare as your health care provider and join a Medicare Managed Care (HMO) plan provided by a private health insurance company. Here Medicare pays an insurance company a set amount of money each month, and the insurance company becomes responsible for the payment of the benefits that you would receive under both Parts A and B of Medicare.

Since the variables are too numerous to mention, we will simply urge you to check out any other private plans (their benefits, their costs, their financial stability, their claims history and a host of other factors) with extreme caution before you forgo your Medicare coverage. Although there may be perceived benefits (prescription drug coverage), there are also compensating factors, such as finding physicians and hospitals that accept the Medicare Managed Care plan you may select.

The Medicare website (**www.medicare.gov**) has a valuable interactive search tool called Medicare Health Plan Compare that allows you to compare various plans that are pertinent to your geographic area. For further information, you may want to refer to the Appendix where we have reproduced from the Medicare website the description of Medicare Plan Choices.

Long Term Care Insurance

Long term care insurance is becoming an increasingly popular insurance product. The purpose of this insurance is what it sounds like - to provide a means of payment for long term care when it is required due to chronic illness or a condition such as Alzheimer's Disease, shifting the risk of loss from the individual or family to an insurance company. This type of coverage also makes someone more attractive as a prospective resident to a nursing home as the home has a guaranteed source of payment and at the higher private pay (not Medicaid) rates.

If, for any reason, you or you parents are uncomfortable with the idea of being dependent on Medicaid for financing long term care or your parents (like many senior citizens of modest means) refuse to shelter or gift out their assets so as to qualify for Medicaid benefits and (and I stress the word "and") they have sufficient income to pay the somewhat substantial annual premiums and can qualify for the purchase of this type of coverage, then a long term care insurance policy should absolutely be considered.

As a result of the Health Insurance Portability and Accountability Act of 1996 (HIPAA), there are long term care insurance policies that are Tax Qualified which means that the benefits received are not taxable as ordinary income for federal income tax purposes, and the premiums paid may be included as part of the insured's medical deduction.

The purchase of long term care insurance policy is usually not contingent on a medical exam, but is issued on the basis of a review of the medical records of the proposed beneficiary. It is better to purchase this type of insurance at an earlier age because the older one gets, the more likely someone will be found uninsurable due to declining health, or, if deemed insurable, the cost of a policy goes up. Nevertheless, even at the highest level, an annual premium will still be substantially less than the cost of nursing home care for a one-year period, and usually is roughly equivalent to the cost of one to two months at a nursing home. Also, ask about discounts that are sometimes made available when spouses purchase coverage together, or when a healthy person purchases coverage.

One of the most important aspects of policy coverage is guaranteed renewability. Do not buy a policy where the insured can be dropped except for non-payment of the premium. And the policy should provide that the requirement to pay the premium is waived when the insured begins to receive benefits.

Usually long term care policies anticipate coverage for care received outside of a hospital setting, such as care in a nursing home, or home health care at home or in a personal care home or assisted living facility.

A long term care policy should cover all levels of care. In the order of lowest to highest, the levels of care are "custodial" which is the type of care most residents of nursing homes receive, "intermediate" and "skilled".

The qualification for receipt of benefits, or the policy's trigger, is usually based on medical necessity. This may be defined as the inability to perform a couple or more activities of daily life without assistance, such as bathing, dressing, etc. Or, it may be a function of a cognitive impairment that hampers or prevents the performance of certain activities of daily life. For tax-qualified status (meaning that the payment of benefits is non-taxable to the insured), one of the triggers must be a certification that the insured requires assistance with two or more activities of daily life.

You are going to have to shop around for the policy that is best for your needs and budget. Policies differ in terms of the nature of services covered, the location where services are to be delivered, the duration of benefits, and when and under what circumstances benefits will be triggered.

Most policies also contain a number of variables that will affect the price of the coverage and the amount of the premiums. Here are a number, some of which we have already touched upon, that you should consider when purchasing coverage –

- *Guaranteed renewability* – a guarantee that the policy will not be terminated, non-renewed or cancelled, as long as the premiums are being paid, due to the declining health of the insured or the age of the insured.

- *Waiver of Premium* – the obligation to pay premiums is waived while insured is receiving benefits of the policy.

- *Daily Benefits* - the amount of the daily benefits payable may vary from $50 a day (which will not cover much in a nursing home setting) on up. Expect that daily benefits for home care will be substantially less than daily benefits for nursing home care.

- **Inflation protection** - though it may cost more, this feature is worth serious consideration as this will increase, or mitigate a decrease in, the amount of the benefits over time. This can be accomplished as a fixed percentage or a compounded basis, which costs more. This option should also allow the insured to increase the benefit level from time to time without the need to provide evidence of insurability.

- **Elimination Period** - the length of the elimination period, comparable to a deductible, from 0 days to 365 days. Obviously, the longer the elimination period before the benefits are payable, the lower the cost of the policy.

- **Coverage Period** – this is usually in terms of the number of years that the policy will pay benefits, from 1 year through lifetime coverage. Again, the longer the coverage period, the more expensive the policy.

- **Nature of Coverage** – nursing home care, with or without other possible venues and types of care such as home health services, homemaker or companion services, personal care, assisted living facility, adult day care, and the like.

- **Nonforfeiture Benefits** – this provision comes into play when someone ceases to pay premiums before they have begun to receive benefits under the policy. With this type of provision, the insured will receive some value for the money they have paid into the policy, either through reduced coverage or benefit period, or a return of premium. This benefit can substantially increase the amount of premiums payable for the coverage.

Some other optional features to be considered include –

- No requirement that insured be hospitalized prior to receipt of benefits for nursing home or home health care

- No requirement that the insured be receiving skilled nursing home care before receipt of benefits for lower levels of care such as custodial or home health care

- Number of deductibles required to be paid – a single lifetime deductible is best

- Coverage without a waiting period for pre-existing conditions that are disclosed on the insurance application

- Coverage for home health or nursing home care should not be limited to skilled care but should include coverage for custodial care (assistance with ADL's such as bathing, usually the first ADL with which a person requires assistance)

- The right to cancel and receive a full refund within 30 days of purchase.

You also need to do your homework with respect to the insurance company writing the policy. There is a lot of competition in the market place for this type of product and not all insurance carriers are created equally. You will want to know about their payment history on claims, and how long they have been writing this type of insurance. You will want to know their financial strength which is a function of their ratings such as through Standard and Poors or A.M. Best Co. as you want a company that will still be in business when a claim is made down the road. And you should find out more about their history of rate and price increases. The list of websites at the end of this book includes sites for a number of insurance rating bureaus.

Hospice Care and Medicare

Here we are in the middle of a chapter that discusses Medicare and Medigap and ways to pay for health care and we are switching gears to discuss hospice care. Why this digression? Because Medicare will pay for most hospice patient care. The nature of this type of care program will be handled in more detail later.

Briefly, hospice care is for the terminally ill, those persons with less than 6 months of life. This type of care, which is designed to comfort, and not treat in an effort to cure, the terminally ill, can be provided in a hospital, skilled nursing home or at home, or anywhere in between. But more on that later. Let's talk about Medicare coverage.

The federal regulations require that a qualified hospice program include an interdisciplinary team consisting of a doctor, registered nurse, medical social worker and pastoral or other counselor. In order to be eligible for reimbursement by Medicare, the hospice provider must create a plan of care for the patient that is implemented and maintained by the hospice team's medical director, all of the members of the interdisciplinary team and the patient's family.

Medicare will pay for a wide variety of components that make up a hospice program, including intermittent nursing care; doctors; medical social services; physical, speech and occupational therapy; counseling including dietary and spiritual; home health aides and homemaker services; drugs (except for a small co-pay); medical supplies and durable equipment; respite for caregivers and continuous care for the patient; trained volunteers and bereavement services.

Medicare recipients must elect hospice care, the result of which is that they agree to forgo traditional medical/hospital treatment and efforts to cure their condition. This election is made by the patient filing an "election statement" with the hospice provider. The patient, directly or though his representative, is required through the election statement to acknowledge that s/he understands that the hospice will provide palliative and not curative care for the terminally ill patient. The hospice election can be revoked at any time by filing a signed and dated statement of revocation, and full Medicare hospitalization benefits will then resume. However, the Medicare recipient will not be able to resume hospice care until the expiration of the hospice period, which cannot be more than 6 months, since a hospice period totals 240 days.

Medicare coverage for hospice care is divided into four time periods theoretically totaling 240 days. There are two periods of 90 days, a third period of 30 days and the final period of 30 days or more. So even though the program is designed to begin and end in a 240-day period, hospice will continue until the patient actually dies, provided that they are still periodically found to be eligible (still terminally ill according to their attending physician) and as long as they have not revoked hospice care as we discussed above.

At the end of each of the first three periods, a patient is reevaluated to determine if s/he is still eligible for the hospice care benefit. Eligibility is determined by a diagnosis of a terminal illness certified by a physician. The patient also needs to be qualified to receive Medicare Part A benefits in order to be eligible for hospice benefits.

So what do I do now?

Well, having examined the ways to finance long term care, what do you do if you have a parent of modest means who cannot afford (or want to pay) the annual premiums of from $6,000 to $10,000 per year for long term care insurance, or who cannot qualify for this type of insurance regardless of cost? Although the annual premium is roughly equivalent to one to two months in a nursing home, if your folks rely on Social Security benefits and have perhaps a small portfolio of investments that throw off some additional income, there still is probably no or little wiggle room in their fixed income for this type of coverage. Medicaid planning may be your only hope of salvaging any of their estate.

Medicaid Eligibility

Well, if you thought Medicare was confusing, wait until we get through the Medicaid rules on eligibility. That requires its own chapter.

Chapter 7

Financial and Medicaid Planning:

What You Need To Know About Shifting the Cost of Long Term Care

Dad at age 82 has finally reached the point where nursing home care is no longer just an option to consider. He has been diagnosed with a number of chronic conditions none of which are terminal but since your Mother passed away, there is no one in a position to care for him and he can no longer live alone. He owns a house worth $100,000, and stocks and bonds of $50,000. He has no long term care insurance. He has another bout of congestive heart failure and goes into the hospital for treatment and is then discharged to a nursing home for rehabilitation. You then realize that he cannot go back to his home alone, and he cannot live with you for a number of reasons. You learn from the nursing home that Medicare will stop paying benefits because he has reached a level where no further rehabilitation is justified, and, because of his assets, he is not eligible for Medicaid. If he wants to stay at the nursing home, he will be required to liquidate and dissipate his assets for the payment of his care. At around $72,000 per year, he will have enough money to privately pay for about two years of nursing home care before he is eligible for Medicaid. He becomes distraught with the idea that everything he and your Mom worked so hard to accumulate will have to be spent on his care. He had wanted you and your children to have a little something when he passed away and he now realizes that he most likely will die a pauper, ultimately dependent on welfare (Medicaid) for his end of life care, should he outlive his resources. And you and your kids will get $0.

Well, even though it may be too late to plan for long term care, there are some options and that is explored in this chapter. (For one answer to the dilemma we just described, see "Half a Loaf" Gifting below.)

Medicaid Planning

Although we are going to give you the basics, this is like those crazy stunts you see on television with the warning "Don't Try This At Home". You are going to want to speak with someone with expertise in Medicaid financial planning in order to properly develop a plan that will work for your parents and their assets, and conforms to the Medicaid rules of the state where your parents will seek eligibility, and is consistent with their overall estate plan.

Just because your parents have done financial planning from an estate tax, inheritance tax or gift tax point of view, that type of financial planning does not necessarily include and may actually be at cross purposes from a Medicaid planning point of view. If a long term care life insurance policy is not in the cards due to cost or ineligibility or otherwise, your parents should consider restructuring the ownership of their assets, unless they are financially able and emotionally prepared to personally fund all costs of their long term care.

All of this is of real significance to those seniors of modest means; with the average cost of nursing home care being in the range of $70,000 a year, it will take little time to consume every dime of a senior citizen's nest egg for nursing home care. Most parents want to leave something behind for their kids and grandkids. However, they might not be able to do this if some catastrophic illness or chronic condition strikes and they are not financially prepared.

Essentially, Medicaid planning anticipates that someone eventually may need long term health care in a skilled nursing home, and they do not want their hard earned assets to be fully dissipated before being able to utilize Medicaid benefits. After years of working hard to accumulate and preserve assets, a potential Medicaid applicant must shift gears completely and seek ways to:

- eliminate (or spend down) assets, or

- transform countable assets into non-countable or excluded assets, or

- transfer ownership of countable assets.

It is like tax planning – it is no longer illegal and has never been immoral to structure your affairs so that the government either does not eat it up with estate taxes at your death or require you to dissipate it for your care before your death. In some situations and for some families, it just makes good business sense especially since the average nursing home can cost about $6,000 per month, and the average life span continues to increase as medical technology finds even more ways to extend life.

(Fortunately, in 1996 the "Granny Goes to Jail" law (Section 217 of the Health Insurance Portability and Accountability Act of 1996 (HIPAA), 42 U.S.C. Section 1320(a)(6)) was repealed. The lawyer or other advisor then became at risk under Section 4737 of the Balanced Budget Act of 1997 (42 U.S.C. Section 1320a7(a)(6))– the "Granny's Attorney Goes to Jail" provision making it illegal if someone for a fee knowingly and willfully assisted another to become eligible for Medicaid benefits. Although it is still on the books as a criminal offense, this law was held unconstitutional in violation of the First Amendment Freedom of Speech in <u>New York State Bar Association v. Reno</u>, No. 97-CV-1760 (N.D.NY 1998).)

First, let me say that although good planning should be done before someone actually is in need of nursing home care, it is nevertheless possible to shelter assets after someone enters a home. There are "look back" periods for asset transfers for less than fair market value, or gifts, and transfers in trust, and transfer penalties to calculate as determined by your state's law. But, if you are dealing with an estate, even if modest, it is still possible to perhaps salvage some resources. We will take a more detailed look into this later in this chapter.

In the following chapter, we will refer sometimes to the "Institutionalized Spouse" and the "Community Spouse". For Medicaid purposes the "Institutionalized Spouse" is someone who is institutionalized in a hospital or nursing home for at least 30 consecutive days and is married to someone who is not institutionalized but who lives in the community. The "Community Spouse" is the spouse of an Institutionalized Spouse".

Medicaid Basics
Excluded and Available Assets

But first things first – the Medicaid basics. The primary rule is that all non-excluded assets, income and resources are to be considered available to pay for care in determining someone's eligibility for Medicaid benefits.

Assets that an applicant or applicant's spouse has the beneficial use of, whether owned or not, are, unless specifically exempted, "available resources" (or countable) that must be "spent down" to not more than $2,000 before someone is eligible for Medicaid. In the case of those deemed to be "Categorically Needy", that is, age 65 or older, blind or disabled and who is eligible for Supplemental Security Income (SSI) which is a needs based program with strict income and resource eligibility tests, the maximum amount is $2,400.

Resources, including income, are defined by state law but essentially include any real or personal property (not credit) which someone can use or make available for partial or total support, including partial or beneficial interests in property.

Available (or Countable) Resources include:

- Cash or cash equivalents, including checking, savings, Christmas Club, Vacation Club and credit union accounts, certificates of deposit, money market accounts, stocks, bonds, trust funds, savings bonds, mutual funds, loans, mortgages, annuities, and the like of more than $2,000

- Real estate other than a primary residence

- Business interests including limited partnership interests and partnerships

- Personal property including motor vehicles, boats, trailers

- Cash value of whole life insurance policies of more than $1,500

- Viatical settlements of life insurance, that is, selling or assigning the policy to a third party at a discount in order to "pre-pay" the death benefit prior to the death of the insured

- Pension plan and other retirement benefits, including IRA's, 401ks, Keoghs, veterans' benefits

- Revocable trusts

- Certain irrevocable trusts where a nursing home resident or spouse is designated discretionary income or principal beneficiary

- Reverse mortgages

- Inheritances.

The Medicaid application process requires the disclosure of the above types of assets, and other information such as the title and ownership of the assets and value.

So what's "exempt?"

"Exempt" means that the government will not count the resource as available for purposes of determining eligibility. However, if any of the following "exempt" property is sold, transferred or conveyed while someone is receiving Medicaid benefits, the proceeds of the sale are not exempt but instead become resources available to pay for the cost of care.

- One residential property occupied by the applicant, applicant's spouse, dependent relative or disabled child, or occupied by the unmarried applicant if the applicant intends to return home

- One automobile

- Life insurance policies having no cash surrender value (that is, Term Life Insurance); or life insurance policies having a cash surrender value but not exceeding a total face value of $1,500; or if the total face value is more than $1,500, then a total cash surrender value of $1,000 is excluded and the rest is included

- Prepaid (irrevocable) burial fund; burial spaces and marker for applicant and applicant's immediate family, revocable burial reserve of up to $1,500 reduced by certain insurance policy amounts

- Household goods and personal effects including clothing, jewelry, recreational equipment, musical instruments, hobby items, and certain other property including tools, equipment and uniforms used in connection with applicant's or applicant's spouse or dependent's employment or self-support without regard to value

- Pension funds (IRA, 401k) and other deferred compensation retirement funds owned by and other income received by applicant's spouse who remains in the community

- Community Spouse's Resource Allowance (CSRA) (more on this below) and Community Spouse's Minimum Monthly Maintenance Needs Allowance (MMMNA) (more below)
- Certain irrevocable trusts.

Well, there's exempt and then there's exempt. For instance, a home used as a primary residence by an applicant (without a Community Spouse) is exempt *if* the applicant plans to return to the home after receiving nursing home care. What that means is that the value of the residence will not be counted for purposes of determining Medicaid eligibility. If, however, the applicant never returns to the residence and dies after a stay in the nursing home on Medicaid's dime or receipt of other Medicaid benefits, then an amount up to the fair market value of the home may be subject to recapture by the State from the estate of the Medicaid beneficiary for the cost of the nursing home care or other benefits paid by Medicaid.

Remember that eligibility for receipt of Medicaid benefits does not mean that the government will never scarf up the value of the exempt or excluded assets. It just means that the State will not factor in the fair market value of the excluded assets in determining eligibility for receipt of Medicaid benefits at the get-go. Instead, the State will wait until the Medicaid recipient has died and those assets have become part of the recipient's estate, and then the State will move in for the kill in a matter of speaking under various State estate recovery laws.

What about Asset Transfers before a Medicaid application is filed?

Look Back Dates and Look Back Periods

Well, if you are going to transfer assets of a potential Medicaid applicant, you need to time it properly.

Assets transferred to an individual for less than "fair market value" (gifts) in the 36 months prior to the date of the Medicaid application must be disclosed on the application, and may create a period of ineligibility determined by a mathematical formula. (By the way, you don't want to lie on these application forms.)

Transfers, or contributions, of assets to a trust have a 60-month "look back" period for purposes of determining the ineligibility period.

The "look back date" is the date that is either (1) 36 months for transfers to individuals (this number can be increased by a State), or (2) 60 months for transfers to a trust, before the first date as of which the applicant is both institutionalized for thirty consecutive days *and* has applied for medical assistance (sometimes called the "baseline date"). So, in other words, the "look back period" is the period that begins with the look back date and ends with the baseline date.

Spousal Transfers

Transfers of assets to a spouse are not subject to transfer penalties and cause no period of ineligibility for the Institutionalized Spouse seeking Medicaid benefits. For example, provided that Medicaid eligibility has been established for the Institutionalized Spouse, the transfer of the principal residence, owned jointly by the Institutionalized Spouse and the Community Spouse, to the Community Spouse alone enables the Community Spouse to retain 100% of the sale proceeds when the home is sold, or pass to the heirs of the Community Spouse should the

Community Spouse die before the death of the Institutionalized Spouse.

However, if the Community Spouse owns 100% of the primary residence and dies before the Institutionalized Spouse, the real property may transfer back to the Institutionalized Spouse under the Community Spouse's will, or the Institutionalized Spouse may be attributed under state estate laws to have what is known as an "elective share" interest even if the Community Spouse has named other beneficiaries. This unwanted inheritance could render them ineligible for Medicaid.

In addition to transferring some jointly held assets to the Community Spouse, another Medicaid planning strategy to avoid transfer penalties is to use or "spend down" cash or other liquid assets to purchase excluded resources (such as a new automobile for the Community Spouse), or to enhance the value of excluded assets (necessary repairs to the family residence, pay off the mortgage for the home), or a purchase of an asset for the sole benefit of the Community Spouse for fair value (payment of an entry fee for a continuing care community where the Community Spouse will reside, or an annuity, if your particular state permits.)

The potential benefits of spousal transfers can outweigh the potential pitfalls, and, because of these Medicaid rules, it is often prudent to consider the transfer of various jointly held assets to the Community Spouse. Just make sure that the Institutionalized Spouse has been "disinherited" by the spouse or other relatives so that Medicaid eligibility is not interrupted by an unwanted inheritance.

At the risk of being redundant, remember that you have to be careful with spousal transfers, and should definitely consult with an elder or health care law attorney in your State about these issues.

Other Exempt Transfers of a Principal Residence

Besides transfers to a spouse, a Medicaid beneficiary can also transfer his or her principal residence without suffering a period of ineligibility if the transfer is to –

- A child under age 21 or a child at any age who is blind or disabled

- A sibling who has an equity interest in the property and who has resided there for at least one year immediately prior to the date the Medicaid beneficiary is institutionalized

- An adult child who has lived with and provided care for the Medicaid beneficiary for at least 2 years before institutionalization.

What is fair market value?

According to the State Medicaid Manual published by the federal government, "fair market value" is an estimate of the value of an asset if sold at the prevailing price at the time it was transferred. The state is directed to use the same criteria in establishing the value of transferred assets as it does in assessing Medicaid eligibility of an applicant. If an asset is transferred for some "valuable consideration" even if less than fair market value, then the value or amount of the valuable consideration is used to determine the "uncompensated" fair market value.

So what is "valuable consideration"?

"Valuable consideration" essentially means that the person transferring the asset, in exchange for his or her right in the transferred asset, has received some act, object, service or other benefit having a tangible or intrinsic value to the transferor. Therefore, no period of ineligibility will result if liquid assets (cash and cash equivalent) are spent to make improvements to the principal residence, purchase excluded resources such a new automobile for the Community

Spouse, prepay funeral arrangements, or pay entry fees for the Community Spouse to move into a retirement community. These types of expenditures can hasten the Medicaid eligibility of an Institutionalized Spouse. But be attentive to the timing of these expenditures – you may want to wait until after someone has been admitted to a nursing home so that the Community Spouse's "Resource Allowance" (more on this topic later) is not diminished as a result of these expenditures.

The Medicaid Manual specifically disclaims transfers for "love" as not involving valuable consideration. The government presumes that care provided by members of the family are provided for free, that is, without valuable consideration, so a transfer to a relative (not a spouse) for care provided in the past is a transfer of assets for less than fair market value.

Since relatives can legitimately be compensated for these types of caregiving services, it then is up to the applicant to rebut the presumption that such services were provided for free with tangible evidence, a pay back or other written agreement that had been in place at the time the services were provided spelling out the compensation arrangements. Get your ducks in a line at the get-go and in writing if there are any oral agreements or understandings with a family member for whom care is provided. And be mindful of any tax consequences, as payments for care provided to relatives is income for purposes of income tax.

So what is a period of ineligibility?
The Divestment Penalty rules.

A period of ineligibility, or the "Penalty Period", is a certain number of months that must expire before an applicant for Medicaid benefits will qualify for receipt of such benefits because he has transferred an asset without receiving adequate compensation for the asset during the look-back period. To figure out the "period of ineligibility", you need to know the uncompensated fair market value of the transferred asset.

Let's assume that a boat with a fair market value of $50,000 was transferred for $10,000, that leaves $40,000 in uncompensated fair market value. Divide that number ($40,000) by the average monthly cost to a private pay patient for nursing home care in the State where benefits are sought, or at the option of the State, the community where the patient is institutionalized (this number is actually determined by each particular state or the specific facts of the applicant's care arrangements. For our example, we will use $5,000 as the "Penalty Divisor" which amount is a reasonable but rough average monthly figure for nursing home care in the U.S.) - $40,000 divided by $5,000 = 8 months of ineligibility.

So, just because you have transferred an asset to an individual during the look-back period does not mean that you are ineligible for Medicaid benefits for the full look-back period. The period of ineligibility, the Penalty Period, is only for a certain number of months where those funds for which value was not received by the applicant could have been used to privately pay for care instead of relying on Medicaid benefits. Obviously, the higher the dollar amount of the transferred assets, the longer the period of ineligibility until you hit the maximum of either 36 months (transfers to individuals) or 60 months (transfers to a trust).

The timing of the application for Medicaid benefits is also a crucial factor to be considered in determining an ineligibility period. Let's go back to that 8-month period that we started with in this section. If the applicant described above had filed for Medicaid benefits 8 months after he had transferred that $50,000 boat for $10,000, he would be immediately eligible for Medicaid benefits since the period of ineligibility, the Penalty Period, starts to run from the date the applicant transfers the assets, not from the date he files the application for Medicaid benefits.

Multiple Transfers

Before we leave this topic, let's talk a bit about "Multiple Transfers", that is transfers of different assets or amounts of assets at different times. This sometimes results in overlapping Penalty Periods. The Medicaid Manual suggests that the value of all transferred assets be added together, and, using the applicable state's Penalty Divisor (the average monthly cost of nursing home care), arrive at a single Penalty Period. Or, in the alternative, you can calculate the individual penalty periods and impose them sequentially to determine the Penalty Period.

Unmarried Nursing Home Residents

For unmarried Medicaid applicants (that's everyone who does not have a Community Spouse), the Medicaid eligibility rules are pretty grim. With very limited exceptions, just about all available resources must be "spent down" until available resources fall below $2,000 ($2,400 for those found to be categorically needy) before becoming eligible for Medicaid benefits. Since there is no Community Spouse to whom to transfer assets, if they have not planned properly they may be ineligible for Medicaid benefits for some time while they spend down the assets they had earmarked as the family inheritance.

If the unmarried applicant expresses an intent to return to his home, then the residential real estate and items of personal property may be preserved (not required to be spent down) by filing a written statement of intent to return home, usually a box on the Medicaid application. However, you should determine if your state also requires a physician's certificate that the unmarried applicant is likely to return home six months from the date they enter the nursing home.

Where such a certificate is required and filed, then the monthly real estate maintenance costs for six months is payable out of the beneficiary's income, and not used toward his nursing home costs in a spend down. In some states, if this certification is not made, then the residence can still be maintained, but none of the applicant's income can be used to pay taxes, insurance, utilities or maintenance on the residence while he is receiving Medicaid benefits.

Bear in mind that under the various State estate recovery laws, implemented under federal mandate, Medicaid liens on the applicant and his property will continue to accrue until the Medicaid beneficiary dies and his assets are transferred to his estate.

Community and Institutionalized Spouses: Even More Rules

So you have a Mom and a Dad and they are still legally married, living together or apart. If one them requires nursing home or hospital care for more than thirty consecutive days, that spouse, as discussed earlier, is called the "Institutionalized Spouse", and the other spouse still living in the community, be it at home, a personal care home or assisted living facility, is called the "Community Spouse". So why is this important? Because the Medicaid rules apply differently to married couples and unmarried individuals.

A system for the allocation of assets between the Institutionalized Spouse and the Community Spouse was established by Medicare Catastrophic Coverage Act of 1988 (MCCA). This law is also known as the "Spousal Anti-Impoverishment Act" as it is designed to limit the "spending down" of marital assets for nursing home care in order to prevent the total impoverishment of the Community Spouse. It does, however, require some spending down of marital resources and what the government considers to be minimum impoverishment of the Community Spouse.

Assets:
The Community Spouse's Resource Allowance

Under MCCA, all non-excluded resources owned by the applicant or the applicant's spouse at the time the

Institutionalized Spouse enters a nursing home for a period of 30 consecutive days (the snapshot date) are considered available to pay for the care of the Institutionalized Spouse, less a "Community Spouse Resource Allowance" (CSRA).

The CSRA is the lesser of (i) one-half of the total spousal assets (not including excluded assets) or (ii) $89,280 (2002/Pennsylvania), but not less than $17,856 (2002/Pennsylvania). The actual amount of the CSRA is not determined by the applicant or his spouse, but is determined by the state after an Institutionalized Spouse has filed for Medicaid and a full disclosure of spousal assets has been made.

This is one of those times when it may be better to have more assets on the table rather than less when filing for Medicaid benefits so that the Community Spouse's Resource Allowance is at the highest amount. However, there is no typical situation and no standard solution, and every family's assets and long and short term needs require careful analysis.

Income:
The Community Spouse's Minimum Monthly Needs Allowance

Under MCCA, states are provided with the discretion to establish an allowance for the Community Spouse, adjusted annually for inflation, while the Institutionalized Spouse receives Medicaid benefits. This monthly allowance is called the Minimum Monthly Maintenance Needs Allowance (MMMNA), is not a countable asset for Medicaid purposes, and is equal to a percentage of the federal poverty level, indexed annually, for a family of two.

The MMMNA is the sum of

- an amount of income sufficient to insure the Community Spouse's income is 1/12 of the annual federal poverty level income for a family of two, as defined by the federal Office of

Management and Budget, at $1,493, effective July 2002, plus

- an excess shelter allowance to cover higher housing costs as determined by the Community Spouse's actual shelter costs.

The MMMNA cannot, however be more than $2,232 per month for 2002 (a percentage of the federal poverty level).

The excess shelter allowance is the amount by which the sum of all of the Community Spouse's monthly shelter costs (rent, mortgage, including principal and interest, real estate taxes, home owners insurance, utilities, and where applicable, monthly maintenance charges) exceeds 30% of the minimum protected monthly amount, currently $1,493, or $448.

If the Community Spouse's actual income is less than the MMMNA, then the Community Spouse may be able to receive additional income by deducting income of the Institutionalized Spouse, if there is any such income.

Once approved for Medicaid, all of the income of the Institutionalized Spouse is considered available to pay for nursing home care except for (i) an income contribution to the Community Spouse discussed above to bring the Community Spouse's actual income up to the MMMNA, (ii) cost of health insurance premiums or other medical expenses, and (iii) a personal needs allowance of $30 per month.

Revocable Trusts and Irrevocable Trusts

Some basics first.

A trust is an arrangement by which a grantor, the creator of the trust, transfers property owned by the grantor to a trustee with the intent that such property be held, managed or administered by the trustee for the benefit of the grantor or the designated beneficiaries. In order to be valid, the trust must be evidenced by trust documents that conform to the requirements of state law.

The beneficiaries of a trust are the individuals designated in the trust document to receive benefits from the trust, whether in the form of income or the principal of the trust.

The trustee is an individual or entity that manages a trust and has fiduciary duties including duties of loyalty and care in rendering accountings of the trust property, dealing prudently with the trust assets and performing acts required by law and the trust instrument.

A trust which can be revoked by the grantor, or modified or terminated by a court upon petition by the grantor or his representative, or which terminates by its own terms upon the occurrence of a condition within the control of the grantor or his representatives, is considered to be a Revocable Trust.

As for Revocable Trusts, the Medicaid rules provide that the trust property (sometimes called the trust corpus) is to be counted as an available resource of the grantor; payments made to the grantor as a trust beneficiary from the trust are counted as income to the beneficiary; and payments from the trust to beneficiaries who have not contributed property to the trust are considered assets transferred for less than fair market value, that is, a gift.

An Irrevocable Trust is a trust that cannot be revoked by the grantor, the original owner of the assets that are contributed to the trust.

As discussed above, if a transfer of assets to a trust has been made by the Medicaid applicant or his spouse more than 60 months prior to the date Medicaid eligibility is sought, the assets transferred to an Irrevocable Trusts can be excluded for purposes of determining Medicaid eligibility. The trust assets may still be considered in determining Medicaid eligibility if the grantor has retained rights to receive principal or interest from the trust, but only to the extent of the retained interest.

Although it may be better than gifting or giving away the assets outright to children or other proposed heirs, the problem with Irrevocable Trusts in many cases is the unwillingness of the parent either to part with control over the assets placed in trust, or to deny the Community Spouse enjoyment of the stream of income such assets may generate. And, if the "Grantor" (the one who establishes the trust) retains control of the principal ("trust corpus") as the Trustee, then it ceases to be considered Irrevocable and is part of the mix of assets and income used to determine Medicaid eligibility, even if the trust was established 6, 10 or 100 years before an application for Medicaid is filed.

There are, however, ways to overcome some of the control issues (remember, you still have the five year look back). For example, an Irrevocable Trust (established more than five years before a Medicaid application is filed) can be established where only the income is distributable to the grantor or his spouse. This is called an "income-only trust", and it allows the principal of the trust to be preserved for distribution at a later date to children and heirs. In these cases, the grantor of the trust is permitted to retain a "limited power of appointment" over the trust principal either during his life (intervivos) or through his Will (testamentary), without jeopardizing Medicaid eligibility.

In addition to the control issue, there may be tax benefits of an income only trust, such as a stepped up basis for the trust assets at the time of the death of the income beneficiary. Also, the income beneficiary (the parent) is more likely than not taxed at a lower rate. And, the trust principal may not be reachable by creditors or spouses of the grantor's children assuming they are the beneficiaries of the trust principal.

If you considering the formation of any trusts, please consult with an attorney in your state.

Annuities

These are tricky. An annuity is a right to receive fixed, periodic payments for life or for some designated period of time; it is a contract with four parties – the owner, the annuitant, the beneficiary and the insurance company. The owner and the annuitant may, or may not, be the same person. When purchasing an annuity, however, the medical condition and age of both the owner and annuitant will be important factors as their deaths will result in various tax consequences and settlement options that need to be carefully considered.

There are two phases of an annuity contract. The accumulation phase during which payments (which may be tax deferred) are made to the insurance company, and the annuitization phase during which the insurance company pays income to the beneficiary.

An annuity contract consists of a number of standard provisions including, for example, interest rates, charges, fees, maximum age that annuitization begins, payment of premium, withdrawals and settlement options.

Typically, there are five settlement options to consider, all of which are designed to insure that the annuitant does not outlive the income stream created by the annuity–

- Life Annuity. Payments are made by the insurance company to the annuitant for the life of the annuitant. The risk here is if the annuitant dies shortly after the income payments begin, the cost of the annuity will exceed the amount of annuity benefits paid by the insurance company

- Life with a period guarantee. Here, the insurance company agrees to pay the annuity benefit for the longer of the life of the annuitant or a designated number of years which, in some instances, may not exceed the life expectancy of the annuitant

- Refund Life Annuity. The insurance company pays the annuity benefit for the life of the annuitant, and, at the annuitant's death, if the accumulation amount is more than the benefits paid, will pay a lump sum amount to the beneficiary equal to accumulation amount of annuity less all installments of income paid to the annuitant during the annuitant's life

- Joint and Survivor Annuity. Here the annuity benefits are paid during the lives of two persons and for so long as one of the two continues to live. When one annuitant dies, the survivor continues to receive all or a part of the annuity benefit, depending on the annuity contract terms, for the remainder of the survivor's life

- Fixed Amount Annuity. The insurance company pays annuity benefits of a fixed amount until the annuity's accumulation value plus interest has been exhausted

- Fixed Period Annuity. The insurance company pays the annuity benefits to the annuitant for a fixed number of years.

According to the State Medicaid Manual published by the federal Centers for Medicare & Medicaid Services, the purchase of an annuity is considered to be a transfer of an asset (namely, the cash used to buy the annuity) for which fair consideration (the purchase price) is given to the extent the length of the payout is reasonable considering the life expectancy of the beneficiary (which, in many cases, is the Community Spouse). Therefore, strictly speaking, the purchase of an annuity should not result in a transfer penalty or create any period of ineligibility for a Medicaid applicant. However, individual States are not in agreement on this issue and anyone considering the purchase of an annuity would be well advised to check on his State's position on this before making such an investment if the possible impact on Medicaid eligibility is a concern.

Gifts

Everyone knows what a gift is. For Medicaid purposes, if any asset is transferred to an individual for free with no expectation of repayment (that is, for no consideration, and hence, a gift), that ugly "look back" period comes into play for purposes of determining Medicaid eligibility. If the gift is for more than $10,000 each year, the donor/giver, not the donee/recipient, may also have a federal gift tax liability, but that is an issue for tax accountants and attorneys and financial planners.

"Half a Loaf" Gifting

Another way to reduce the amount of assets that will be countable for determining Medicaid eligibility is something called Half a Loaf gifting. Someone entering a nursing home is still able to gift out his assets to his heirs, and reduce the ineligibility period.

Let's say a Medicaid applicant has $100,000 in cash in the bank at the time he entered the nursing home and he gives his son one-half, or $50,000. This is a transfer of an asset to an individual for no consideration with a 36-month look back. Before this person would be eligible for Medicaid benefits, how many months of nursing care would he have to pay for privately? Ten months. ($50,000 divided by the Divestiture Penalty Divisor of $5,000 = 10 months). In other words, after the gift is made, the Medicaid applicant should still have enough cash to privately pay a nursing home through the ineligibility period.

Remember that the Divestiture Penalty varies from state to state and changes from year to year, so check the state where your folks would be filing for Medicaid benefits. (Don't forget that gifts of more that $10,000 per individual per year may be subject to federal gift taxes payable by the donor so make sure there's enough money available to satisfy any tax liability.)

Burial Funds or Trusts

These funds or trusts can take a variety of forms, and if done right, should not be considered transfers for purposes of the transfer penalty rules discussed above and, therefore, should be excluded from the list of countable assets.

You can assign life insurance proceeds to the funeral home, or establish a trust with the funeral director as trustee, both of which must be irrevocable and the amount, reasonable.

You can deposit funds into a bank under a special Burial Fund Agreement (statement on a passbook may be insufficient), making funds payable to funeral home or to an estate; again, this must be irrevocable and in a reasonable amount – usually, the average cost of a funeral plus 25%.

Or you can prepay the funeral home outright; here you need to be careful that you know and trust the funeral home in question to actually be in a position to honor the commitment down the road. Later in this work, we deal in more depth with "preneed funeral contracts", so you may want to skip ahead.

Estate Recovery

Federal law (OBRA-93) requires that with respect to a deceased Medicaid recipient age 55 or older at the time benefits were received, states are required to seek recovery from the recipient's estate of an amount for benefits correctly paid under Medicaid for nursing home services, home and community based services, related hospital and prescription drug services. Recovery is limited to the probate estate of the deceased beneficiary; and if there are no or little assets in the estate, then the state can only recover a portion of the Medicaid benefits actually paid, if that.

The "estate" includes all real and personal property and other assets included within an individual's estate as defined by a particular state's probate laws. Each state has the option of including other property in which the deceased had legal title or an interest at death including assets conveyed to a successor, heir or assign through joint tenancy, tenancy in common, survivorship, living trust, life estate or other arrangement.

This is where it can get a little sticky. **Be aware that the executor or administrator of the estate is personally liable for the amount of property transferred by the executor or administrator before satisfying the obligation to the state for Medicaid benefits paid.** The executor or administrator of the estate is required to determine if the deceased received any Medicaid benefits before his death, and to notify the state so that the state may make its claim on the estate assets.

Chapter 8

Essential Documents

Let's say that your mother is diagnosed with a terminal condition. She has refused to sign a living will and a durable power of attorney. Before she lapses into a coma, her last spoken words to her doctor, in response to the question "what kind of treatment do you want?, are "I want the full monty!"

So what happens next? Her physical condition begins to rapidly deteriorate. Feeding tubes are inserted to bring nutrition and hydration into her system, and ventilators to assist her breathing. She is heavily sedated to limit her ability to pull out any of the tubes. Her mobility is restricted due to her poor health and the medical devices that sustain her. She develops pressure ulcers (commonly known as bedsores) that become infected. That is followed by aggressive antibiotic treatments to bring her infection under control. She goes into cardiac arrest, once, twice – you begin to lose track of how many times she has coded. Each time she is revived through cardiopulmonary resuscitation (CPR), the result of which includes some broken ribs and a punctured lung. More pain. You stand by helplessly and watch as medical technology keeps her body alive. Day after day, you watch the monitors that are attached to the various pieces of equipment that sustain her. The doctors do test after test. Her blood count, usually around 10, is down to 7. She is bleeding internally. They transfuse her to bring her blood count up. She seems to need blood every few days. The hemorrhaging cannot be stopped because she is too weak for treatment, surgery or even diagnostic testing. More tubes, more transfusions. The doctors have done CAT scans and determined that she still has brain function. Every now and then, when she is due for her sedation, she wakes up and stares at you, and you watch as tears stream down her sunken cheeks. She squeezes your hand, not the squeeze of an able bodied person, but an almost imperceptible pressure that would be hardly noticeable to anyone else. She is unable to speak because of the medical devices that are keeping her alive. You stand by and cannot hold back your own tears, helpless to intervene on her behalf, unable to end the misery. And she continues in a semi-vegetative state, and you wonder just how long the human body can survive. And each day you agonize as the process of her death is interrupted and delayed through medical intervention. Day after day. Week after week. And weeks become months. There is no possibility of her physical condition ever returning to anything that would resemble a normal life. You have no power to speak for her and she has refused to speak for herself through a living will. Without someone with the authority to issue a "Do Not Resuscitate" order, your mother, trapped in a body that has ceased to function on its own accord, will be brought back to life. Every time her heart stops, they will break every rib in her chest to revive her. Eventually, the body will fail and she will die, even with all of the medical technology available. But what an ugly death. And you realize that being alive can be worse than being dead.

The above narrative is not out of a horror novel. It is the story of a number of folks who have failed or refused to address their own mortality. It happens every day in hospitals throughout the country. Valuable medical resources are misspent trying to keep bodies alive, prolonging death, resulting in pain and misery for the recipient of the medical treatment and their families and loved ones.

What a way to go! Thanks, but no thanks!

I am going to die. You are going to die. Everyone is going to die. And to refuse to deal with this absolutely irrefutable fact of life by empowering those you claim to love with the power to end your misery and their anguish is the single most selfish and arrogant thing someone can do.

Absolutely every senior should have both a durable power of attorney and a living will in place.

Through the durable power of attorney, an individual appoints another person or persons to act on his behalf and to speak for him with respect to designated medical and/or financial issues.

With a living will, also known as an advance medical directive, an individual states his preferences for certain types of medical treatments if he is in a terminal condition or can no longer speak for himself. A living will can also go a long way towards alleviating the guilt of family members who armed with a Power of Attorney can issue that "Do Not Resuscitate" order when death become inevitable.

Powers of Attorney

A power of attorney allows the person designated as the proxy or agent to make certain decisions, execute certain documents, handle property or conduct certain affairs on behalf of the grantor of the power. Powers of attorney can be general or limited in scope; they can take effect immediately, at some specified future date, for a designated period of time or upon the occurrence of some condition in the future. The grantor decides when and for how long and under what circumstances the power is effective.

However, ordinary powers of attorney require both the agent and grantor to be competent and, therefore, automatically expire if the grantor becomes incompetent or incapacitated.

Durable Powers of Attorney

A durable power of attorney (DPA) is specifically designed to survive the incompetence or incapacity of the grantor; hence, the term "durable". Durable powers of attorney can be limited to health care decisions or can be broad enough to allow the agent (the person designated as the grantor's proxy or "attorney-in-fact") to make financial decisions, such as the sale of property, or the granting of gifts, as well.

With the execution of a durable power of attorney, the grantor decides "who" he wants to act on his behalf, and the scope of that authority. In the absence of this type of document, in a crisis situation, a person may have to rely on guardianship laws and procedures for protection; this can be a time consuming and expensive process. Under those circumstances, a court has the authority to appoint someone of its choice to act as agent to make decisions for and on behalf of someone who is unable to do so for himself. This is not a very comforting thought, and it is why most people would prefer to personally appoint a family member or trusted friend of their own choice to act as agent for them through the execution of a durable power of attorney.

In many cases, a health care durable power of attorney is signed in conjunction with a living will or advance directive. Something to consider is whether the agent under the durable power of attorney has the discretion to act contrary to the instructions contained in the living will, or is required to act in strict accordance with the terms of the advance directive. This is largely a matter of personal preference.

Although durable powers of attorney survive the incompetence of the grantor, they must be executed while the grantor is still competent. You cannot wait until Mom or Dad is unable to handle his/her own affairs to put this document into place.

When is a DPA Effective?

The conditions for the effectiveness of a durable power of attorney are within the grantor's discretion. The grantor can decide when and upon what conditions it will become effective, and for how long it will remain effective.

In some cases, it may be appropriate to have a Durable Power of Attorney effective immediately. In this way, it is available whenever it may be needed and for whatever reason including simply for the convenience of the grantor. The risk in this situation is that it is effective in the absence of any necessity when the grantor is capable of handling all of his own affairs. Many persons, including loving parents who trust their kids, may nevertheless be reluctant to grant such broad power over their affairs to anyone in the absence of a compelling need.

In many cases, durable powers of attorney came into effect only upon the grantor's incapacity or inability to make decisions on his own. This is called a "springing" power of attorney. Usually, the document will specify that there be a determination of incapacity or disability of the grantor by the grantor's physician.

Regardless of the timing of the effectiveness of the power of attorney, many parents think this is a power grab. They are giving their children the power and authority to sell their house, stocks or bonds, withdraw money from their bank accounts. This makes them nervous. You need to handle this topic carefully and thoughtfully. No one wants to deal with the thought that they will no longer be in a position to control their own affairs and their destiny. However, this is not an optional document if your parents are getting on in years. If your parents do not already have a lawyer that they trust, you should make an appointment to see a lawyer together so that the attorney can explain the importance of this document to your parents.

For information purposes only, a general form of springing durable power of attorney that is broad enough to encompass health-related decisions can be found in the Appendix. Please consult with an attorney in your particular state so that the power of attorney that is put into place meets all of your needs and any local requirements. Some jurisdictions require that the power of attorney be filed with the county, especially where it is used as part of a real estate transaction. Some states require it to be notarized, and in others, witnesses are sufficient. Some require specific notices to be acknowledged by the grantor and terms of acceptance by the agent. And others require that a copy be given to the grantor's physician in the case of a health care power of attorney. You get the point.

Qualifications of Agent

Although you should check with an attorney about your state's particular requirements for proxy qualification, as a general matter a proxy or designated agent –

- Must be at least 18 years old; and

- Cannot be an employee or owner of the health care provider (except if also a relative) providing care to the individual.

Multiple Agents

The grantor has a lot of flexibility with respect to the to appointment of agents for a durable power of attorney. For example, he may appoint a single agent with or without naming a successor agent, if the first is unable or unwilling to act; two or more co-agents that may or may not be able to act alone; or other variations on the theme.

There are some things to consider. Appointing a single agent can be risky. Life is uncertain, and if the designated agent is unable to serve for any reason, the grantor may no longer be able to appoint another. Therefore, naming one or more successor agents is prudent.

If you name two or more persons as co-agents, you need to decide if both are required to make a decision, or if either one of the two is empowered alone to make a decision. Again, if both are required, there is a risk that one may not be available when most needed.

Living Wills/ Advance Directives

Since 1991, the federal Patient Self-Determination Act of 1990 has required hospitals and certain other health care providers to inform all patients at the time of admission of their rights:

- to make medical decisions and advance directives regarding care,

- to accept or refuse treatment,

- to have their current medical records note prominently whether or not there is an advance directive (living will) in place for them, and

- to be transferred to the care of another physician or facility if the doctor or hospital is unable to comply with the medical directive.

The states have since enacted laws that deal more specifically with these health care directives. You should consult with an attorney licensed to practice in the state where medical treatment will most likely be sought about that state's requirements for a living will; for example, the requirement for witnesses or notarization may differ from state to state.

You can also check **www.partnershipforcaring.org** where state-specific forms of living wills and medical powers of attorney can be found.

Some states require that a copy or an original of the living will and the durable health care power of attorney to be given to someone's personal or attending physician in order to be effective. But whether or not it is a legal requirement in your state, it just makes good sense to give your doctor a copy for your medical records so that he is aware of your wishes and the identity of your designated health care agent and how to contact them.

What is a Living Will?

A living will and advance directive are two different names for the same thing, and the terms are used interchangeably. Generally speaking, it is a written statement of a person's desires with respect to the nature and scope of medical treatment if s/he becomes unable to actively participate in the decision making process.

Most living wills take effect when someone is incapacitated and unable to speak for themselves for any number of reasons and in a permanent state of unconsciousness or has been diagnosed with a terminal condition, often understood to mean less than six months to live.

The process of preparing a living will forces people to consider their worst case scenarios and what treatment they want or do not want in those situations. This document also can help to alleviate the guilt experienced by friends and relatives when the time comes to make the really hard decisions about the continuation of life.

Things to consider when making an advance directive – What the health care agent needs to know.

The issues typically dealt with in a living will are the same issues you should discuss with your parents if you have been designated their agent for medical matters under a durable power of attorney. There is no good time to have this chat. Obviously, it is better to undertake this line of questioning when your folks are still in good health. Delaying it until you are faced with a medical crisis is certainly not prudent.

You are going to need to discuss what your parents fear - loss of independence, loss of mobility, loss of cognitive abilities (memory), pain. What treatments they would want and not want if they were to be diagnosed with a terminal condition, or irreversible dementia. Some living wills, like the one you can find in the Appendix, are a series of questions, each of which needs to be addressed from the perspective of having been diagnosed with a terminal illness or being in a state of permanent unconsciousness.

Some questions to consider include the following:

I do or do not want -

- a **feeding tube** for feeding and hydration purposes (this commonly involves one of two types – for short term purposes (1 to 4 weeks), a nasogastric (NG) tube is put through the nose and down the throat and into the stomach. For long term purposes, a PEG tube or g-tube, is inserted into the wall of the stomach. Some of the risk factors of this procedure include liquid entering the lungs, coughing, pneumonia, infections, pain, nausea, vomiting. Obviously, while the patient has a tube down his throat, he will be unable to vocalize his needs and wishes.)

- placement on a **ventilator or other mechanical breathing device** if my breathing fails (this involves a tube being inserted down the throat of the patient, leaving her completely unable to verbally communicate. As a short-term remedial measure, to get through a specific crisis while there is promise of a return to a life of quality, this procedure is an obvious lifesaver. As a long term condition the ventilator would have to be replaced with a tracheotomy, a tube placed directly into the throat, but again in most cases, this leaves a patient unable to vocalize and eat. This may also mean that a feeding tube will need to be inserted. Bear in mind that procedures like this and feeding tubes are so invasive and uncomfortable that many patients also need to be sedated to minimize their agitation, or physically restrained to deter them from pulling out the tubes.)

- **cardiopulmonary resuscitation** (CPR) if my heart fails or I stop breathing (this involves a great deal of pressure being exerted on the chest and electrical stimulation to the chest. The physical pressure of the procedure may cause ribs to break or a lung to collapse. Placement on a ventilator is very common after a patient has "coded". The survival rate is not very optimistic for those already debilitated by illness, and the physical `consequences following this procedure promise, in the best of cases, additional discomfort and possibly pain to the person revived.)

- **antibiotics** (this sounds deceptively benign, however, many people with terminal illnesses do not actually die as a result of the diagnosed disease. They contract a bacterial infection like sepsis (blood infection) that causes death either because they or their medical agent decided against the use of antibiotics, or because the infection is resistant to antibiotics, an increasingly disturbing problem that is a result of our abuse and overuse of antibiotics. Delivering antibiotics when death is near sometimes merely serves to prolong the process of death.)

- **dialysis** if my kidneys fail (clearly, no fun but a fairly non-restrictive treatment, unlike feeding tubes and ventilators).

All of this is scary stuff, but these are the kind of things you may have to deal with if a medical crisis occurs and you find one of your parents in an emergency ward or intensive care unit.

Health Care Proxies – Do's and Don'ts

So, you have been designated as the agent under a durable power of attorney (DPA) for your parents and you are now in a position to make medical and perhaps financial decisions for them. Now what?

Well, obviously, you need to read the DPA that has been executed to determine what duties you have assumed. Is its scope financial or health care or both? Hopefully, you have been part of the planning process and have participated in the development of the document after conversations with Mom or Dad and a discussion of what their wishes are under various scenarios.

Your duties may begin when the grantor loses the ability to make decisions for himself. This usually means that the grantor is in a state of unconsciousness or is otherwise incompetent or incapacitated due to health conditions. Some times there needs to be a certification of the disability by a physician for the power to take effect.

In many cases, the DPA may be activated in a crisis situation – that is not the best time to pull out the document and read it for the first time. Or, even worse, find that you do not have a copy of it handy. Something awful happens, someone calls 911, and you find yourself sitting in an emergency ward at the hospital in the dead of night. Hopefully, your folks have also signed a Living Will so that you understand their preferences and wishes with respect to medical treatment, and whether you have any discretion to override their expressed wishes.

Mom or Dad needs immediate treatment by the medical staff and someone with a cool head to make decisions on their behalf. Put away the tissues and pull yourself together. This is often the first step in your rite of passage to adulthood.

You now have the same rights to information and to direct or decline medical treatment that your parent would have if s/he were competent and able to make their own decisions. Use them. Some of these rights include –

- The right to receive medical information regarding their condition, including the right to review their medical charts,

- to confer with the doctors and nurses administering treatment and care,

- to ask questions and get answers including available treatment options,

- to request consultations and get second opinions,

- to consent to or decline medical tests and treatment, including life sustaining measures, and

- to authorize the transfer to another doctor or facility such as a nursing home.

Do Not Resuscitate

One of the hardest decisions that you may have to make is the issuance of a "do not resuscitate" order (DNR) -- when it becomes apparent to you that the wishes of your parent under the circumstances would be that heroic measures not be implemented and life-sustaining treatment be declined or discontinued.

There comes a time when you will have to let Mom and Dad go; when to do otherwise is only to prolong the process of death rather than provide an opportunity for life with a measure of quality and dignity. The topic of death will be dealt with in more detail in another chapter.

Guardianships

So, what happens if you have completely dropped the ball and Mom or Dad becomes incompetent and unable to manage his or her affairs due to health or mental reasons (e.g. stroke, car accident) before you have had a chance to put a durable power of attorney into effect? At that point, you may need to obtain that power over their affairs through state judicial proceedings known as guardianships.

The laws of every state provide for a proceeding where the court has the power to appoint a guardian to manage the affairs of a party, called the "ward", the court finds to be incompetent. Because the court must actually make a determination of competency or lack thereof, this is not a legal road that anyone should go down unless circumstances truly demand it – where there is the potential for harm to the proposed ward unless someone intercedes. If you find yourself in this situation, you will need to retain an attorney to help you through this difficult process.

Chapter 9

Hospitalization

Monitoring Medical Treatment

When a loved one becomes seriously ill and ends up in a hospital, there are certain general things you may want to know, especially if you have been designated someone's representative under a durable power of attorney.

First, you need to determine the facts surrounding their condition. Find out what the doctors know or do not know. What do the doctors suspect might be the condition? What specialists are being called in and why? What is the medical condition or what do they believe might be the condition based on the symptoms? What tests are being done and why? What will the test results show? What are the risk factors associated with a test?

Once the condition has been diagnosed, what are the treatment options for the condition? What is the likelihood of a cure? What are the risks and side effects associated with the treatment? What do the doctors recommend and why?

If you have been entrusted with someone's medical proxy, you need to gather the facts and evaluate them in light of the instructions you have received as the agent. What would he or she (not you or other members of the family) want done or not done under the circumstances at hand? Do you have any discretion? You might want to refer back to the section on do's and don'ts for health care proxies.

ICU (Intensive Care Unit)

Entering an Intensive or Critical Care Unit of a hospital is like being transported to another world. When a loved one becomes ill enough to warrant this level of care, you need to be prepared to learn a lot of medical jargon, quickly. Since you won't have time to get a medical degree, you will need to be or become assertive with the medical team assigned to your loved one and make them educate you.

Many medical professionals will make the time to help you as they consider it a part of their job. Others will be resentful and haughty and try to make you feel stupid. Do not allow them to cow you into ignorance. Even the most complicated medical condition or treatment can be laid out in understandable layman terms. If you do not understand something, it may not be you, but rather the doctor who "explained" it to you may have made no or little effort to spell it out. Although many in the medical community may take exception, we believe part of a doctor's job includes helping families and loved ones to understand the condition and prognosis of an ill loved one.

Be sensitive to the fact that the medical team does not have the time to explain the same things and answer the same questions over and over again to a number of family members. If there is no one designated under a durable power of attorney as the medical proxy, then decide among the concerned members of the family or friends who will be the spokesperson for the group. Then have that person accumulate the questions of the group and present them to the appropriate member of the medical team, preferably the attending physician or on duty nurse. That designated person then has the responsibility of reporting his findings to the group.

Ask questions. Take notes. What does that monitor mean? Why is that tube in – is it for hydration or the delivery of medication. What medication? What is it designed to treat? Heart monitors, ventilators – they each provide valuable information that you need to understand in order to track the progress of the patient. You need to know their baseline (where were they from a medical perspective when they entered) so that you can monitor the effectiveness of treatments and track improvements or declines.

Blood (CBC), kidney (creatinine) and a host of other test results depending on the particulars of your patient need to be understood. Small, incremental improvements can make you joyful and bad test results can make you grieve in anticipation of the worse.

There is a website (**www.labtestsonline.org**) that can be a valuable resource in helping you understand what is going on if you know the name of the clinical test in question.

If your loved one is in ICU for more than a few days, from a non-clinical point of view, you will begin to notice familiar faces – in the elevators, the waiting rooms, the dining area. You will see the families of other patients day in and day out. As a result of this, you become familiar with the other patients and their conditions. This impromptu network can provide great comfort to you and other family members.

Finally, a little sick room etiquette – some medical professionals contend, and we believe, that even though someone may appear to be drugged, asleep, comatose or on the verge of death, it is nevertheless important when in their presence to speak directly to them and not speak about them in the third person. They may be more aware than they appear. Your words should be comforting and encouraging. And your touch (a kiss on the check, a squeeze of the hand) can be revitalizing.

Heroic Measures

In an earlier chapter, we discussed living wills and advance directives. We even included a rather grim example (based on our personal experience) of what can happen if there is no living will in place. We do have to mention, however, that there are instances when someone can actually be terminally ill without having been diagnosed with a terminal condition. This leaves you in a kind of never-never land. In this type of situation, measures that would be considered heroic if there was a diagnosis of a terminal condition are, in fact, remedial.

When you are faced with a life and death situation and do not have any objective data to support invoking a living will, what do you do? There is no right or wrong answer to the question. When we were faced with this dilemma with Dad, we all agreed that a ventilator (without which he would have died then and there) was a remedial measure that had to be undertaken. In the absence of facts, we trusted our instincts.

He was on the ventilator for ten very long days. A few days into the ordeal, he became alert enough to let us know that he absolutely hated the ventilator and wanted off immediately. When he was finally liberated and able to articulate again, he made it abundantly clear that under no circumstances were we ever to do that to him again, regardless of the consequences. Although we would later learn that he had inoperable cancer, we were so grateful for the few extra months with him that a short time on a ventilator gave to us. Did we do the right thing? Based on the information we had at the time, yes, we made the right decision.

Social Services

When we hear from friends that their Mom or Dad is in a hospital for other than outpatient care or testing, our initial advice to them is find the social services department at the hospital and start to plan for the discharge. The social services folks know the ins and outs of Medicare, and what can and cannot be paid for by Medicare, and how to qualify.

They are also familiar with the local nursing and rehabilitation homes and their reputations, as well as which ones accept Medicaid patients. They can arrange for clergy to visit your parent to provide spiritual support during hospitalization. If your parent's situation is terminal, they are also there to help you arrange hospice care. The social services folks are an under appreciated and invaluable resource at both hospitals and nursing homes.

Use them. They are your new best friends when Mom or Dad become hospitalized or transferred to a nursing home for post-hospital rehabilitation.

Final Chapter

No one gets out of here alive

We are all going to die. The death process is as varied as the life process. And, there are some things that are worst than death. There are times when forgoing available medical treatment and not artificially prolonging the process of death becomes the right decision for a loved one. This can involve the discontinuation of treatment and procedures, like feeding tubes, and/or the refusal to accept treatment, like CPR or antibiotics.

Hopefully, your loved one has had the foresight to execute a living will or advance directive, making their wishes known and alleviating guilt that you and other family members might experience in deciding to not take or to discontinue steps that will prolong the process of death. If a loved one has entrusted you with a medical power of attorney, hopefully, you have had ample opportunity to discuss her wishes about her end of life health care, so you can comfort yourself with the notion that you have made her (not your) wishes a reality.

Terminal Illness

A terminal illness is generally understood to be a condition that will result in death within six months or less. A diagnosis of a terminal condition is a life altering experience for everyone affected, the patient and the family. Time becomes finite, death becomes imminent, advance directives/living wills kick in and "Do Not Resuscitate" orders are often issued.

A not too uncommon problem is when the family is advised of the condition before the patient is made aware. This can be due to a number of reasons, but in many cases it is because the patient is too sick to be told or to comprehend the gravity of their physical condition. The dilemma then becomes who, what, when and if to tell a loved one that death is near. Although they certainly have the right to know, do they need to know, and what good will come of them knowing?

In this situation, there simply is no right or wrong answer. Some people would want to know and others would not.

From our personal experience, when Dad's cancer was finally diagnosed, we as a family believed he was too ill to be told. And, looking back, at the time he was too ill to be told. As a result of radiation treatments given to halt the bleeding and not in an effort to cure, he slowly came back on line. We continued the charade that he was going to get better when he was transferred to rehab, and then when he was released to home (which he actually did under a hospice program). When he was home again, we learned that he had known all along that he had cancer but he had pretended not to know in an effort to spare our feelings. Can you believe it? He wanted to minimize *our* pain.

The diagnosis of a terminal condition is difficult for everyone. However, you can still find joy during final days and deepen your emotional bond with your loved one and other members of your family. Like everything in life, it is a matter of your attitude.

Hospice

Not that many years ago, most folks died in nursing homes, or in or on their way to a hospital. Dying was a nasty business that was best kept out of our homes, if at all possible. Also, dying at home was not an option especially for those who suffered from illnesses or chronic conditions that required skilled care. Fortunately, our attitudes toward death and dying have changed, and hospice care is in some ways either the reason for or the result of this change in attitude.

Hospice is not a place, but is a holistic program of care for the terminally ill and their families and caregivers provided by an interdisciplinary team consisting of doctors, nurses, medical social workers and pastoral or other spiritual counselors. Hospice recognizes that death is inevitable, and, therefore, supporting and comforting the patient and their loved ones, and easing the pain and discomfort of the patient, are the primary goals. No measures to cure the disease are undertaken in a hospice program.

Hospice care is available wherever the patient chooses to spend his or her final days, in their own or a relative's home or a nursing home or other health care facility, and as discussed in more detail in another chapter, Medicare covers virtually all of the costs, except for small co-pays for medicines.

The hospice interdisciplinary team performs and coordinates a number of functions:

- the physician provides or supervises the provision of medical care to the patient, with an emphasis on alleviation of pain and discomfort through the use of appropriate drugs;

- the registered nurse assists the doctor in providing medical care, evaluates the need for medical supplies, equipment, therapy and counseling;

- the medical social worker assesses the needs of the patient and his family, including psychological, legal, financial and spiritual; and

- the pastoral counselor provides emotional and spiritual support to the patient and his family in facing death and managing grief.

By federal law, at least 5% of the total patient hours consisting of administrative or direct patient care must be provided by volunteers of the hospice. In many cases, this requirement is satisfied through the counseling efforts of members of the clergy and religious organizations.

Hospice services are available 24 hours a day, 7 days a week, and are primarily provided in a patient's home. A visiting caregiver or home health aide trained by the hospice and usually trained in nursing provides personal care for the patient. This may include bed baths and other personal hygiene and grooming matters such as shaving and shampoos, changing linens, taking temperatures and pulse readings.

Hospice care at home for a terminally ill patient who is surrounded by family and friends is a great alternative to dying among strangers in an institutional setting. You may question the use of the word "great" in connection with such sad circumstances. However, although death is never pretty or easy, for the dying or their families, there is a dignity and sense of peace that comes with a passing of a loved one that occurs in a hospice setting.

The members of the hospice team become invaluable friends and allies, a source of information, strength and support that can only be provided by persons knowledgeable about the process of death. Upon death, the first call made by the family of the deceased is to the hospice, if they are not already present at the time of death. The hospice team will arrive quickly, bath and prepare the body of the deceased for transportation to a funeral home, and assist the family in arrangements for the removal of medical equipment in an effort to return the household to a state of normalcy as quickly and efficiently as possible. The hospice team is also available after death to provide bereavement support services to the family.

From a purely practical and economic point of view, hospice care is far more cost effective and sensible than the wanton squandering of valuable medical resources in no-win situations with individuals who have absolutely no chance of recovery. From an emotional point of view, it can help you as a survivor develop coping skills that will be invaluable when death finally arrives.

Letting Go and Saying Goodbye

Many people in health care and especially hospice care have said, and it is our personal experience, that loved ones, especially parents, need to be told that they can go, that you will be all right, that even though you love them and will miss them that it is okay for them to die. Sometimes, as in the case of our beloved Aunt Mottie (Uncle Henry's wife), they need to be reassured that someone they love will be cared for when they are gone. You need to pick the right moment because this is a very hard thing to do.

We recently bumped into an old business associate and we were talking about the death of my Dad and his Mom. The conversation turned to the concept of letting them go, and how we each had told our folks that it was okay for them to die before they were able to let go of life peacefully. We agreed that there seemed to be something to this notion. He went on to tell us that shortly after his own Mother's death he had run into an old boyhood friend of his. He had shared this idea with his friend whose Mom was then in the hospital. A few months later he had the opportunity to meet this fellow again, and was immediately chewed out about his poor advice. Apparently, this guy proceeded to the hospital and promptly told his Mom that it was okay for her die. Instead of it being the moment of emotional release that had been described to him, his Mom threw him out of her hospital room, cursing at him for wanting her to move on before she was ready, chastising him for his arrogance, informing him in no uncertain terms that she was not ready to go anywhere and he had no say in the when and where of her demise, and accusing him of wanting to her die so he could get to her substantial assets.

The moral here is pretty obvious – pick your moment carefully, when death is imminent. Trust me when I say, you'll know when the time has come. Even if your loved one is non-responsive or in a coma, we do believe that they can still hear your words when you speak from the heart.

Funerals

You are not really a grownup until you have buried a loved one. Funeral details are a matter that is best dealt with in advance of a loved one's death, if possible, before they become ill. Perhaps this topic can be raised in conjunction with a discussion about a living will, establishing a burial fund or other legal matter.

You need to determine if your parents have any special wishes regarding their burial arrangements. Sometimes, they are the ones who initiate the discussion. If this is the case, let them express themselves and listen to and hear what they are saying. Do not put off the discussion because you are uncomfortable. There will come a day (sooner than you think) when you will be grateful that they had the foresight to discuss this delicate subject.

As painful as it is, you will need to know their views and desires. Do they want to be buried or cremated? Do they have a cemetery plot? Where is it? Do they have any special wishes regarding a viewing? What do they want to wear? Do they want any religious ceremony? Do they want flowers or donations to a favorite charity?

Funerals and Kids

There is no general rule on whether or not, or the extent to which, children and teenagers should be involved in the funeral arrangements for elderly family members. Some kids are close to their grandparents and will naturally feel grief at the loss. Others kids are not close and may feel nothing at the passing of an elderly relative. However, parents need to be sensitive to the emotional reaction of their own children when a family member passes away.

Parents also need to be able to help their children work through their grief while in a grief-stricken state themselves. You may have lost a Mom or Dad, but your child has lost a grandparent. Their grief is as real as yours, except that they may lack the emotional maturity to deal with it as effectively as an adult.

As awful as you may feel or as busy as you may be making final arrangements, make the time, or have another family member or friend take the time, to talk to the kids and ask them how they feel. Answer their questions as honestly as their age and maturity dictate. Watch them closely for signs of depression including behavioral changes, and problems at school. And get professional help for your kids if your instincts tell you that they are having more difficulty accepting and adjusting to the loss than you are able to handle.

It has become popular these days to do photograph/collage memorials commemorating the life of the deceased for presentation at their funerals. Going through old photos and remembering happier days of the deceased, as well as seeing an elderly loved one when they were a child or young adult, can help the grieving process for children as well as adults.

Preneed Funeral Contracts

Preplanning a funeral is not the same as prepaying for a funeral. There may be a number of good reasons to prepay for these services such as Medicaid eligibility and locking in prices.

Like any other consumer purchase, you should know who you are dealing with – the funeral director should be licensed by the state and have a good reputation in the community.

If you decide to prepay for a funeral, this arrangement will need to be documented in the form of what is called a "Preneed Contract". A preneed contract is a written agreement for the purchase and delivery of funeral goods and services in the future.

There are guaranteed and non-guaranteed preneed contracts. With guaranteed contracts, the delivery of selected goods and services is guaranteed to be delivered for a specified amount of money regardless of the actual costs at the time of delivery. Under a non-guaranteed contract, the funeral director promises to deliver the specified goods and services at the prevailing rate at the time of delivery.

These contracts may be revocable, that is, you can cancel the contract and all or a portion of the payment and interest will be refunded, or irrevocable, which means that you cannot cancel the agreement and receive any monies back. Irrevocable agreements are often used for setting aside funds for funeral arrangements when someone is seeking Medicaid eligibility.

Preneed contracts can be funded through trusts, insurance policies or annuities. The method of funding should be spelled out in the preneed contract.

With a preneed funeral trust, the goods and services are purchased in advance of the need and all or the majority of the money paid is deposited with a financial institution. If funds are to be placed in trust, then the contract should identify the institution with which the funds will be deposited, when the deposit will be made, and the amount of the deposit, who will receive any interest income, and any trustee fees or other administrative costs to be deducted from the trust, and who is responsible for taxes on interest income.

If an insurance policy is to be used, a copy of the policy should be attached to the preneed contract. Preneed insurance policies are purchased specifically for the payment of funeral goods and services and these policies direct payment of death benefits to the funeral director. You should also determine if the policy can be surrendered for less than face value or transferred to another funeral director, and if the benefits are adjusted for inflation.

In addition to identifying who is the recipient of the benefits of the contract, the contract should also contain some basic provisions including –

- A detailed description of the goods and services to be provided;

- The costs of the goods and services;

- Whether the prices are guaranteed or not; if guaranteed, the contract should state that if any of the goods or services are unavailable at the time of need, then goods or services of equal or greater value shall be substituted at no additional cost;

- If the contract is revocable or not; if revocable, the time period for revocation and the amount of monies to be refundable should be stated in the contract as well as any revocation fees payable to the funeral director;

- The method of funding the purchase price such as trusts, insurance or other means; and

- The geographical boundaries of the funeral director's service area and the circumstances under which the contract is transferable to another funeral director should internment be made outside the boundaries.

Funeral homes and preneed contracts are regulated by state law, so you should check your state's particular requirements before entering into this type of agreement.

Probating a Will

The final step in your caregiving duties may be the opening of an estate or probating the Last Will and Testament of your now deceased care recipient if you have been named Executor or Executrix of the Will, or are the next-of-kin, or other appropriate relative, if your care recipient died without a Will.

The laws of individual states govern wills and estates, so although we will discuss some very basics in this chapter, you really need to consult with an attorney licensed to practice in the state where a Will is to be probated or the state where assets of the deceased person who has died without a Will are located.

Here are some basic terms –

- Intestate – someone who has died "intestate" has died without a valid Will

- Testate – someone who has died "testate" has died with a valid Will

- Executor (male) or Executrix (female) – the person who has been named in a Will as the administrator of the estate

- Probate – the process set forth in state law of filing a Will (with a copy of the death certificate) with the appropriate state Court and petitioning the Court for authority to administer the estate and handle the assets of the deceased as Executor or Executrix, as the case may be

- Administrator (male) or Administratrix (female) – the personal representative appointed by the appropriate court to administer the estate and handle the assets of a person who has died without a valid Will

- Letters Testamentary (where there is a valid Will) or Letters of Administration (where there is no Will) – authority granted by the appropriate Court to the designated personal representative of an estate as Executor or Executrix (or Administrator or Administratrix, as the case may be) to handle the affairs of an estate, such as closing bank accounts, selling stocks and bonds, transferring cars. Some states require that the granting of these types of Letters be advertised in newspapers as notice to those who may have an interest in the estate, such as creditors of the deceased.

The personal representative of an estate has a number of duties and responsibilities. Generally, these duties include

- Identifying the assets of an estate which may include cash and funds in bank accounts, stocks, bonds, cars, real estate, personal valuables in safes or safe deposit boxes;

- Taking appropriate steps to safeguard, collect and protect the assets of the deceased (changing locks on real estate, renting and depositing valuables in a safe deposit box, obtaining and maintaining adequate insurance on real estate and cars);

- Using estate assets to pay the debts and obligations of the deceased and his/her estate;

- Communicating with the beneficiaries of a Will or the heirs of an estate where there is no Will;

- Preparing and filing appropriate tax returns and paying taxes including income, inheritance and estate taxes, if any;

- Preparing and filing various documents with the appropriate Court having jurisdiction over the estate, such as an inventory of the assets, status reports to the Court;

- Making final distributions of the estate to beneficiaries and heirs.

All of this can be pretty hairy stuff, so, again, consulting with an attorney is strongly advised.

Grief

The topic of grief seems like a fitting conclusion to this work. So, despite the fact that there is a plethora of information on this subject, we will touch on it briefly.

Grief is a normal and healthy response process to a loss with a variety of stages – shock, anger, denial, guilt, and depression. The process can take days, weeks, months or even years. Grief manifests itself through emotions (sadness, shock, anger, guilt, relief, anxiety), through physical reactions (heart palpitations, digestive problems, fatigue) and behavioral problems (sleep and appetite disorders, crying, confusion). The illness and death of a loved one is stressful, and stress causes a chemical depression of the human immunity system, which can result in even more problems such as colds and headaches.

Another less openly discussed result of the death of a loved one is a sense of relief that often is experienced by the primary caregiver. This is a legitimate reaction and in no way diminishes the love and affection felt by the caregiver toward the deceased care recipient.

Although you may never get over the sense of loss that results from the death of a loved one, the fog will eventually lift and you will find a way to accept the loss as a fact of life. With acceptance is the resolution of the grief process and the ability to again live and enjoy life. Although life will never be the same, you will find ways to discover and experience happiness again, but in a different way.

In addition to dealing with your own loss upon the death of a parent, you may also have to deal with the surviving parent's grief and efforts to live life without their spouse. Here our advice is pretty straightforward – let your Mom or Dad grieve in their own way, but reassure them that you are there to help. Do not cause them further disorientation by making plans for them to move or to sell their house. At a time of loss, they need as much stability as is possible, and familiar surroundings can be comforting. Do not force them to purge their world of the deceased spouse's belongings. They will know when the time is right to go through Dad's closet and dispose of his clothes, and if at all possible, you should assist them in this very difficult task. You should have a pretty good idea of the division of labor in your parent's household, that is, who did what. If Dad kept the checkbook, then Mom may need some help with this task. If Mom did all of the grocery shopping, then help Dad get acquainted with the local food market. Step in and do what you can do as long as it does not create any additional stress for your surviving parent.

As for your own sense of loss, give yourself time to grieve. Allow yourself some time to feel sad and depressed. Lower your expectations of yourself for a while. And then, get on with the business of living your life.

For caregiver children, there is another facet to the grieving process, and that is the recognition of your own mortality and self-grief when your last parent has passed on. As long as Mom or Dad is alive, you are buffered from the harsh reality of your own inevitable demise. With Mom and Dad gone, you are now the grownup and next in line for purposes of being the one who will need to be cared for rather than the one providing care for another, and the next to die.

It is the cycle of life and, short of dying young, you will grow old and become infirm and find yourself at the mercy of your own children. Your kids are watching you and how you treat your parents and handle your issues as a caregiver. In caring for your parents, you are creating the standard by which your own children when they become adults will probably measure their caregiving duties and obligations. The quality of care and affection you give to your folks during their lifetime will most likely become the measure for your own care down the road.

So, ask yourself, "what lessons am I teaching my own kids now about how to care for elderly loved ones?"

WEBSITES

There is an abundance of websites that deal with issues of aging, caregiving, and related topics. We have compiled a number of websites that we found to be the most comprehensive. We recommend these sites as good starting points for your research because a number of them have great locators and databases and hyperlinks to related sites.

Nevertheless, we cannot endorse these sites as we have no control over their content, and inclusion in this work should not be considered an endorsement of the site or any products or services offered or mentioned at these sites. In addition, although we have endeavored to be as accurate as possible, website addresses and links may be modified or changed since the date of this writing.

Also included in the Appendix is a good part of the *Resource Directory for Older Persons* compiled by the National Institute on Aging and the Administration on Aging which also has tons of website addresses, email addresses, street addresses and phone numbers for a vast number of organizations, some of which overlaps with the information in this section of the book.

Government Resources:

www.cms.hhs.gov (formerly *www.hcfa.gov*)
In July 2001, there was a change of name for the Health Care Financing Agency (HCFA) which is the agency within the U.S. Department of Health and Human Services responsible for the Medicare and Medicaid programs at the federal level. This agency is now known as the Centers for Medicare & Medicaid Services (CMS), and information for the HCFA site is being migrated to the CMS site. Both website name addresses are usable as of this writing.

www.cms.hhs.gov/manuals
You can find the official Web version of the Medicaid Manuals referred to from time to time in this work at this location.

www.cms.hhs.gov/regs/default.htm
Federal Medicare/Medicaid laws and Regulations. See comment above regarding HCFA's change of name.

www.medicare.gov
This is absolutely one of the best sources of information on a number of issues affecting the elderly. This site has useful information on Medicare coverage and a comparison of private insurers who contract with the government to provide health coverage for Medicare eligible persons who select this HMO/managed care option for their medical coverage. Some of the information has been reproduced and is included in the Appendix. It also has a listing of each State's Ombudsman Office, and a variety of on-line search tools.

This site also has a feature that compares the 17,000 nursing homes in the U.S. that are Medicare/Medicaid qualified (**www.medicare.gov/NHCompare/home.asp**). Unfortunately, we have found that much of the survey information is stale. If you have narrowed your search to a selection of nursing homes, do not rely on the survey information at this website, but instead request a copy from the nursing home of their latest state survey and plan of correction (the home's response to a negative survey).

This site also provides links to each State Health Insurance Counseling and Assistance Programs to provide assistance with decisions regarding Medicare or managed care options, appealing payment denials, and Medigap issues, to name a few. (**www.medicare.gov/Contacts/Ships.asp**)

Also at this site you can find a very helpful questionnaire, which has been reproduced for inclusion in the Appendix of this work, to help you assess a nursing home (**www.medicare.gov/nursing/checklist.asp**).

www.aoa.gov
This is an incredible site sponsored by the Administration on Aging which was established as a result of the Older Americans Act of 1965. The goal of the agency is to help the elderly maintain their independence and remain in their own homes for as long as possible. The AOA works in cooperation with the more than 650 Area Agencies on Aging. It has an eldercare locator data base that is a nationwide directory assistance service designed to help locate local support services for the elderly and their caretakers. It also has a resource directory that is the most comprehensive that we have ever seen. It is definitely a site worth visiting and book marking.

www.va.gov
This site is sponsored by the Department of Veterans Affairs and has lots of information on benefits available to veterans, including health care and nursing home care. If Mom or Dad is a vet, you should make sure they are getting all of the benefits to which they are entitled and this is a good place to start your investigation.

www.nih.gov
This site is sponsored by the National Institute of Health (NIH), one of the federal health agencies that operates under the Department of Health and Human Services and which serves as a focal point for health research for the

United States. Within the NIH are almost 30 Institutes and Centers, including the National Institute on Aging (NIA).

www.nia.nih.gov
The National Institute on Aging site contains valuable health information, as well as the *Resource Directory for Older People*, an incredible directory of links to a huge variety of resources of interest to seniors arranged alphabetically by name of organization, with telephone and fax numbers, street and website addresses and a general subject list. This directory has been reproduced in part and is included in the Appendix **(www.nih.gov/nia/health/resource/rd2001)**. This site also has links to other sites relevant to aging, including Alzheimer's Disease Education and Referral (ADEAR) Center.

www.ssa.gov
This is the official website for the Social Security Administration with valuable forms, publications and links.

www.dhhs.gov
This is the website sponsored by the United States Department of Health and Human Services (DHHS) – the primary U.S. agency for protecting the health of and providing human services to Americans. Not the best site for obtaining substantive information but it does have links to related sites and sources.

www.hud.gov
This is the website for the U.S. Department of Housing, and it includes information of interest to seniors on its Senior Citizen Page such as reverse mortgages and housing assistance for low-income seniors.

www.cdc.gov
The Center for Disease Control (CDC) website is a source generally for national health statistics (**www.cdc.gov/nchs**), but of more interest to those with elder care issues, it also contains the National Nursing Home Survey (NNHS) which has tons of statistical data about nursing homes and residents, as well as other health care related surveys.

www.health.state.mn.us/library/otherhds.htm
This site is sponsored by the Minnesota Department of Health and it has the website addresses of state health departments and agencies for every state in the U.S.

Health:

www.healthfinder.gov
Another must see site if you have health related questions. This site, sponsored by the U.S. Department of Health and Human Services, includes a medical encyclopedia, a medical dictionary, prescription drug information, information on a variety of diseases, and loads of other helpful info on aging topics, and Alzheimer's Disease.

www.nim.nih.gov/medlineplus/druginformation.html
This is a guide within the National Institutes of Health (NIH) site that contains information for more than 9,000 prescription and over-the-counter medications.

www.fda.gov/medwatch
The website for the Food and Drug Administration (FDA) has a reporting program for adverse events associated with and safety information regarding a variety of types of medical devices, medications and medical products.

www.webmd.com
One of the preeminent commercial sites for medical information.

www.labtestsonline.org
This site can be a valuable resource in helping you understand the purpose and results of a variety of clinical tests.

www.medicinenet.com
This is a commercial website for an online healthcare media publishing company with tons of medical information, including diseases and conditions, medical procedures and tests, medications and a medical dictionary.

www.mayo.edu
This is the website maintained by the famous Mayo clinic. It is a premier site for medical and health information.

www.alz.org
This site is sponsored by the Alzheimer's Association, one of the largest voluntary national health organizations, and contains valuable information for those suffering with the disease and their caregivers as well as related links.

www.alzheimer.org
This is the site maintained by the Alzheimer's Disease Education and Referral Center (ADEAR), a service of the National Institute on Aging (NIA) and contains valuable information about the disease, clinical trials and links to related sites.

Geriatric Care Managers:

www.caremanager.org
This site is provided through the National Association of Professional Geriatric Care Managers, and has a lot of useful information and links to regional sites that might be helpful in your search for a GCM.

www.careguide.net
This site has information on Geriatric Care Managers and other topics of interest to caregivers.

Home Health Care, Caregiving and Housing:

www.nahc.org
This site sponsored by the National Association for Home Care (NAHC) has tips on finding home health care and hospice care.

www.nfcacares.org
This site provides tips on caregiving and is sponsored by the National Family Caregivers Association (NFCA) and addresses the common needs and concerns of family caregivers.

www.caregivers.com
This site has a lot of helpful information with respect to many issues faced by caregivers.

www.caregiving.com
Another great site for caregivers. This site also hosts online support groups.

www.caregiver.org
This site is sponsored by the Family Caregiver Alliance, and it has excellent internet resources on a variety of elder care issues, diseases, services and support groups.

www.careguide.com
This is a commercial site sponsored by a care management company with pertinent housing, healthcare, housing and other information for caregivers.

www.elderweb.com
This site has information on many issues faced by caregivers as well as information on housing for seniors.

www.extendedcare.com
This site (a commercial site sponsored by a software vendor) has useful information for care recipients and givers and a data base of extended care providers for consumers.

www.wellspouse.org
This site offers support group services to spouses of care recipients.

www.aahsa.org
This is the website of the American Association of Homes and Services for the Aging site whose members apparently include more than 5,600 not-for-profit nursing homes, assisted living and senior housing facilities.

www.ccaconline.org
The Continuing Care Accreditation Commission (CCAC) is a site sponsored by the American Association of Homes & Services for the Aging (AAHSA). The CCAC offers an accreditation program available to continuing care and other retirement communities.

www.aarp.org
The American Association of Retired Persons (AARP) sponsors this site which has information of a variety of topics of interest to elders, including housing and health.

www.hud.gov
This is the website for the U.S. Department of Housing, and it includes information of interest to seniors on its Senior Citizen Page such as reverse mortgages and housing assistance for low-income seniors.

Hospice Care, Death and Grief:

www.hospicefoundation.org
This site is sponsored by the Hospice Foundation of America and promotes hospice care and also contains information on caregiving, terminal illness and grief.

www.NHPCO.org
This site is sponsored by the National Hospice and Palliative Care Organization and contains helpful information on hospice programs and end-of-life care.

www.growthhouse.org
The stated mission of this site is to be an "international gateway to resources for life-threatening illness and end of life care" with categories such as hospice and home care, palliative care, pain management, grief, and death with dignity.

www.aarp.org/griefandloss
The AARP site addresses many issues of aging, including grief and coping with the loss of a loved one.

www.widownet.org
This site offers information, support and resources for surviving spouses.

www.elderhope.com
This site also offers information, support and resources for caregivers and those coping with the loss of a loved one.

www.lastacts.org
This site has an annotated data base of internet links and other resources on death and dying, and a guide for preparing for death.

Insurance Rating Services:

www.ambest.com
www.fitchratings
www.moodys.com
www.standardand poors.com
www.weissratings.com

Miscellaneous:

www.partnershipforcaring.org
This national nonprofit corporation offers on its site state-specific forms of living wills and medical powers of attorney (though inclusion in this list should in no way be considered an endorsement or opinion as to the legal adequacy of any of this site's forms.) It also has an extensive library of links to other internet resources on aging, illnesses, caregiving, pain and death.

www.law.stetson.edu/excellence/elderlaw
This site was established and is maintained by the Elder Law Center at Stetson University College of Law in Florida, and it has a variety of information pertinent to elders and tons of links to related sites.

www.geroserver.iog.wayne.edu/GeroWeb
Wayne State Institute of Gerontology in Michigan is the designer and sponsor of this online virtual library resource on aging and related issues.

www.ink.org/public/keln/
The Kansas Elder Law Network, an affiliate of the University of Kansas, claims to be "the nations' most comprehensive site devoted to topics of interest to America's senior citizens and their advocates." It is an impressive site with national data bases and a variety of elder law resources.

www.healthlaw.org
The sponsor of this site is the National Health Law Program (NHeLP) a non-profit organization that provides consumer health care research and assistance for legal service organizations for low income persons.

www.seniorlaw.com
This site is sponsored by a NY law firm and has links to eldercare attorneys with web addresses, and additional resources on estate planning, elder abuse, Medicare and Medicaid. However, it does not appear to be regularly updated.

www.abanet.org
This is the official site of the American Bar Association. Although access to most of the site is limited to members, there are some general public resources available, including a national lawyer referral service.

www.nafep.com
This site is sponsored by a private association, the National Association of Financial and Estate Planning, and has available consumer information about estate planning and asset protection.

www.estateplanninglinks.com
This site is sponsored by a NC law firm and contains an extensive selection of links to various estate planning topics.

www.viatical.org
This is the site sponsored by the Viatical Settlement Association of America where you can find a list of viatical settlement providers and other information.

www.friendly4seniors.com
This site has an extensive data base with links to a number of sites and resources of interest to seniors with a number of categories such as housing and government agencies.

www.elderabusecenter.org
This is the National Center on Elder Abuse website, and it is funded by government and private sources to provide information on and research of elder abuse, as well as to provide assistance to the public.

Sources

FEDERAL LAWS:

Medicare: 42 U.S.C. Sections 1395-1395ccc; 42 CFR Section 483

Medicaid: 42 U.S.C. Sections 1396-1396s: 42 CFR Section 431

Federal Nursing Home Reform Law, passed as part of the Omnibus Budget Reconciliation Act of 1987, as amended; Regulations, 42 C.F.R. Sections 483.5 – 483.75

Medicare Catastrophic Coverage Act of 1988 (MCCA), 42 U.S.C. Section 1396 et.seq. (1988), as amended (Spousal Anti-Impoverishment Act)

Health Insurance Portability and Accountability Act of 1996 (HIPAA), as amended, 42 U.S.C. Section 1320

The Omnibus Budget Reconciliation Act of 1993, as amended

Medicaid Manuals

Advance Directives and Patient Rights: The Patient Self-Determination Act of 1990, Omnibus Budget Reconciliation Act of 1990, Pub. L. No. 101-508, 42 USC Section 1395cc(f) – Advance Medical Directives

Domestic Elder Abuse and Neglect: U.S. Administration on Aging, The National Elder Abuse Incidence Study, 1996 – see **www.aoa.gov/abuse/report** for the full report.

Appendices

AoA Elder Abuse Factsheet – A

Living Will Form – B

Durable Power of Attorney Form – C

Medicare Nursing Home Checklist – D

Medicare Website Information – E

Medicare Plan Choices – F

AoA/NIA Resource Directory for Older Persons – G

Appendix A
AoA Elder Abuse Factsheet

Reproduced from the Administration on Aging website at
www.aoa.gov/factsheets/abuse.html)

Elder Abuse Prevention

Elder Abuse Is a Serious Problem

Each year hundreds of thousands of older persons are abused, neglected and exploited by family members and others. Many victims are people who are older, frail, and vulnerable and cannot help themselves and depend on others to meet their most basic needs.

Legislatures in all 50 states have passed some form of elder abuse prevention laws. Laws and definitions of terms vary considerably from one state to another, but all states have set up reporting systems. Generally, adult protective services (APS) agencies receive and investigate reports of suspected elder abuse.

National Elder Abuse Incidence Study

Reports to APS agencies of domestic elder abuse increased 150 percent between 1986 and 1996. This increase dramatically exceeded the 10 percent increase in the older population over the same period.

A national incidence study conducted in 1996 found the following:

- 551,011 persons, aged 60 and over, experienced abuse, neglect, and/or self-neglect in a one-year period;

- Almost four times as many new incidents of abuse, neglect, and/or self-neglect were not reported as those that were reported to and substantiated by adult protective services agencies;

- Persons, aged 80 years and older, suffered abuse and neglect two to three times their proportion of the older population; and

- Among known perpetrators of abuse and neglect, the perpetrator was a family member in 90 percent of cases. Two-thirds of the perpetrators were adult children or spouses.

Generally Accepted Definitions

Physical abuse is the willful infliction of physical pain or injury, e.g., slapping, bruising, sexually molesting, or restraining.

Sexual abuse is the infliction of non-consensual sexual contact of any kind.

Psychological abuse is the infliction of mental or emotional anguish, e.g., humiliating, intimidating, or threatening.

Financial or material exploitation is the improper act or process of an individual, using the resources of an older person, without his/her consent, for someone else's benefit.

Neglect is the failure of a caretaker to provide goods or services necessary to avoid physical harm, mental anguish or mental illness, e.g., abandonment, denial of food or health related services.

The Role of the Administration on Aging

The Administration on Aging (AoA) is the only federal agency dedicated to policy development, planning, and the delivery of supportive home and community-based services to our nation's diverse population of older persons and their caregivers.

We provide critical information and assistance and programs that protect the rights of vulnerable, at-risk older persons through the national aging network. State elder abuse prevention activities include:

Professional training, e.g., workshops for adult protective services personnel and other professional groups, statewide conferences open to all service providers with an interest in elder abuse, and development of training manuals, videos, and other materials.

Coordination among state service systems and among service providers, e.g., creation of elder abuse hotlines for reporting, formation of statewide coalitions and task forces, and creation of local multi-disciplinary teams, coalitions and task forces;

Technical assistance, e.g., development of policy manuals and protocols that outline the proper or preferred procedures; and

Public education, e.g., development of elder abuse prevention education campaigns for the public, including media public service announcements, posters, flyers, and videos.

AoA funds the National Center on Elder Abuse as a resource for public and private agencies, professionals, service providers, and individuals interested in elder abuse prevention information, training, technical assistance and research. The website includes a state-by-state listing of statewide toll-free telephone numbers.

What Happens After You Report?

The APS agency screens calls for potential seriousness. The agency keeps the information it receives confidential. If the agency decides the situation possibly violates state elder abuse laws, the agency assigns a caseworker to conduct an investigation (in cases of an emergency, usually within 24 hours). If the victim needs crisis intervention, services are available. If elder abuse is not substantiated, most APS agencies will work as necessary with other community agencies to obtain any social and health services that the older person needs.

The older person has the right to refuse services offered by APS. The APS agency provides services only if the older person agrees or has been declared incapacitated by the court and a guardian has been appointed. The APS agency only takes such action as a last resort.

You Have Questions About the APS Services

If you have questions about the services provided to an older person by a local APS agency, call the Director of the local APS agency or the State APS agency. Give them the name and address of the older person and ask them to look into the matter. The AoA does not have oversight responsibility for APS.

Working in close partnership with its sister agencies in the Department of Health and Human Services, the Administration on Aging provides leadership, technical assistance, and support to the national aging network of 57 State Units on Aging, 655 Area Agencies on Aging, 225 Tribal and native organizations representing 300 American Indian and Alaska Native Tribal organizations and 2 organizations serving Native Hawaiians, plus thousands of service providers, adult care centers, caregivers, and volunteers.

For more information about the Administration on Aging, please contact:

Administration on Aging
U.S. Department of Health
and Human Services
Washington, DC 20201

Phone: (202) 619-0724
Fax: (202) 401-7620
E-mail: aoainfo@aoa.gov
Website: http://www.aoa.gov

**Eldercare Locator: 1-800-677-1116,
Monday – Friday, 9 a.m. to 8 p.m. ET**

Appendix B

Living Will Form

The following is a form used for the Commonwealth of Pennsylvania. You should consult with an attorney for the requirements of your particular state.

LIVING WILL DECLARATION

I, _____
being of sound mind willfully and voluntarily make this declaration to be followed if I become incompetent. This declaration reflects my firm and settled commitment to refuse life-sustaining treatment under the circumstances indicated below.

I direct my attending physician to withhold or withdraw life-sustaining treatment that serves only to prolong the process of dying, if I should be in a terminal condition or in a state of permanent unconsciousness.

I direct that treatment be limited to measures to keep me comfortable and to relieve pain, including any pain that might occur by withholding or withdrawing life-sustaining treatment.

In addition, if I am in the condition described above, I feel especially strong about the following forms of treatment:

I ( ) do ( ) do not want cardiac resuscitation.
I ( ) do ( ) do not want mechanical respiration.
I ( ) do ( ) do not want tube feeding or any other artificial or invasive form of nutrition (food) or hydration (water).
I ( ) do ( ) do not want blood or blood products.
I ( ) do ( ) do not want any form of surgery or invasive diagnostic tests.
I ( ) do ( ) do not want kidney dialysis.
I ( ) do ( ) do not want antibiotics.

I realize that if I do not specifically indicate my preference regarding any of the forms of treatment listed above, I may receive that form of treatment.

Other instructions:

_____
_____
_____

SURROGATE DESIGNATION

I ( ) do ( ) do not want to designate another person as my surrogate to make medical treatment decisions for me if I should be incompetent and be in a terminal condition or in a state of permanent unconsciousness.

Name and address of surrogate (if applicable):

_____
_____
_____

Name and address of substitute surrogate (if surrogate designated above is unable to serve):

_____
_____
_____

ANATOMICAL GIFT DONATION

I ( ) do ( ) do not want to make an anatomical gift of all or part of my body, subject to the following limitations, if any:

_____
_____

DECLARANT SIGNATURE

I made this declaration on the _____ day of _____, 200___.

Declarant's signature:

_____

Declarant's address:

_____

_____

_____

WITNESS SIGNATURES

The declaration of the person on behalf of and at the direction of the declarant knowingly and voluntarily signed this writing by signature or mark in my presence.

Witness signature:

_____

Witness address:

_____

Witness signature:

_____

Witness address:

_____

Appendix C

Durable Power of Attorney Form

The following is a form used for the Commonwealth of Pennsylvania. You should consult with an attorney for the requirements of your particular state.

DURABLE POWER OF ATTORNEY
PENNSYLVANIA REQUIRED NOTICE

THE PURPOSE OF THIS POWER OF ATTORNEY IS TO GIVE THE PERSON YOU DESIGNATE (YOUR "AGENT") BROAD POWERS TO HANDLE YOUR PROPERTY, WHICH MAY INCLUDE POWERS TO SELL OR OTHERWISE DISPOSE OF ANY REAL OR PERSONAL PROPERTY WITHOUT ADVANCE NOTICE TO YOU OR APPROVAL BY YOU.

THIS POWER OF ATTORNEY DOES NOT IMPOSE A DUTY ON YOUR AGENT TO EXERCISE GRANTED POWERS, BUT WHEN POWERS ARE EXERCISED, YOUR AGENT MUST USE DUE CARE TO ACT FOR YOUR BENEFIT AND IN ACCORDANCE WITH THIS POWER OF ATTORNEY.

YOUR AGENT MAY EXERCISE THE POWERS GIVEN HERE THROUGHOUT YOUR LIFETIME, EVEN AFTER YOU BECOME INCAPACITATED, UNLESS YOU EXPRESSLY LIMIT THE DURATION OF THESE POWERS OR YOU REVOKE THESE POWERS OR A COURT ACTION ON YOUR BEHALF TERMINATES YOUR AGENT'S AUTHORITY.

YOUR AGENT MUST KEEP YOUR FUNDS SEPARATE FROM YOUR AGENT'S FUNDS.

A COURT CAN TAKE AWAY THE POWER OF YOUR AGENT IF IT FINDS YOUR AGENT IS NOT ACTING PROPERLY.

THE POWERS AND DUTIES OF AN AGENT UNDER A POWER OF ATTORNEY ARE EXPLAINED MORE FULLY IN CHAPTER 56 OF TITLE 20 OF THE PENNSYLVANIA CONSOLIDATED STATUTES.

IF THERE IS ANYTHING ABOUT THIS FORM THAT YOU DO NOT UNDERSTAND, YOU SHOULD ASK A LAWYER OF YOUR OWN CHOOSING TO EXPLAIN IT TO YOU.

I HAVE READ OR HAD EXPLAINED TO ME THIS NOTICE AND I UNDERSTAND ITS CONTENTS.

_____
Signature

Date: _____

DURABLE POWER OF ATTORNEY

I, _____ of the County of _____, State of _____, with a Social Security Number of _____ do hereby constitute and appoint _____ _____ ("Primary Agent"), my true and lawful attorney for me, and in my name, place and stead, or in the event Primary Agent shall predecease me or be unable or unwilling to serve in this capacity, then I hereby constitute and appoint _____, my true and lawful attorney for me, and in his/her name, place and stead ("Secondary Agent") (hereinafter the Primary Agent and Secondary Agent shall be referred to as "Agent"):

1. **ASSETS AND PROPERTIES; SALES, TRANSFERS AND COLLECTIONS**. To enter upon and take possession of any lands, tenements and hereditament that may belong to me, or the possession of which I may be entitled; to ask, collect and receive any rents, profits, issues of income of any and all such lands, tenements and hereditament or of any part or parts thereof; to make, execute and deliver any deed, mortgage or lease, whether with or without covenants and warranties, in respect of any lands, tenements and hereditament, or of any part or parts thereof, and to manage any such lands, and to manage, repair, rebuild or reconstruct any buildings, houses or other structures, or any part thereof, that may now or hereafter be erected upon any such lands; to extend, renew, replace or increase any mortgage or mortgages now or hereinafter affecting any of my lands, tenements and hereditament and/or personal property belonging to me, and for any such purposes, to sign, seal, acknowledge and deliver any bond or bonds, or to make, sign and deliver any note or notes, and any extension, renewal, consolidation or apportionment agreements, or any other instruments, whether sealed or unsealed, that may be useful or necessary to accomplish any of the foregoing purposes.

2. **TAX AUTHORITY**. To pay any and all taxes, charges and assessments that may be levied, assessed or imposed upon any of my lands, buildings, tenements or other structures; to disclaim as my agent shall deem appropriate and in my best interest, property receivable my me by reason of gift, devise, or operation of law, consistent with applicable state and federal laws, rules and regulations; to settle tax disputes; to make any and all tax elections available to me, and to make, execute and file on my behalf any federal and/or state income or intangible tax return, declaration of estimated tax required, or tax power of attorney. I hereby request permission from the District Director of the Internal Revenue Service in the internal revenue district in which I am a legal resident to permit my aforenamed Agent to make, execute, and file the aforesaid returns and declarations.

3. **INSURANCE**. To obtain insurance of any kind, nature or description whatsoever, on any of my lands, tenements and hereditament and/or on any personal property belonging to me and/or in respect of any rents, issues and profits arising therefrom, and to make, execute and file proof or proofs of all loss or losses sustained or claimable thereunder, and all other instruments in and about the same, and to make, execute and deliver receipts, releases, or other discharges therefor, under seal or otherwise.

4. **BANKING AUTHORITY**. To make, execute, endorse, accept, collect or deliver any and all bills of exchange, checks, drafts, notes and trade acceptance, and to enter any safe deposit box, or boxes in my name; to pay all sums of money, at any time or times, that may hereafter be owing by me upon all bill of exchange, check, draft, note or trade acceptance made, executed, endorsed, accepted and delivered by me or for me, and in my name, by my said attorney; to conduct banking transactions to receive on my behalf, all monies due and owing to me, including, but not limited to my paycheck, disability payments, insurance proceeds, dividend, and interest income, to write checks on all of my personal checking accounts, to withdraw funds

from any and all of my savings accounts, certificates of deposit, money market funds, or any other place I may have financial resources, and to sign any and all documents necessary to effectuate the receipt of said sums or withdrawals of said monies, to hold all monies received or collected under this Paragraph and not used in paying my ongoing bills, in trust for me until my recovery or death; and

5. **SECURITIES AND BENEFITS AUTHORITY**. To sell, mortgage or hypothecate any and all shares of stock, bonds or other securities now or hereafter belonging to me, and to make, execute and deliver an assignment or assignments of any such shares of stocks, bonds or other securities, either absolutely, or as collateral security; to open and close accounts with any dealer of securities; to pay commissions and other fees and expenses in connection with any securities transaction; to execute stock powers for the purpose of transfer of securities; to purchase, receive, accept or otherwise acquire U.S. Treasury bonds redeemable in payment of federal estate taxes, upon such term as my said attorney shall deem advisable, and to borrow money for the purpose of purchasing such bonds, upon such terms as my said attorney shall deem advisable; to create an employee benefit plan (including a plan for a self-employed individual) for my benefit, to select payment options under any IRA or employee benefit plan in which I am a participant or to change options I have selected; to make voluntary contributions to such plans, to make roll-overs of plan benefits, and otherwise to waive rights, borrow money, purchase assets, make and change beneficiary designations, and grant consents.

6. **LITIGATION AUTHORITY**. To defend, settle, adjust, compound, submit to arbitration and compromise all actions, suits, accounts, reckonings, claims and demands whatsoever that are now, or hereafter shall be, pending between me and any person, firm, association or corporation, in such manner and in all respects as my said attorney shall think fit; to file any proof of debts, or take any other proceedings, under the Bankruptcy Act, or under any law of any state or territory of the United States, in

connection with any such claim, debts, money or demand and, in any such proceeding or proceedings, to vote in the election of any trustee or trustees, or assignee or assignees, and to demand, receive or accept any dividend or dividends, or distribution or distributions that may be or become payable therein or thereunder; to demand, sue for, collect, recover and receive all goods, claims, debts, monies, interest and demands whatsoever now due, or that may hereafter be due or belonging to me (including the right to institute any action, suit or legal proceeding for the recovery of any land, buildings, tenements or parts thereof, to the possession whereof I may be entitled), to make, execute and deliver receipts, releases or other discharges therefor, under seal or otherwise, and to other commence, prosecute, enforce, defend, answer, oppose, compromise, refer to arbitration, submit to judgment any such action or proceeding in which I may in any way be interested or concerned.

7.   **HIRING OF THIRD PARTIES**. To hire accountants, attorneys-at-law, clerks, workmen and others, and to remove them and appoint others in their place, and to pay and allow to the persons to be so employed such salaries, wages and other compensation as my said attorney shall think fit.

8.   **GUARDIAN**. If it shall become necessary for a court to appoint a guardian of my person or property, then and in such event, I hereby designate my Agent as guardian.

9.   **HEALTH CARE AUTHORITY**. To authorize, arrange for and consent to, my medical, therapeutic or surgical treatment and procedures if I should be physically or mentally incapacitated or otherwise unable to make such authorization for myself, including authorization for emergency care, hospitalization, surgery, therapy, dental, psychiatric, or any other kind of treatment, which s/he, in his sole discretion, thinks necessary; to enter into any contract or agreement with an institution or physician of his/her choice for my long term care and medical treatment; to apply for public benefits, including bit not limited to,

Medicare and Medicaid for me, to defray or pay the costs of health or custodial care; to have access to my clinical records and authorize the release of information and records to appropriate persons; to seek Court orders providing for the withholding and withdrawal of life-prolonging or death delaying procedures in accordance with a living will or other directive and declaration I may have made or hereafter make; to authorize the release of my body from any hospital or any other authority having possession of my body at the time of my death and to make all decisions necessary or incident to the removal and transportation of my body from the place of my death, to make all decisions necessary for the performance of funeral and burial services, if any, to have published in any newspaper an obituary notice containing whatever information he/she may choose, to contract with any competent person or company for the rendering of professional services by any funeral director of his/her choosing, to make all decisions necessary for the interment or cremation of my body, including, but not limited to, the selection of a casket or urn, the selection of a gravesite, and the selection of a gravestone and the inscription thereon, to contract with any person or company for the provision of care and tendering of my gravesite; and to be accorded first priority in visitation should I be a patient in any institution and unable to express a preference on account of my illness or disability.

My Agent shall not be liable or responsible for any costs or expenses of my medical treatment or care and my Agent's signature on any admission papers for a health care facility shall not make the Agent liable or responsible for any costs and expenses incurred for my care at such health care facility, it being understood that the Agent acts for me and in my stead, and I, alone, would be liable or responsible for such costs and expenses.

10. **GIFT AUTHORITY**. To make gifts on one or more occasions to one or more charitable organizations and individuals who are determined by my said attorney to be the natural objects of my bounty (and I hereby specifically declare that my Attorney-in-Fact himself or herself is one of

the natural objects of my bounty, and I specifically authorize my said attorney to make gifts to himself or herself), provided, however, that in no event shall the total gifts to any one individual in any one calendar year exceed the federal gift tax annual exclusion in effect at the time of such gift.

11. **FUNDING OF TRUSTS** (with Medicaid Provision). To transfer from time to time and at any time to the trustee or trustees of any revocable trust agreement or other trust created by me before or after the execution of this instrument, as to which trust I am, during my lifetime, a primary income and principal beneficiary, any and all cash, property, or interest in property, including any rights to receive income from any source; and for this purpose to enter and remove from any safety deposit box of mine (whether the box is registered in my name alone or jointly with one or more other persons) any of my cash or property and to execute such instruments, documents, and papers to effect the transfers described herein as may be necessary, appropriate, incidental, or convenient; to make such transfers absolutely in fee simple or for my lifetime only with the remainder or reversion (of the property transferred) remaining in me so that such property will be disposed of at my death by my Will or by the intestacy laws of the state in which I shall die as a resident. If I would qualify for governmental long term care benefits, except for my income, to establish an irrevocable income trust within the contemplation of the applicable federal tax or other laws, as amended, and the regulations administering or interpreting such provisions, and to transfer to the Trustee or Trustees of any such Trust, any and all pension income, Social Security benefits, or other income received by me, as "other income".

12. **GENERAL AUTHORITY**. Without in any way limiting the foregoing, generally to do, execute and perform any other act, deed, matter, or thing whatsoever that ought to be done, executed or performed, of any nature and kind whatsoever, as fully and effectively as I could do, with full power and authority to do and perform all and every act and thing whatsoever requisite and necessary to be done in and

about my estate, property and affairs as fully as I might or could do if personally present, the special powers enumerated above being an explanation of and not a limitation of such general power, and I hereby ratify and confirm all that my said attorney or any substitute for my said attorney shall lawfully do or cause to be done by virtue hereof.

13. **THIRD PARTY PROTECTION; INDEMNIFICATION.** I hereby declare that everything my Agent shall do or cause to be done under the provisions hereof shall be valid and effectual in favor of any person or entity claiming the benefit hereof who relied upon this instrument and had no knowledge or notice of revocation. Additionally, I declare that no revocation, termination or suspension of this Power of Attorney shall occur without actual notice thereof to my Agent; no person who relied in good faith on the authority of my Agent under this instrument shall incur any liability to me, my estate or heirs, successors and assigns. In addition, no person who acts in reliance upon any representations by Agent may make as to (a) the fact that my Agent's powers are then in effect; (b) the scope of my Agent's authority granted under this instrument; (c) my competency or capacity at the time this instrument is executed; (d) the fact that this instrument has not been revoked or amended; (e) the fact that my Agent continues to serve as may Agent, shall incur any liability to me, my estate, or my heirs or assigns for permitting my Agent to exercise any such authority nor shall any person who deals with my Agent be responsible to determine or ensure the proper application of such or property by my Agent. Any party dealing with any person named as Agent may rely upon as conclusively correct an affidavit or certificate of such Agent that (i) my Agent's powers are then in effect; or (ii) the action my Agent desires to take is within the scope of my Agent's authority granted under this instrument; (iii) I was competent and had capacity at the time this instrument was executed; (iv) this instrument has not been revoked; and/or (v) my Agent continues to serve as may Agent. It is further declared that if this Power of Attorney has been made a matter of public record, any revocation, termination, or suspension of this

power shall be ineffective unless documentation of such revocation, termination or suspension is also recorded in the public record of the county or counties where this power has been recorded. Furthermore, no actions taken by my Agent in good faith hereunder, and in furtherance of this purposes and intent of this power, shall give rise to any liability to any third party by my Agent it being expressly understood that the agreement by Agent to act as Agent hereunder and actions taken as Agent hereunder shall be without liability to Agent and no third party shall have a right by virtue of this instrument and the actions taken hereunder by Agent to bring any actions, suits, demands, claims or other recourse against my Agent in his/her individual capacity, and Agent shall have the right to use proceeds and properties within his/her control hereunder to defend and protect himself/herself against any such third party claims, suits, demands .

14. **LIMITATIONS.** Notwithstanding the powers contained in this durable Power of Attorney, my Agent may not perform duties under a contract that requires the exercise of my personal services; make any affidavit as to my personal knowledge; vote in any public election on my behalf; execute or revoke any will or codicil, Trust or amendment thereto, on my behalf; or create, amend, modify, or revoke any documents or other dispositions effective at my death.

I hereby ratify and confirm all whatsoever that my said attorney, or his or her substitute or substitutes shall do, or cause to be done, in or about the premises by virtue of this power.

THIS POWER IS CONTINGENT UPON AN OCCURRENCE OF A DISABILITY SUFFERED BY ME AS DEFINED BELOW, AND SHALL SURVIVE ANY SUCH DISABILITY OCCURRING TO OR SUFFERED BY ME UNLESS OTHERWISE REVOKED BY ME IN WRITING OR EXCEPT AS MAY BE PROVIDED BY STATUTE.

A. **DEFINITION OF DISABILITY.** A principal shall be under a disability if the principal is unable to manage his or her property and affairs effectively for reasons such as mental illness, mental deficiency, physical illness or disability, advanced age, chronic use of drugs, chronic intoxication, confinement, detention by a foreign power or disappearance.

B. **TAKES EFFECT ONLY UPON DISABILITY.** This Power of Attorney will only become effective when (and if) I become disabled (as defined above), which disability shall be verified by a signed, sworn and notarized statement of a Medical Doctor (M.D.) or Doctor of Osteopathy (D.O.)

IN WITNESS WHEREOF, I have hereunto set my hand and seal this _____ day of _____, _____

_____
(Signature)

Signed, sealed and delivered in the presence of

_____
(Signature)

_____
(Signature)

STATE OF _____
                                         ss.
COUNTY OF _____

On this _____ day of _____, _____, before me, a Notary Public in and for the State noted above, the undersigned officer, personally appeared _____ _____ known to me, or satisfactorily proven, to be the person whose name is subscribed to the within instrument, and acknowledged under oath that s/he executed the same for the purposes therein contained and as his or her voluntary act or deed.

_____
Notary Public
My Commission expires:_____

POWER OF ATTORNEY
ACKNOWLEDGEMENT OF AGENT

The undersigned acknowledge that s/he has read the attached Power of Attorney and is the person(s) identified as "Agent" for the principal, and that in the absence of a specific provision in the Power of Attorney, or in state law when I act as Agent:

1. I shall exercise the powers for the benefit of the principal.

2. I shall keep the assets of the principal separate from my assets.

3. I shall exercise reasonable caution and prudence.

4. I shall keep a full and accurate record of all actions, receipts and disbursements on behalf of the principal.

ACKNOWLEDGED AND AGREED THIS_____ day of _____,_____by the undersigned Agent.

_____
Name

_____
Address

_____
Name

_____
Address

Appendix D

Medicare Nursing Home Checklist

(reproduced from the Medicare website
www.medicare.gov/nursing/checklist.asp)

Medicare Nursing Home Checklist

Nursing Home Name:
_____

Address:
_____
_____

Date Visited: _____

1. **Basic Information**

    1. Is the facility Medicare certified?:____(yes) _____(no)

    2. Is the facility Medicaid certified?:____(yes) _____(no)

    3. Is this a skilled nursing facility?:____(yes) _____(no)

    4. Is the facility accepting new patients?:____(yes) _____(no)

    5. Is there a waiting period for admission?:____(yes) _____(no)

    6. Is a skilled bed available to you?:____(yes) _____(no)

Useful Tips

- Generally, skilled nursing care is available only for a short period of time after a hospitalization. Custodial care is for a much longer period of time. If a facility offers both types of care, learn if residents may transfer between levels of care within the nursing home without having to move from their old room or from the nursing home.

- Nursing homes that only take Medicaid residents might offer longer term but less intensive levels of care. Nursing Homes that don't accept Medicaid payment may make a resident move when Medicare or the resident's own money runs out.

- An occupancy rate is the total number of residents currently living in a nursing home divided by the home's total number of beds. Occupancy rates vary by area, depending on the overall number of available nursing home beds.

2. **Nursing Home Information**:

    1. Is the home and the current administrator licensed?:____(yes) _____(no)

    2. Does the home conduct background checks on all staff?:____(yes) _____(no)

    3. Does the home have special services units?:____(yes) _____(no)

    4. Does the home have abuse prevention training?:____(yes) _____(no)

Useful Tips

- **LICENSURE**: The nursing home and its administrator should be licensed by the State to operate.

- **BACKGROUND CHECKS**: Do the nursing home's procedures to screen potential employees for a history of abuse meet your State's requirements? Your State's Ombudsman program might be able to help you with this information.

- **SPECIAL SERVICES**: Some nursing homes have special service units like rehabilitation, Alzheimer's, and hospice. Learn if there are separate waiting periods or facility guidelines for when residents would be moved on or off the special unit.

- **STAFF TRAINING**: Do the nursing home's training programs educate employees about how to recognize resident abuse and neglect, how to deal with aggressive or difficult residents, and how to deal with the stress of caring for so many needs? Are there clear procedures to identify events or trends that might lead to abuse and neglect, and on how to investigate, report, and resolve your complaints?

- **LOSS PREVENTION**: Are there policies or procedures to safeguard resident possessions?

For Sections III through VI, give the nursing home a grade from one to five. One is worst, five is best.

Quality of Life:

	Worst				Best
	1	2	3	4	5
1. Residents can make choices about their daily routine. Examples are when to go to bed or get up, when to bathe, or when to eat.					
2. The interaction between staff and patient is warm and respectful.	1	2	3	4	5
3. The home is easy to visit for friends and family.	1	2	3	4	5
4. The nursing home meets your cultural, religious, or language needs.	1	2	3	4	5
5. The nursing home smells and looks clean and has good lighting.	1	2	3	4	5
6. The home maintains comfortable temperatures.	1	2	3	4	5
7. The resident rooms have personal articles and furniture.	1	2	3	4	5
8. The public and resident rooms have comfortable furniture.	1	2	3	4	5
9. The nursing home and its dining room are generally quiet.	1	2	3	4	5
10. Residents may choose from a variety of activities that they like.	1	2	3	4	5

11. The nursing home has   1   2   3   4   5
outside volunteer groups.

12. The nursing home has   1   2   3   4   5
outdoor areas for resident
use and helps residents to
get outside.

TOTAL: _____

                             (Best Possible Score: 60)

3. Quality of Care:

	Worst				Best
	1	2	3	4	5
1. The facility corrected any Quality of Care deficiencies that were in the State inspection report.					
2. Residents may continue to see their personal physician.	1	2	3	4	5
3. Residents are clean, appropriately dressed, and well groomed.	1	2	3	4	5
4. Nursing Home staff respond quickly to requests for help.	1	2	3	4	5
5. The administrator and staff seem comfortable with each other and with the residents.	1	2	3	4	5
6. Residents have the same care givers on a daily basis.	1	2	3	4	5
7. There are enough staff at night and on week-ends or holidays to care for each resident.	1	2	3	4	5
8. The home has an arrangement for emergency situations with a nearby hospital.	1	2	3	4	5
9. The family and residents councils are independent from the nursing home's management.	1	2	3	4	5
10. Care plan meetings are	1	2	3	4	5

held at times that are easy for residents and their family members to attend.

TOTAL: _____

(Best Possible Score: 50)

Useful Tips

- Good care plans are essential to good care. They should be put together by a team of providers and family and updated as often as necessary.

4. Nutrition and Hydration (Diet and Fluids):

	Worst 1	2	3	4	Best 5
1. The home corrected any deficiencies in these areas that were on the recent state inspection report.					
2. There are enough staff to assist each resident who requires help with eating.	1	2	3	4	5
3. The food smells and looks good and is served at proper temperatures.	1	2	3	4	5
4. Residents are offered choices of food at mealtimes.	1	2	3	4	5
5. Residents' weight is routinely monitored.	1	2	3	4	5
6. There are water pitchers and glasses on tables in the rooms.	1	2	3	4	5
7. Staff help residents drink if they are not able to do so on their own.	1	2	3	4	5
8. Nutritious snacks are available during the day and evening.	1	2	3	4	5
9. The environment in the dining room encourages residents to relax, socialize, and enjoy their food.	1	2	3	4	5

TOTAL: _____

(Best Possible Score: 45)

Useful Tips

- Ask the professional staff how the medicine a resident takes can affect what they eat and how often they may want something to drink.

- Visit at mealtime. Are residents rushed through meals or do they have time to finish eating and to use the meal as an opportunity to socialize with each other?

- Sometimes the food a home serves is fine, but a resident still won't eat. Nursing home residents may like some control over their diet. Can they select their meals from a menu or select their mealtime?

- If residents need help eating, do care plans specify what type of assistance they will receive?

5. Safety

	Worst				Best
	1	2	3	4	5
1. There are handrails in the hallways and grab bars in the bathrooms.					
2. Exits are clearly marked.	1	2	3	4	5
3. Spills and other accidents are cleaned up quickly.	1	2	3	4	5
4. Hallways are free of clutter and have good lighting.	1	2	3	4	5
5. There are enough staff to help move residents quickly in an emergency.	1	2	3	4	5
6. The nursing home has smoke detectors and sprinklers.	1	2	3	4	5

TOTAL: _____

(Best Possible Score: 30)

6. Useful Tips Relating to Information in Nursing Home Compare

Nursing Home Compare contains summary information about nursing homes from their last state inspection. It also contains information that was reported by the nursing homes prior to the last State inspection including nursing home and resident characteristics. If you have questions or concerns about the information on a nursing home, you should discuss them during your visit. This section contains useful tips and questions that you may want to ask the nursing home staff, family members and residents of the nursing home during your visit.

Nursing Home Compare Information on Results of Nursing Home Inspections

- Bring a copy of the Nursing Home Compare inspection results for the nursing home. Ask whether the deficiencies have been corrected.

- Ask to see a copy of the most recent nursing home inspection report.

Nursing Home Compare Information on Resident and Nursing Home Characteristics

1. **For the Measure: Residents with Physical Restraints**

    - Does it appear that there is sufficient staff to assist residents who need help in moving or getting in and out of chairs and bed?
    - Ask the Director of Nursing who is involved in the decisions about physical restraints.

- When physical restraints are used, do the staff remove the physical restraints on a regular basis to help residents with moving, and with activities of daily living?

- Do the staff help residents with physical restraints to get in and out of bed and chairs when they want to get up?

- Do staff help residents with physical restraints to move as much as they would like to?

2. **For the Measure: Residents with Pressure (Bed) Sores**

    - Ask the staff how they identify if a resident is at risk for skin breakdown. Ask them what they do to prevent pressure sores for these residents.

    - Ask the staff about the percentage of their residents that have pressure sores and why.

    - Do you see staff helping residents change their positions in wheelchairs, chairs, and beds?

3. **For the Measure: Residents with Bowel and Bladder Incontinence**

Does the nursing home smell clean?

Ask the staff what steps they take to prevent bowel and bladder incontinence for residents who are at risk.

4. **For the Measure: Residents Who Are Very Dependent in Eating**

    - Look at your response to Question 2 in Section V above.

    - Observe residents who need help in eating. Are they able to finish their meals or is the food returned to the kitchen uneaten?

5. **For the Measure: Residents Who Are Bedfast**

    - Ask the Director of Nursing how staff are assigned to care for these residents.

6. **For the Measure: Residents With Restricted Joint Motion**

    - Ask the Director of Nursing how the nursing home cares for residents with restricted joint motion.

    - Do the residents get help with getting out of chairs and beds when they want to get up?

7. **For the Measure: Residents with Unplanned Weight Gain or Loss**

    - Look at your responses to Questions 2, 3, 4, 5, 8, and 9 in section V above.

8. **For the Measure: Residents with Behavioral Symptoms**

- What management and/or medical approaches for behavioral symptoms are being used by the nursing home?

- How does staff handle residents that have behavioral symptoms such as calling out or yelling?

- Ask whether residents with behavioral symptoms are checked by a doctor or behavioral specialist.

- Ask whether staff get special training to help them to provide care to residents with behavioral symptoms.

Nursing Home Compare Information on Nursing Staff

Caring, competent nursing staff who respect each resident and family member are very important in assuring that residents get needed care and enjoy the best possible quality of life. Adequate nursing staff is needed to assess resident needs, plan and give them care, and help them with eating, bathing and other activities. Some residents (e.g., those who are more dependent in eating or who are bedfast) need more help than other residents depending on their conditions.

The combinations of registered nurses (RNs), licensed practical and vocational nurses (LPNs/LVNs), and certified nursing assistants (CNAs) that nursing homes may have vary depending on the type of care that residents

need and the number of residents in the nursing home.

- Look at your responses to Questions 2 and 5 in section III above and Questions 4, 5, and 10 in section IV above. Also look at your responses to Questions 2 and 7 in section V above.

- Are nursing staff members courteous and friendly to residents and to other staff?

- Do nursing staff respond timely to residents calls for assistance such as help getting in and out of bed, dressing and going to the bathroom?

- Observe meal times. Do all residents who need assistance with eating get help? Do staff give each resident enough time to chew food thoroughly and complete the meal?

- Which nursing staff members are involved in planning the resident's individual care? (Are they the same ones who give the care to residents?)

- Ask questions about staff turnover. Is there frequent turnover among certified nursing assistants (CNAs)? What about nurses and supervisors, including the Director of Nursing and the Administrator? If staff changes frequently, ask why.

- While the number of nursing staff is important to good care, also consider other factors, such as education and training. How many registered nurses (RNs) are on the staff, and how many available on each shift? What kind of training do certified nursing assistants (CNAs) receive? How does the nursing home ensure that all staff receive continuing education and keep their knowledge and skills up-to-date?

Appendix E

Medicare Website Information

(reproduced from the Medicare website – www.medicare.gov)

What is Medicare?

Medicare is a Health Insurance Program for:

- People 65 years of age and older.
- Some people with disabilities under age 65.
- People with End-Stage Renal Disease (permanent kidney failure requiring dialysis or a transplant).

Medicare has Two Parts:

- **Part A (Hospital Insurance)**
  Most people do not have to pay for Part A.
- **Part B (Medical Insurance)**
  Most people pay monthly for Part B.

Part A (Hospital Insurance)

Helps Pay For:

Care in hospitals as an inpatient, critical access hospitals (small facilities that give limited outpatient and inpatient services to people in rural areas), skilled nursing facilities, hospice care, and some home health care. Information about your coverage under Medicare Part A can be found in the Your Medicare Coverage database.

Cost:

Most people get Part A automatically when they turn age 65. They do not have to pay a monthly payment called a premium for Part A because they or a spouse paid Medicare taxes while they were working.

If you (or your spouse) did not pay Medicare taxes while you worked and you are age 65 or older, you still may be able to buy Part A. If you are not sure you have Part A, look on your red, white, and blue Medicare card. It will show "Hospital Part A" on the lower left corner of the card. You can also call the Social Security Administration toll free at 1-800-772-1213 or call your local Social Security office for more information about buying Part A. If you get benefits from the Railroad Retirement Board, call your local RRB office or 1-800-808-0772.

For More Information About Medicare Part A Coverage:
Visit the Your Medicare Coverage database.
Call your Fiscal Intermediary about Part A bills and services. The phone number for the Fiscal Intermediary in your area can be found in the Helpful Contacts section.

Part B (Medical Insurance)

Helps Pay For:

Doctors' services, outpatient hospital care, and some other medical services that Part A does not cover, such as the services of physical and occupational therapists, and some home health care. Part B helps pay for these covered services and supplies when they are **medically necessary**. Information about your coverage under Medicare Part B can be found in the Your Medicare Coverage database.

Cost:
You pay the Medicare Part B premium of $58.70 per month in 2003. This amount may change January 1, 2003. In some cases this amount may be higher if you did not choose Part B when you first became eligible at age 65. The cost of Part B may go up 10% for each 12-month period that you could have had Part B but did not sign up for it, except in special cases. You will have to pay this extra 10% for the rest of your life.

Enrolling in part B is your choice. You can sign up for Part B anytime during a 7-month period that begins 3 months before you turn 65. Visit your local Social Security office, or call the Social Security Administration at 1-800-772-1213 to sign up. If you choose to have Part B, the premium is usually taken out of your monthly Social Security, Railroad Retirement, or Civil Service Retirement payment. If you do not get any of the above payments, Medicare sends you a bill for your part B premium every 3 months. You should get your Medicare premium bill by the 10th of the month. If you do not get your bill by the 10th, call the Social Security Administration at 1-800-772-1213, or your local Social Security office. If you get benefits from the Railroad Retirement Board, call your local RRB office or 1-800-808-0772.

For More Information About Medicare Part B Coverage:
Visit the Your Medicare Coverage database.
Call your Medicare Carrier about bills and services. The phone number for the Medicare Carrier in your area can be found in the Helpful Contacts section.

You may have choices in how you get your health care including the Original Medicare Plan, Medicare Managed Care Plans (like HMOs), and Medicare Private Fee-for-Service Plans.

Who is Eligible for Medicare?

Generally, you are eligible for Medicare if you or your spouse worked for at least 10 years in Medicare-covered employment and you are 65 years old and a citizen or permanent resident of the United States. You might also qualify for coverage if you are a younger person with a disability or with End-Stage Renal disease (permanent kidney failure requiring dialysis or transplant).

Here are some simple guidelines. You can get Part A at age 65 without having to pay premiums if:

- You are already receiving retirement benefits from Social Security or the Railroad Retirement Board.

- You are eligible to receive Social Security or Railroad benefits but have not yet filed for them.

- You or your spouse had Medicare-covered government employment.

If you are under 65, you can get Part A without having to pay premiums if:

- You have received Social Security or Railroad Retirement Board disability benefit for 24 months.

- You are a kidney dialysis or kidney transplant patient.

While you do not have to pay a premium for Part A if you meet one of those conditions, you must pay for Part B if you want it. The Part B monthly premium in 2003 is $58.70. It is deducted from your Social Security, Railroad Retirement, or Civil Service Retirement check. If you do not get any of the above payments, Medicare sends you a bill for your Part B premium every 3 months.

If you have questions about your eligibility for Medicare Part A or Part B, or if you want to apply for Medicare, call the Social Security Administration. The toll-free telephone number is: 1-800-772-1213. The TTY-TDD number for the hearing and speech impaired is 1-800-325-0778. You can also get information about buying Part A as well as part B if you do not qualify for premium-free part A.

Copy of Initial Enrollment Package

The Initial Enrollment Package includes four (4) separate documents:

7. A <u>Message About Medicare</u> from the Federal Medicare Agency,

8. Medicare: <u>What You Need to Know</u> About Medicare and Other Health Insurance,

9. <u>Social Security</u>: You May Be Able to Get SSI,

10. <u>Form CMS-40</u>: The Complete Medicare Card Form.

A Message About Medicare from the Federal Medicare Agency

Welcome to Medicare!

You have been enrolled automatically in Part A and Part B of the Medicare program because you are a Social Security beneficiary. Part A helps pay for hospital expenses and Part B helps pay for medical expenses, such as doctor visits. This package will help you learn about the Medicare program. It contains your red, white, and blue Medicare card. Your Medicare card shows that you have hospital insurance (Part A) and medical insurance (Part B). Your card also shows the dates your coverage begins.

Your Part A is free. There is a monthly premium for your Part B medical insurance. In 2002, Part B costs $54.00 each month. If your income is low, your state may pay your Part B monthly premium. Read the section "Assistance for Low-Income Medicare Beneficiaries" in the enclosed booklet.

You have three important decisions to make:

1) Do you want to keep Medicare Part B?

2) If you keep Medicare Part B, how do you want to receive your Medicare-covered services?

3) Do you need supplemental insurance to pay for services and products that Medicare does not cover?

1) DECISION: Do you need Part B?
Before you make a decision, you should read the information about Part B in the enclosed booklet, "What You Need to Know about Medicare and Other Health Insurance". You must keep Part B if you want to be able to join any of the Medicare managed care plans (such as HMOs), Medicare medical savings accounts, or other Medicare health insurance options. If you do not keep Part B, you will only be eligible to receive Medicare hospital coverage.

If you are turning 65 or are older, you can delay taking your Part B medical insurance if: (1) you or your spouse (of any age) continue to work **and** (2) **you** are covered under a group health plan from that current employment.

If you are under age 65 and disabled, you can delay your Part B if (1) you, or any member of your family is currently working, **and** (2) **you** have group health plan coverage from that current employment.

You can find out how your group health plan works together with Medicare by contacting your employer or health benefits representative.

IMPORTANT: If you do not have group health plan coverage based on current employment and you delay taking Part B, your monthly premium may be higher. Your premium **will increase by 10 percent** for each 12 months that you could have had Part B, but did not take it. For example, if you delayed your Part B for 12 months at the current rate, you may have to pay $59.40 each month for Part B, instead of $54.00. If you do not keep Part B now, you will only have a chance to sign up for Part B once a year -- between January 1 and March 31. Your Part B insurance will start the following July. If you choose to delay taking Part B because you currently have group health plan coverage, you may be able to avoid paying this higher premium by signing up for Part B while you have this coverage or within eight months after the employment ends or the group health coverage ends, whichever comes first.

If you want to keep Part B, cut out the enclosed card and keep it with you. No further action is necessary. Your premium will begin to be deducted from your Social Security payment the month your Part B starts. If you do not get monthly Social Security benefits, you will receive a bill every three months for your Part B. **Do not send any money now.**

If you do not want to keep Part B, sign the enclosed form and check the block after "I do not want medical insurance". Return the entire form in the enclosed envelope. Do this before the date shown on the card so you will not owe a monthly premium. We will send you a new card that shows you have Part A only.

2) DECISION: How do you want to receive your services?
3) DECISION: Do you need supplemental insurance?

If you have any questions or need more information, you can call Social Security at 1-800-772-1213.

Enrolling in Medicare - How Do I Sign up for Medicare Part A & B?

Medicare Has Two Parts. They are:

- **hospital insurance** or Medicare Part A (hospital insurance), which helps pay for care in a hospital and skilled nursing facility, home health care and hospice care; and

- **medical insurance** or Medicare Part B (medical insurance), which helps pay for doctors, outpatient hospital care and other medical services.

Most people do not have to pay for Medicare Part A.

Most people pay for Medicare Part B.

General Enrollment Period for Medicare Part B

If you did not take Part B when you were first eligible for Medicare, you may sign up during the General Enrollment Period. The General Enrollment Period runs from January 1 through March 31 of each year.

Remember, the cost of your Part B may go up 10% for each 12-month period that you could have had Part B but did not take it, and you will have to pay this extra amount as long as you have Part B, except in special cases.

If you already have Medicare Part A and need Part B you can sign up for Part B at your local Social Security office or by calling 1-800-772-1213.

Help to Pay Your Health Care Costs

Most of your health care costs are covered if you have Medicare and you qualify for Medicaid. Medicaid is a joint federal and state program that helps pay medical costs for some people with low incomes and limited resources. Medicaid programs vary from state to state. People on Medicaid may also get coverage for nursing home care and outpatient prescription drugs which are not covered by Medicare. You can find more information about Medicaid on cms.hhs.gov.

States also have programs that pay some or all of Medicare's premiums and may also pay Medicare deductibles and coinsurance for certain people who have Medicare and a low income. To qualify, you must have:

- Part A (Hospital Insurance),
- Assets, such as bank accounts, stocks, and bonds that are not more than $4,000 for a single person, or $6,000 for a couple, and
- A monthly income that is below certain limits.

For more information on these programs, look at the Medicare Savings Programs publication.

There are also Prescription Drug Assistance Programs available. These programs offer discounts or free medications to individuals in need.

Your Medicare Card

Need a Replacement Card? Order a Medicare Card by Phone or Online

If you lose your Medicare card, you can obtain a replacement card from the Social Security Administration one of the following ways:

- Call the Social Security Administration's toll-free number at 1-800-772-1213.

- Make sure you have your Medicare number ready when you call. You should receive your new card in about four weeks.

- Order Online by visiting the Medicare Card Replacement section of the Social Security Administration's Website.

Their Online business hours are:

Monday - Friday: 6 a.m. until 1 a.m
Saturday: 8 a.m. until 11 p.m.
Sunday: 8 a.m. until 8 p.m.
To make your online request, you will need the following information:

- Your name as it appears on your most recent Social Security card
- Your Social Security Number
- Your date and place of birth
- Your mother's maiden name (to help identify you)

- Your phone number in case Social Security needs to contact you about your request
- Your e-mail address (optional)
- Your last payment amount or the month and year you last received a payment if you have received benefits in the last 12 months.

- Contact your local <u>Social Security Office</u>.

    If you get benefits from the Railroad Retirement Board, call your local RRB office, or call 1-800-808-0772.

    Make sure you have your Medicare number ready when you call. You should receive your new card in about four weeks.

New to Medicare?

You will receive your Medicare card in the mail 3 months prior to eligibility. The Medicare card will include your name, Medicare claim number, the type of coverage you have (Part A, Part B, or both), and the date your coverage starts.

Using Your Medicare Card

Show your card whenever you get medical care. This will assure that a claim for payment is sent to Medicare. Make sure to use your exact name and claim number. If you are married, your spouse will have his or her own card and claim number. Never let anyone else use your Medicare card, and keep the number as safe as you would a credit card number. Take your card with you when you travel, and have it handy when you call about a Medicare claim.
Note: CMS began using cards displaying the 1-800-Medicare number. If you have a card that shows something different, it is still valid and can be used to get medical care.

Medicare Premium Amounts for 2002

Part A: (Hospital Insurance) Premium
- Most people do not pay a monthly Part A premium because they or a spouse has 40 or more quarters of Medicare covered employment.
- $319.00 per month (Note: This premium is paid only by individuals who are not otherwise eligible for premium-free hospital insurance and have less than 30 quarters of Medicare covered employment).
- The Part A premium is $175.00 for those individuals having 30-39 quarters of Medicare covered employment.

Part B: (Medical Insurance) Premium
- $54.00 per month.

Original Medicare Plan Deductible and Coinsurance Amounts for 2002

Part A: (Hospital Insurance)
Deductible
- $812.00 (Per Benefit Period)

Coinsurance
- $203.00 a day for the 61st - 90th day each benefit period.
- $406.00 a day for the 91st - 150th day for each lifetime reserve day (total of 60 lifetime reserve days - non-renewable).

Skilled Nursing Facility Coinsurance
- up to $101.50 a day for the 21st - 100th day each benefit period.

Part B: (Medical Insurance)

Deductible

- $100.00 per year. (Note: You pay 20% of the Medicare approved amount for services after you meet the $100.00 deductible.)

See Medicare & You for additional information about Original Medicare Plan coinsurance and copayment amounts.

Medicare Premium Amounts for 2003

Part A: (Hospital Insurance) Premium

- Most people do not pay a monthly Part A premium because they or a spouse has 40 or more quarters of Medicare covered employment.
- $316.00 per month (Note: This premium is paid only by individuals who are not otherwise eligible for premium-free hospital insurance and have less than 30 quarters of Medicare covered employment).
- The Part A premium is $174.00 for those individuals having 30-39 quarters of Medicare covered employment.

Part B: (Medical Insurance) Premium
- $58.70 per month.

Original Medicare Plan Deductible and Coinsurance Amounts for 2003

Part A: (Hospital Insurance)

Deductible
- $840.00 (Per Benefit Period)

Coinsurance
- $210.00 a day for the 61st - 90th day each benefit period.
- $420.00 a day for the 91st - 150th day for each lifetime reserve day (total of 60 lifetime reserve days - non-renewable).

Skilled Nursing Facility Coinsurance
- up to $105.00 a day for the 21st - 100th day each benefit period.

Part B: (Medical Insurance)
> Deductible
>> • $100.00 per year. (Note: You pay 20% of the Medicare approved amount for services after you meet the $100.00 deductible.)

See <u>Medicare & You</u> for additional information about Original Medicare Plan coinsurance and copayment amounts.

Address Changes

If you need to change your address, call the Social Security Administration at 1-800-772-1213, or call your local Social Security office. They will make the change for you. If you get benefits from the Railroad Retirement Board, call your local RRB office, or call 1-800-808-0772.

Appendix F

Medicare Plan Choices

(reproduced from the Medicare web site –
www.medicare.gov/nursing/checklist.asp)

Medicare Plan Choices

What are Medicare Health Plans?

Medicare offers you different ways to get your Medicare benefits. These different options are called Medicare health plans. One option is the Original Medicare Plan. Some private companies contract with the Medicare program to offer Medicare health plans. These are called Medicare + Choice ("Medicare plus Choice") plans. How you get your health care in the Medicare program depends on which plan you choose. Depending on where you live, you may have more than one plan to choose from.

What types of Medicare health plans are available?

In 2002, Medicare offers the following types of Medicare health plans:

- The Original Medicare Plan (sometimes called fee-for-service) -- Everyone with Medicare can join the Original Medicare Plan. This plan is available nationwide. Many people in the Original Medicare Plan also have a Medigap (Medicare Supplemental Insurance) policy or supplemental coverage provided by their former employer to help pay health care costs that this plan does not cover.

- Medicare + Choice (pronounced "Medicare plus Choice") plans –
- **Medicare + Choice plans include**:

    - Medicare managed care plans (like HMOs), and
    - Medicare Private Fee-for-Service plans.

Medicare + Choice plans provide care under contract to Medicare. They may provide benefits like coordination of care or reducing out-of-pocket expenses. Some plans may offer additional benefits, such as prescription drugs. There are two types of Medicare + Choice plans. They are available in many parts of the country.

To find a list of plans available in your area, look at the <u>Medicare Personal Plan Finder</u>.

Making the Best Choice for You

How you get your Medicare health benefits affects many things, like cost, extra benefits, doctor choice, convenience, and quality. They are all important, but some may be more important to you than others. You need to look at what plans are available in your area, what each plan offers, and make the best choice for you.
Your choice will affect:

Cost - What will my out-of-pocket costs be?

Benefits - Do I need extra benefits and services, like prescription drugs, eye exams, hearing aids, or routine physical exams?

Doctor Choice - Can I see the doctor(s) I want to see? Do I need a referral to see a specialist?

Convenience - Where are the doctors' offices and what are their hours? Is there paperwork? Do I have to file claims myself? Is there a telephone hotline for medical advice from a nurse or other medical staff?

Think about what is most important to you in a health plan. Then look at this chart. It can help you see which types of plans have the things that are most important to you.

		Medicare + Choice Plans	
	Original Medicare Plan	Managed Care Plan (like an HMO)	Private Fee-for-Service Plan
Costs Total Out-of-Pocket Costs	**High**	**Low to Medium**	**Medium to high**
Extra Benefits In addition to Medicare covered benefits.	**None**	**Most** Like prescription drugs, eye exams, hearing aids, or routine physical exams.	**Some** Like foreign travel or extra days in the hospital.
Doctor Choice	**Widest** Choose any doctor or specialist who accepts Medicare.	**Some** Usually must see a doctor or specialist who belongs in your plan.	**Wide** Choose any doctor or specialist who accepts the plan's payment.
Convenience	**Varies** Available nationwide.	**Varies** Available in some areas. May require less paperwork and have phone hotline for medical advice.	**Varies** Available in some areas. May require less paperwork and have phone hotline for medical advice.

Help with Health Care Coverage

Before making a health plan decision, it is important to learn more about what the different health plans cover and how that may affect your out-of-pocket costs. For example, the Original Medicare Plan does not pay for or cover everything. To get extra coverage, you may buy a Medigap policy, or join a Medicare + Choice plan. You may also have or qualify for:

- Employer or union health coverage,
- Veteran's benefits,
- TRICARE for Life (for military retirees and their spouses and survivors),
- Help from your state (i.e., Medicare Savings Programs and Medicaid),
- Prescription Drug Assistance Programs,
- PACE,
- Other insurance, like long-term care insurance.

The way each of these types of insurance work varies. **Remember:** Whether you get your Medicare health care coverage from the Original Medicare Plan or another Medicare health plan, you are still in the Medicare program.

Quality Data to Help You Choose

Research shows that Medicare health plans differ on quality. The Medicare program measures the quality of care that people like you get. This information is available to everyone. You can view quality information in the detailed results section of the Medicare Personal Plan Finder.

When can I Join a Medicare + Choice Plan?

Generally, you may join a Medicare + Choice plan at any time. However, some Medicare + Choice plans limit the number of members in their plans. These plans may not accept new members when they reach their limit. A plan can tell you if it is signing up new members. Also, if you are in an institution (like a nursing home), check with the plan to see if you may be able to join at other times.

When can I leave A Medicare + Choice Plan?

You may leave your plan at anytime, for any reason.

Buying (Joining) Medigap Plans

The best time to buy a Medigap plan is during your Medigap open enrollment period. Your Medigap open enrollment period lasts for 6 months. It starts on the first day of the month in which you are both:
- Age 65 or older, and
- Enrolled in Medicare Part B.

In some situations, you have the right to buy a Medigap policy outside of your Medigap open enrollment period. These rights are called "Medigap Protections" or "Guaranteed Issue Rights." Medigap Protections are important because without them, if you are not in your Medigap open enrollment period, an insurance company can refuse to sell you a policy, or you may be charged more for the policy. In addition, if you drop your Medigap policy, you may not be able to get it back except in very limited situations. For more information on Medigap Protections, look at the Choosing a Medigap Policy publication below.

To find a list of Medigap Policies offered in your area, look at the Medicare Personal Plan Finder

Health Plan References and Materials

Listed below are some additional publications that can help you learn about Medicare's health plan options and guide you in choosing the best plan for you. You can view the publication by clicking on its title below or call 1-800-MEDICARE (1-800-633-4227, TTY/TDD: 1-877-486-2048 for the hearing and speech impaired) to get free copies of these publications.

Appendix G

AoA/NIA

Resource Directory for Older Persons

(reproduced in part from the nih website – www.nih.gov/nia/health/resource/rd2001)

Resource Directory for Older People
Introduction

Knowledge is of two kinds. We know a subject ourselves, or we know where we can find the information. ~Samuel Johnson~

The *Resource Directory for Older People* is designed to help people find the information they need. A cooperative effort of the National Institute on Aging (NIA) and the Administration on Aging (AoA), the directory is intended to serve a wide audience including health and legal professionals, social service providers, librarians, and researchers, as well as older people and their families. The directory contains organizational names, addresses, phone numbers, and fax numbers, as well as email and website addresses.

The directory lists Federal agencies, AoA-supported resource centers, professional societies, private groups, and volunteer programs. Some deal mainly with older people and their families, while others serve professionals who work with older adults, and still others target people of all ages. Inclusion in the directory does not imply an endorsement by NIA or AoA.

The directory is arranged alphabetically by organization name, and there is a general subject index. Every effort was made to publish a brief but accurate overview about each listed organization. Readers should contact each organization directly if they want more detailed information.

We welcome comments, suggestions, and additions for future editions. Updates, as well as information on any national group serving older people that is not included in this edition, should be sent to:

Editor, *Resource Directory for Older People*
National Institute on Aging

Office of Communications and Public Liaison
Building 31, Room 5C27
31 Center Drive, MSC 2292
Bethesda, MD 20892-2292
(301) 496-1752

Administration on Aging (AoA)
Department of Health and Human Services (DHHS)
330 Independence Avenue, SW
Washington, DC 20201
Public Inquiries: 202-619-0724
202-619-7501
Eldercare Locator: 1-800-677-1116 (toll-free)
Fax: 202-401-7620
Website: http://www.aoa.gov
Working in close partnership with its sister agencies in DHHS, the AoA is the Federal agency dedicated to policy development, planning and the delivery of supportive home- and community-based services to older persons and their caregivers. The AoA works through the national aging network of State and Area Agencies on Aging, Tribal and Native organizations, and thousands of service providers, adult care centers, caregivers, and volunteers.

Agency for Healthcare Research & Quality (AHRQ)
Publications Clearinghouse
PO Box 8547
Silver Spring, MD 20907-8547
Phone: 1-800-358-9295 (toll-free)
Website: http://www.ahrq.gov
AHRQ, part of the Federal Government, provides an information clearinghouse service that distributes *Evidence-Based Summaries and Reports*, *Clinical Practice Guidelines*, and other medical statistics and information. Call to order copies of guidelines on topics such as cardiac rehabilitation, treatment of pressure sores, or other publications on elder and long term health care, health insurance, and minority health data. Visit the website to download *Clinical Practice Guidelines* on topics such as urinary incontinence, screening for Alzheimer's disease, and post-stroke rehabilitation.

AIDS Clinical Trials Information Service (ACTIS)
PO Box 6421
Rockville, MD 20849-6421
Phone: 1-800-TRIALS-A (874-2572) (toll-free) (English, Spanish, Portuguese)
301-519-0459
TTY: 1-888-480-3739 (toll-free)
Fax: 301-519-6616
Email: actis@actis.org
Website: http://www.actis.org
ACTIS, funded by the Federal Government, is a central resource providing current information on Federally and privately sponsored clinical trials for HIV/AIDS patients. Free, confidential information is available in English, Spanish, or Portuguese.

Alliance for Aging Research
2021 K Street, NW, Suite 305
Washington, DC 20006
Phone: 202-293-2856
Fax: 202-785-8574
Website: http://www.agingresearch.org
The Alliance is a national, citizen advocacy organization offering free publications including *Investing in Older Women's Health*, *Meeting the Medical Needs of the Senior Boom*, *Delaying the Diseases of Aging*, and other aging-related subjects such as menopause, how to age with ease, and health care options under Medicare.

Alzheimer's Association
919 North Michigan Avenue, Suite 1100
Chicago, IL 60611
Phone: 1-800-272-3900 (toll-free)
312-335-8700
TTY: 312-335-8882
Fax: 312-335-1110
Email: info@alz.org
Website: http://www.alz.org
The Association is a nonprofit organization offering information and support services to people with Alzheimer's disease (AD) and their families. Contact the 24-hour, toll-

free telephone line to link with local chapters and community resources. The Association funds research to find a cure for AD and provides information on caregiving. A free catalog of educational publications is available in English and Spanish.

Alzheimer's Disease Education and Referral (ADEAR) Center
PO Box 8250
Silver Spring, MD 20907-8250
Phone: 1-800-438-4380 (toll-free) (English, Spanish)
301-495-3311
Fax: 301-495-3334
Email: adear@alzheimers.org
Website: http://www.alzheimers.org
The ADEAR Center, funded by the National Institute on Aging, distributes information about Alzheimer's disease (AD) to health professionals, patients and their families, and the public. Contact the Center for information about the symptoms, diagnosis, and treatment of AD; recent research; and referrals to State and other national services. On its website, the Center offers searchable publications and databases, including the AD Clinical Trials Database of studies accepting volunteers.

American Academy of Dermatology (AAD)
930 North Meacham Road
Schaumburg, IL 60173-4965
Phone: 1-888-462-3376 (toll-free) (automated ordering system)
847-330-0230
Fax: 847-330-0050
Website: http://www.aad.org
AAD, an association of doctors specializing in dermatology, provides pamphlets and general information about skin cancers, contact allergies (like poison ivy), shingles (herpes zoster), and other skin conditions. Audio-cassettes, news releases, and public service announcements on dermatology topics also are available. Contact AAD for referrals to certified dermatologists.

American Academy of Family Physicians (AAFP)
11400 Tomahawk Creek Parkway
Leawood, KS 66201
Phone: 1-800-274-2237 (toll-free)
913-906-6000
Fax: 913-906-6094
Email: fp@aafp.org
Website: http://familydoctor.org (information for the public)
AAFP, a national association of doctors in family practice, offers education and information on health care and disease prevention. Contact the AAFP for referrals to certified doctors. Publications on topics such as sensible eating, preventive health services and family practice, and a health care guide are available free from AAFP-certified doctors or for a fee from AAFP. The website offers free fact sheets on specific diseases, questions and answers about common health issues, self-care flow charts, and databases on drugs and drug reactions.

American Academy of Neurology (AAN)
1080 Montreal Avenue
St. Paul, MN 55116
Phone: 651-695-1940
Fax: 651-695-2791
Website: http://www.aan.com
The Academy is an association of doctors specializing in disorders of the brain and central nervous system. Contact AAN for information about neurology. Visit the Academy's website for referrals to accredited neurologists. Publications include the AAN's *Patient Information Guide* on neurological disorders and treatment.

American Academy of Ophthalmology (AAO)
PO Box 7424
San Francisco, CA 94120-7424
Phone: 1-800-222-3937 (toll-free)
415-561-8500
Fax: 415-561-8567
Website: http://www.eyenet.org
AAO is an association of doctors specializing in eye diseases. The Academy's Eye Care America helpline

provides information and publications and connects eligible older people with ophthalmologists who provide free eye care in their community. US citizens qualify for free care at age 65 if they have no health insurance and have not seen an eye doctor for at least 3 years.

American Academy of Orthopaedic Surgeons (AAOS)
6300 North River Road
Rosemont, IL 60018-4262
Phone: 847-823-7186
Fax: 847-823-8125
Website: http://www.aaos.org
AAOS is a nonprofit organization of doctors specializing in bones, joints, muscles, ligaments, and tendons. Contact AAOS for information on orthopaedic medicine including arthritis, osteoporosis, artificial joints, and prevention of hip fractures. Publications on orthopaedic medicine, many specifically for older people, are available.

American Academy of Otolaryngology–Head and Neck Surgery, Inc. (AAO)
1 Prince Street
Alexandria, VA 22314
Phone: 703-836-4444
TTY: 703-519-1585
Fax: 703-683-5100
Email: webmaster@entnet.org
Website: http://www.entnet.org
The Academy is an organization of doctors specializing in ear, nose, and throat problems and diseases of the head and neck. Contact AAO for referrals to specialists and publications on topics such as cosmetic facial surgery, head and neck tumors, treatments for certain types of hearing loss, and balance disorders.

American Academy of Physical Medicine and Rehabilitation (AAPMR)
One IBM Plaza, Suite 2500
Chicago, IL 60611-3604
Phone: 312-464-9700
Fax: 312-464-0227

Email: info@aapmr.org
Website: http://www.aapmr.org
The Academy is an organization of physicians who treat people with disabilities. Contact AAPMR for referrals to physiatrists or for information and publications about rehabilitation medicine.

American Association for Geriatric Psychiatry (AAGP)
7910 Woodmont Avenue, Suite 1050
Bethesda, MD 20814-3004
Phone: 301-654-7850
Fax: 301-654-4137
Email: aagpgpa@aol.com
Website: http://www.aagpgpa.org
The Association works to improve the mental health and well-being of older people. Contact AAGP for information on geriatric psychiatry and to receive referrals to specialists. Available publications include *Growing Older, Growing Wiser: Coping with Expectations, Challenges and Changes in Later Years*, and brochures on topics such as Alzheimer's disease, depression, and the role of the geriatric psychiatrist. Some consumer publications are free.

American Association for Marriage and Family Therapy (AAMFT)
1133 15th Street, NW, Suite 300
Washington, DC 20005
Phone: 202-452-0109
Fax: 202-223-2329
Email: memberservices@aamft.org
Website: http://www.aamft.org
AAMFT is a professional association of qualified marriage and family therapists. The Association provides referrals to marriage and family therapists and offers publications on topics including divorce, depression, and sexual problems.

American Association of Cardiovascular and Pulmonary Rehabilitation (AACVPR)
7600 Terrace Avenue, Suite 203
Middleton, WI 53562-3174
Phone: 608-831-6989

Fax: 608-831-5122
Email: aacvpr@tmahq.com
Website: http://www.aacvpr.org
AACPR is an organization of certified heart, lung, and blood specialists that provides information on diagnosis, treatment, and disease prevention. Information and publications are available on consumer guidelines for cardiac rehabilitation and purchasing fitness equipment. Visit the website for a free brochure.

American Association of Critical-Care Nurses (AACN)
101 Columbia
Aliso Viejo, CA 92656-4109
Phone: 1-800-899-AACN (899-2226) (toll-free)
949-362-2050
Fax: 949-362-2020
Email: info@aacn.org
Website: http://www.aacn.org
AACN is a nonprofit professional association dedicated to meeting the needs of its members who care for acutely and critically ill patients and their families. The Association provides practice and educational resources as well as professional support for its members. Contact AACN for publications and audiovisual materials on critical care.

American Association of Homes and Services for the Aging (AAHSA)
2519 Connecticut Avenue, NW
Washington, DC 20008-1520
Phone: 202-783-2242
Fax: 202-783-2255
Email: inform@aahsa.org
Website: http://www.aahsa.org
AAHSA is a national, nonprofit organization providing older people with services and information on housing, health care, and community involvement. Visit the AAHSA website for information for seniors and caregivers.

American Association of Retired Persons (AARP)
601 E Street, NW
Washington, DC 20049

Phone: 1-800-424-3410 (toll-free)
202-434-2277
Fax: 202-434-6973
Website: http://www.aarp.org
AARP is a nonprofit organization that advocates for older Americans' health, rights, and life choices. Local chapters provide information and services on crime prevention, consumer protection, and income tax preparation. Members can join group health, auto, life, and home insurance programs, investment plans, or a discount mail-order pharmacy service. The AgeLine database, available on CD-ROM, contains extensive resources on issues of concern to older people. Publications are available on housing, health, exercise, retirement planning, money management, leisure, and travel.

American Bar Association
Commission on the Legal Problems of the Elderly
740 15th Street, NW
Washington, DC 20005-1022
Phone: 202-662-8690
Fax: 202-662-8698
Email: abaelderly@abanet.org
Website: http://www.abanet.org/elderly
The Commission examines and responds to law-related needs of older people. It makes referrals and maintains a listing of legal aid offices where older people can get free or low-cost legal assistance. The Commission's website lists available publications and videos.

American Brain Tumor Association (ABTA)
2720 River Road, Suite 146
Des Plaines, IL 60018
Phone: 1-800-886-2282 (toll-free) (Patient Line)
847-827-9910
Fax: 847-827-9918
Email: info@abta.org
Website: http://www.abta.org
ABTA is a nonprofit organization, offering free social work consultations, a nationwide database of established support groups, mentorship for people who want to start a support

group, a resource listing of specialist physicians, and referrals to organizations providing services for brain tumor patients. Publications on brain tumors, treatment, and coping with disease are available.

American Cancer Society (ACS)
1599 Clifton Road, NE
Atlanta, GA 30329
Phone: 1-800-ACS-2345 (227-2345) (toll-free)
404-320-3333
Fax: 404-329-5787
Website: http://www.cancer.org
ACS is a national, community-based volunteer health organization, providing information on cancer and its prevention. The Society sponsors a variety of programs such as Man to Man (education and support for men with prostate cancer) and workshops such as Taking Charge of Money Matters which addresses financial concerns arising from cancer treatment. Local ACS offices sponsor services for cancer patients and their families, including self-help groups, transportation programs, and limited financial aid. Contact the ACS for free publications. Spanish language resources are available.

American Chiropractic Association (ACA)
1701 Clarendon Boulevard
Arlington, VA 22209
Phone: 1-800-986-4636 (toll-free)
703-276-8800
Fax: 703-243-2593
Email: memberinfo@amerchiro.org
Website: http://www.amerchiro.org
ACA is a professional organization of chiropractors. It offers educational programs on spinal problems, posture, physical fitness, and occupational safety. Contact the ACA to buy publications and materials on spinal health and safety. Visit the website to find a chiropractor.

American College of Obstetricians and Gynecologists (ACOG)
409 12th Street, SW

PO Box 96920
Washington, DC 20090-6920
Phone: 202-863-2518 (resource center)
Website: http://www.acog.org
ACOG is a professional society of doctors specializing in women's health care. Contact ACOG for referrals. For free pamphlets on osteoporosis, menopause, and hormone replacement therapy, send a self-addressed, stamped envelope.

American College of Physicians–American Society of Internal Medicine (ACP-ASIM)
190 North Independence Mall West
Philadelphia, PA 19106-1572
Phone: 1-800-523-1546 (toll-free)
215-351-2400
Fax: 215-351-2829
Email: interpub@mail.acponline.org
Website: http://www.acponline.org
ACP-ASIM is the nation's largest medical specialty society. Members of ACP-ASIM specialize in a variety of areas such as in internal medicine, cardiology, infectious diseases, rheumatology, gastroenterology, and oncology. Contact the ACP-ASIM for referrals. ACP-ASIM produces *Healthscope*, a film series on public health.

American College of Sports Medicine (ACSM)
PO Box 1440
Indianapolis, IN 46206
Phone: 317-637-9200
Fax: 317-634-7817
Website: http://www.acsm.org
ACSM is a scientific and medical association of health professionals interested in exercise. It offers training and certification. ACSM's Active Aging Partnership, focuses on education, research, and improving practice for those committed to working with older adults. For free information on exercise for older people, send a self-addressed, stamped envelope.

American College of Surgeons (ACS)
633 North St. Clair Street
Chicago, IL 60611-3211
Phone: 312-202-5000
Fax: 312-202-5001
Website: http://www.facs.org
ACS is a national organization offering educational materials and information about qualified surgeons and surgical treatments for many illnesses and injuries. Contact ACS to locate board-certified surgeons. Public education materials are available on frequently performed types of surgery.

American Council of the Blind (ACB)
1155 15th Street, NW, Suite 1004
Washington, DC 20005
Phone: 1-800-424-8666 (toll-free)
202-467-5081
Fax: 202-467-5085
Email: info@acb.org
Website: http://www.acb.org
ACB is a national organization that advocates for blind and visually impaired people. It provides educational programs, health care services, information about Social Security benefits for visually impaired people, vocational training, and other health and social services. Toll-free information, referrals, and free educational materials are available.

American Counseling Association (ACA)
5999 Stevenson Avenue
Alexandria, VA 22304
Phone: 1-800-347-6647 ext. 222 (toll-free)
703-823-9800
Fax: 703-823-0252
Website: http://www.counseling.org
ACA offers information to older people on adult psychological development and aging. A catalog of publications and videos is available.

American Dental Association (ADA)
211 East Chicago Avenue
Chicago, IL 60611

Phone: 312-440-2593
312-440-2500
Fax: 312-440-2800
Website: http://www.ada.org

ADA is a professional organization that conducts dental research and evaluates findings from dental science for the public. State and local ADA chapters provide referrals to dentists. Publications are available on subjects such as tooth decay, dentures, smoking, diet, and mouth care. Online publications cover topics such as gum disease, finding a dentist, and resolving disputes over treatment.

American Diabetes Association (ADA)
1701 North Beauregard Street
Arlington, VA 22311
Phone: 1-800-DIABETES (342-2383) (toll-free)
703-549-1500
Website: http://www.diabetes.org

ADA provides information and educational materials on preventing, treating, and living with diabetes. The Association has specific outreach programs for minority communities including the Diabetes Assistance and Resources Program, providing information in English and Spanish to the Hispanic community, the African American Program, and Awakening the Spirit, which disseminates diabetes to the Native American community. Local ADA chapters offer support and referrals to community agencies and services.

American Dietetic Association (ADA)
216 West Jackson Boulevard
Chicago, IL 60606-6995
Phone: 1-800-366-1655 (toll-free) (Consumer Nutrition Hotline)
312-899-0040
Fax: 312-899-4899
Website: http://www.eatright.org

ADA is a professional society of registered dieticians and other dietetic professionals who provide nutrition information, education, counseling, and care. One of ADA's professional practice groups focuses on the special needs of older people and offers nutrition counseling and indirect assistance through State and local meal programs. Call ADA to locate a registered dietician.

American Federation for Aging Research (AFAR)
1414 Sixth Avenue, 18th Floor
New York, NY 10019
Phone: 212-752-2327
Fax: 212-832-2298
Email: amfedaging@aol.com
Website: "http://www.afar.org
http://www.infoaging.org
AFAR is a nonprofit organization dedicated to supporting basic aging research. AFAR funds a wide variety of cutting-edge research on the aging process and age-related diseases. Visit the website for a list of free publications.

American Foundation for the Blind (AFB)
11 Penn Plaza, Suite 300
New York, NY 10001
Phone: 1-800-AFB-LINE (232-5463) (toll-free)
TTY: 212-502-7662
Fax: 212-502-7777
Email: afbinfo@afb.net
Website: http://www.afb.org
A national, nonprofit organization, AFB provides services and support for people who are blind or visually impaired. AFB's Technology Information Bank supports the Talking Books program and provides information and mentoring on technology assistance for people who are blind. Books, pamphlets, videos, and periodicals about blindness are available.

American Foundation for Urologic Diseases (AFUD)
1128 North Charles Street
Baltimore, MD 21201
Phone: 410-468-1800
Fax: 410-468-1808
Email: admin@afud.org
Website: http://www.afud.org
http://www.prostatehealth.com

The Foundation works toward the prevention and cure of urologic disease in part by keeping patients, family members, and friends informed about these disorders, treatment options, and recent research findings. AFUD operates six national health education councils that distribute patient education materials on a variety of urologic topics. A specific website addresses prostate health. Online publications are free; publications are available by mail for a fee.

American Geriatrics Society (AGS)
350 Fifth Avenue
New York, NY 10118
Phone: 212-308-1414
Fax: 212-832-8646
Email: info.amger@americangeriatrics.org
Website: http://www.americangeriatrics.org
AGS is a nonprofit organization of physicians and health care professionals supporting the study of geriatrics. Contact AGS for information on geriatrics, long term care, acute and chronic illnesses, rehabilitation, and nursing home care. Publications include the *AGS Complete Guide to Aging and Health* and the *AGS Medical Reference Guide*.

American Health Assistance Foundation (AHAF)
15825 Shady Grove Road, Suite 140
Rockville, MD 20850
Phone: 1-800-437-AHAF (437-2423) (toll-free)
301-948-3244
Fax: 301-258-9454
Website: http://www.ahaf.org
AHAF provides information and supports research on age-related illnesses. The Foundation supports three research programs: Alzheimer's Disease (AD) Research (along with the Alzheimer's Family Relief Program) offers emergency grants of up to $500 to AD patients in need and their caregivers, National Glaucoma Research, and the National Heart Foundation. Contact AHAF for free publications on AD, glaucoma, heart disease, and stroke.

American Health Care Association (AHCA)
1201 L Street, NW
Washington, DC 20005
Phone: 202-842-4444
Fax: 202-842-3860
Website: http://www.ahca.org
AHCA is an organization representing the interests of nursing homes, assisted living centers, and subacute care facilities. Publications are available about nursing homes, guardianship, assisted living, financing, and long term care services.

American Health Foundation (AHF)
1 Dana Road
Valhalla, NY 10595
Phone: 914-592-2600
Fax: 914-592-6317
Website: http://www.ahf.org
AHF is a nonprofit organization conducting research on cancer; preventive medicine; and the effects of lifestyle, environment, and nutrition on health. Contact AHF for information and publications on healthy living, heart disease, cancer, and high cholesterol.

American Heart Association (AHA)
7272 Greenville Avenue
Dallas, TX 75231
Phone: 1-800-AHA-USA1 (242-8721) (toll-free)
1-888-4-STROKE (478-7653) (toll-free)
Fax: 214-706-2139
Website: http://www.americanheart.org
AHA is a nonprofit organization funding research and providing information on the diagnosis, treatment, and prevention of heart diseases and stroke. Contact AHA for its cookbooks, guide to heart attack treatment, and guide to fitness.

American Horticultural Therapy Association (AHTA)
National Office
909 York Street
Denver, CO 80206

Phone: 720-865-3616
Fax: 720-865-3728
Email: ahta@ahta.org
Website: http://www.ahta.org
AHTA is a nonprofit, membership organization that promotes and advances horticultural therapy as a therapeutic intervention and rehabilitation option. The Association provides information related to the principles and practices of horticultural therapy.

American Hospital Association (AHA)
One North Franklin
Chicago, IL 60606
Phone: 312-422-3000
Fax: 312-422-4796
Website: http://www.aha.org
AHA is a national nonprofit association representing all types of hospitals and health care networks, as well as patients and families. AHA provides education for health care leaders and information on health care issues and trends.

American Lung Association (ALA)
1740 Broadway
New York, NY 10019-4374
Phone: 1-800-LUNG-USA (586-4872) (toll-free)
212-315-8700
Fax: 212-265-5642
Email: info@lungusa.org
Website: http://www.lungusa.org
ALA is dedicated to the prevention, cure, and control of lung diseases such as asthma, emphysema, tuberculosis, and lung cancer. The Association offers community service, public health education, advocacy, and research.

American Medical Association (AMA)
515 North State Street
Chicago, IL 60610
Phone: 1-800-621-8335 (toll-free)
312-464-5000
Fax: 312-464-5600

Website: http://www.ama-assn.org
AMA is an organization of licensed doctors that distributes scientific information on health and sets standards on medical law and practice. Local AMA associations can provide referrals to qualified doctors. AMA publishes the *Journal of the American Medical Association*, other subscription medical journals, and books for sale, including an encyclopedia of medicine.

American Medical Directors Association (AMDA)
10480 Little Patuxent Parkway, Suite 760
Columbia, MD 21044
Phone: 1-800-876-2632
410-740-9743
Fax: 410-740-4572
Email: webmaster@amda.com
Website: http://www.amda.com
AMDA is a national professional association representing doctors who care for older people in a variety of long term care settings, including nursing facilities, hospice, home care, continuing care retirement communities, and assisted living. The Association provides education, advocacy, information, and professional development for long term care professionals. AMDA has information on health care policy, regulations, and clinical practice guidelines.

American Menopause Foundation (AMF)
350 Fifth Avenue, Suite 2822
New York, NY 10118
Phone: 212-714-2398
Fax: 212-714-1252
Email: menopause@earthlink.org
Website: www.americanmenopause.org
The Foundation is a nonprofit health organization providing support and assistance on all issues concerning menopause. AMF has information on scientific research and coordinates a network of volunteer support groups for women.

American Music Therapy Association (AMTA)
8455 Colesville Road, Suite 1000

Silver Spring, MD 20910
Phone: 301-589-3300
Fax: 301-589-5175
Email: info@musictherapy.org
Website: http://www.musictherapy.org
AMTA is a nonprofit organization that advocates, promotes, and provides resources and information on the uses and benefits of music therapy. Contact AMTA for referrals as well as for publications and audiovisual materials.

American Nurses Association (ANA)
600 Maryland Avenue, SW, Suite 100W
Washington, DC 20024-2571
Phone: 1-800-274-4262 (toll-free)
202-554-4444
Fax: 202-651-7001
Email: via Website
Website: http://www.nursingworld.org
ANA, a national association of registered nurses, serves as an advocate for nursing practitioners as well as sponsors research and continuing education. Contact the Association for *Facts About Nursing* and other publications. ANA sets standards for the practice of gerontological nursing.

American Occupational Therapy Association, Inc. (AOTA)
4720 Montgomery Lane
PO Box 31220
Bethesda, MD 20824-1220
Phone: 1-800-729-2682 (toll-free) (Association members)
301-652-2682
TTY: 1-800-377-8555 (toll-free)
Fax: 301-652-7711
Website: http://www.aota.org
AOTA offers information on the role of occupational therapy in promoting functional independence, preventing disability, and maintaining health. Contact AOTA for referrals to local practitioners and therapy programs. The Association publishes two periodicals, *OT Practice* and the *American Journal of Occupational Therapy*, as well as many books for educators.

American Optometric Association (AOA)
243 North Lindbergh Boulevard
St. Louis, MO 63141
Phone: 1-800-365-2219 (toll-free)
314-991-4100
Fax: 314-991-4101
Website: http://www.aoanet.org
AOA, a national organization of optometrists, evaluates ophthalmic products and sponsors continuing education programs. It offers VISION USA, a free eye-care program for uninsured or low-income older people and their families. Contact AOA for referrals to certified optometrists and for publications such as *Driving Tips for Older Adults*, *Contact Lenses After 40,* and fact sheets on floaters, macular degeneration, and glaucoma.

American Osteopathic Association
142 East Ontario Street
Chicago, IL 60611
Phone: 1-800-621-1773 (toll-free)
Fax: 312-202-8200
Email: info@aoa-net.org
Website: http://www.aoa-net.org
The American Osteopathic Association represents osteopathic physicians (D.O.'s, doctors of osteopathic medicine), promotes public health, encourages scientific research, and is the accrediting agency for all osteopathic medical schools and health care facilities.

American Parkinson's Disease Association (APDA)
1250 Hylan Boulevard, Suite 4B
Staten Island, NY 10305
Phone: 1-800-223-2732 (toll-free)
Fax: 718-981-4399
Email: info@apdaparkinson.org
Website: http://www.apdaparkinson.org
A nonprofit organization, APDA funds research to find a cure for Parkinson's disease. APDA's toll-free line refers callers to local chapters for information on community services, specialists, and treatments. Publications and educational

materials are available on Parkinson's disease, speech therapy, exercise, diet, and aids for daily living.

American Pharmaceutical Association (APhA)
2215 Constitution Avenue, NW
Washington, DC 20037-2985
Phone: 1-800-237-2742 (toll-free)
202-628-4410
Fax: 202-783-2351
Email: webmaster@mail.aphanet.org
Website: http://www.aphanet.org
http://www.pharmacyandyou.org (consumer information site)
APhA is the national society of licensed pharmacists providing public health information and referrals to resources on medicine and public policy. Available publications include *Managing Medicines As You Grow Older*, *National Medical Awareness Test*, and *Self-Medication Awareness Test*.

American Physical Therapy Association (APTA)
1111 North Fairfax Street
Alexandria, VA 22314
Phone: 1-800-999-2782, ext. 3395 (toll-free)
703-684-2782
Fax: 703-706-8578
Website: http://www.apta.org
APTA is an organization of physical therapists providing referrals to APTA geriatric-certified therapists and information on debilitating ailments like arthritis, stroke, scoliosis, and sudden onset of illness. APTA's Section on Geriatrics offers publications on topics such as osteoporosis; incontinence; neck pain; carpal tunnel syndrome; hip, knee, or shoulder care; and what physical therapists can offer older adults.

American Podiatric Medical Association (APMA)
9312 Old Georgetown Road
Bethesda, MD 20814
Phone: 1-800-FOOT-CARE (366-8227) (toll-free)
301-571-9200
Fax: 301-530-2752

Email: askapma@apma.org
Website: http://www.apma.org
APMA is an association of podiatrists providing services and information on foot problems and foot health. Contact APMA for information on local chapters and referrals to certified podiatrists. Publications on proper foot care and effects of arthritis and diabetes on feet are available.

American Psychiatric Association (APA)
1400 K Street, NW
Washington, DC 20005
Phone: 202-682-6000
Fax: 202-682-6850
Email: apa@psych.org
Website: http://www.psych.org
APA is an association of psychiatrists, physicians specializing in diagnosing and treating people with mental and emotional disorders. Its Council on Aging establishes standards for psychiatric care of older people. Contact the APA for information on elder care issues, including medication use by older people, treatment of Alzheimer's disease, and nursing homes. Contact APA for referrals to local psychiatrists.

American Psychological Association (APA)
750 First Street, NE
Washington, DC 20002-4242
Phone: 1-800-374-2721 (toll-free)
202-336-5500
Email: webmaster@apa.org
Website: http://www.apa.org
APA is a professional society of psychologists that provides assistance and information on mental, emotional, and behavioral disorders. Contact the APA for a list of State chapters, information on the psychosocial aspects of aging, and referrals to APA-member psychologists. The APA's section on older people produces publications on topics such as dementia and dementia research. Publications include a quarterly subscription magazine, *Psychology and Aging*.

American Red Cross
430 17th Street, NW
Washington, DC 20006
Phone: 1-800-HELP-NOW (435-7669) (toll-free) (donations only)
202-639-3269
Fax: 202-639-3520
Email: info@usa.redcross.org
Website: http://www.redcross.org
The Red Cross offers health information programs, health services, blood donation services, disaster relief, and emergency services to the public and the Armed Forces. Local chapters provide programs for older people, including retirement planning, crime prevention instruction, safety courses, health screening clinics, and home nurse care instruction. Publications about programs, information, and services are available.

American Society on Aging (ASA)
833 Market Street, Suite 511
San Francisco, CA 94103
Phone: 1-800-537-9728 (toll-free)
415-974-9600
Fax: 415-974-0300
Email: info@asaging.org
Website: http://www.asaging.org
ASA is a nonprofit organization providing information about medical and social practice, research, and policy pertinent to the health of older people. Membership and subscriptions to *Generations,* a quarterly journal, and *Aging Today*, the Society's bimonthly news magazine, are available to the public. A catalog of books for sale and other educational materials is available on the website.

American Speech-Language-Hearing Association (ASHA)
10801 Rockville Pike
Rockville, MD 20852
Phone: 1-800-498-2071 (toll-free) (ASHA Action Center)
1-800-638-8255 (toll-free)
TTY: 1-800-638-8255 (toll-free)

301-897-0157
Fax: 877-541-5035
Email: actioncenter@asha.org
Website: http://www.asha.org
ASHA represents the interests of medical specialists in speech, language, and hearing science and advocates for people with communication-related disorders. Contact ASHA's toll-free telephone line for information on speech-language legislation, communication disorders, or referrals to specialists. ASHA produces publications and fact sheets on topics such as communication disorders and hearing aids.

American Stroke Association (ASA)
c/o American Heart Association
7272 Greenville Avenue
Dallas, TX 75231
Phone: 1-888-4STROKE (478-7653) (toll-free)
Fax: 214-706-5231
Email: strokeassociation@heart.org
Website: http://www.strokeassociation.org
ASA, a division of the American Heart Association, provides the Stroke Family Warmline, a toll-free information and referral service offering lists of certified doctors who are stroke specialists and volunteer stroke survivors or family members. Callers receive support and can request free information. ASA publishes *Stroke Connection,* a priced subscription magazine for survivors and families.

American Tinnitus Association (ATA)
PO Box 5
Portland, OR 97207
Phone: 1-800-634-8978 (toll-free)
503-248-9985
Fax: 503-248-0024
Email: tinnitus@ata.org
Website: http://www.ata.org
ATA is a volunteer organization supporting research and providing information on tinnitus, a constant buzzing or ringing in the ears or head. ATA sponsors self-help groups

nationwide each offering information, assistance, and referrals to community services and tinnitus specialists.

Arthritis Foundation (AF)
National Office
1330 West Peachtree Street
Atlanta, GA 30309
Phone: 1-800-283-7800 (toll-free)
404-965-7537
Fax: 404-872-0457
Email: help@arthritis.org
Website: http://www.arthritis.org
AF is a nonprofit, volunteer organization focusing on research and information to cure, prevent, or better treat arthritis and related diseases. Contact AF for information on arthritis, related diseases (such as lupus erythmatosus and rheumatism), and referrals to local chapters, specialists, or support groups. Publications and videos are available on topics such as self-help and exercise therapy.

Assisted Living Federation of America (ALFA)
11200 Waples Mill Road, Suite 150
Fairfax, VA 22030
Phone 703-691-8100
Fax: 703-691-8106
Website: http://www.alfa.org
ALFA represents for-profit and nonprofit providers of assisted living, continuing care retirement communities, independent living, and other forms of housing and services. The Federation works to advance the assisted living industry and enhance the quality of life for consumers.

Association for Gerontology in Higher Education (AGHE)
1030 15th Street, NW, Suite 240
Washington, DC 20005-1503
Phone: 202-289-9806
Fax: 202-289-9824
Email: aghetemp@aghe.org
Website: www.aghe.org

AGHE's members are organizations and institutions of higher education. Through conferences, publications, technical assistance, research studies, and consultation with policymakers, AGHE, an educational unit of the Gerontological Society of America, seeks to advance gerontology as a field of study at institutions of higher education.

Better Hearing Institute
5021-B Backlick Road
Annandale, VA 22003
Phone: 1-800-EAR-WELL (327-9355) (toll-free) (Hearing Helpline)
703-684-3391
Fax: 703-684-6048
Email: mail@betterhearing.org
Website: http://www.betterhearing.org
The Institute is a nonprofit, educational organization providing information on medical, surgical, and rehabilitation options for improving hearing loss and on hearing aids. Contact the Institute's Hearing Helpline for facts on hearing loss and a list of publications.

Better Vision Institute (BVI)
1655 North Fort Myer Drive
Arlington, VA 22209
Phone: 1-800-424-8422 (toll-free)
703-243-1508
Fax: 703-243-1537
Website: http://www.visionsite.org
BVI provides news and information on vision health and care. Contact the Institute for facts on the detection, treatment, and prevention of eye diseases. Publications include fact sheets on cataracts, nutrition, care of eyeglasses, diabetes, and vision care.

Beverly Foundation
44 South Mentor Avenue
Pasadena, CA 91106
Phone: 626-792-2292
Fax: 626-792-6117

Email: bf3@ix.netcom.com
Website: http://www.beverlyfoundation.org
The Foundation focuses on mobility and transportation for older people within the community, service delivery within home and institutional settings, and overall life enrichment. It engages in research and education projects and provides information for professionals and caregivers.

B'nai B'rith
1640 Rhode Island Avenue, NW
Washington, DC 20036
Phone: 1-800-500-6533 (toll-free)
202-857-6600
Fax: 202-857-1099
Email: seniors@bnaibrith.org
Website: http://www.bnaibrith.org
B'nai B'rith is the world's oldest and largest Jewish service organization, providing community service, education, and advocacy. Its Center for Senior Housing and Services sponsors housing and travel for senior citizens. A list of publications is available.

Brookdale Center on Aging (BCOA) of Hunter College
1114 Avenue of the Americas, 40th Floor
New York, NY 10036
Phone: 646-366-1000
Fax: 212-481-5069
Email: info@brookdale.org
Website: http://www.brookdale.org
BCOA sponsors a variety of programs including the Institute on Law and Rights of Older Adults which fights for grandparent rights. Other programs focus on elder care services, guardianship, caregiving, Medicare, intergenerational activities, and Alzheimer's disease. Contact BCOA about publications (some available in Spanish) including *Senior Rights Reporter*, *Benefits Checklist for Seniors*, *Help for Seniors*, and *Help for Grandparent Caregivers,* which are for sale.
Captioned Media Program (CMP)

National Association of the Deaf (NAD)
1447 East Main Street
Spartanburg, SC 29307
Phone: 1-800-237-6213 (toll-free)
TTY: 1-800-237-6819 (toll-free)
Fax: 1-800-538-5636
Email: info@cfv.org
Website: http://www.cfv.org
CMP is a free video lending program funded by the Department of Education and administered by NAD. CMP provides open-captioned videos (i.e., they display English text with any TV/VCR). Videos are available for deaf or hard of hearing Americans, their parents, families, teachers, counselors, interpreters, or others. CMP has a wide variety of videos ranging from travel to classic movies; from sign language to hobbies.

Catholic Charities USA (CCUSA)
1731 King Street, Suite 200
Alexandria, VA 22314
Phone: 703-549-1390
Fax: 703-549-1656
Website: http://www.catholiccharitiesusa.org
CCUSA is a network of organizations offering nationwide services to older people, including counseling, homemaker and caregiver services, emergency assistance, group homes, and institutional care. CCUSA advocates for older people's Social Security benefits, employment opportunities, and housing. Publications describe Catholic Charities' programs for older people.

Catholic Golden Age (CGA)
National Headquarters
PO Box 249
Olyphant, PA 18447
Phone: 1-800-836-5699 (toll-free)
Fax: 570-586-7721
Email: info@catholicgoldenage.org
Website: http://www.catholicgoldenage.org
CGA sponsors charitable work and helps older people meet their social, physical, economic, intellectual, and spiritual

needs. Contact CGA for various group insurance plans, discounts on eyeglasses, prescription drugs, and travel. Local CGA chapters provide activities for members, including disease prevention and health promotion programs.

Census Bureau
Special Populations Branch
FB3 Room 2384
Washington, DC 20233
Phone: 301-457-2378
Fax: 301-457-6634
Website: http://www.census.gov
The Census Bureau, part of the Federal Government, collects and provides timely, relevant, and quality data about the people and economy of the US. Contact the Census Bureau for age-related data and statistics about the older populations in the United States.

The Center for Social Gerontology (TCSG)
2307 Shelby Avenue
Ann Arbor, MI 48103
Phone: 734-665-1126
Fax: 734-665-2071
Email: tcsg@tcsg.org
Website: http://www.tcsg.org
TCSG is a nonprofit research, training, and social policy organization. Particular attention is focused on law and aging, tobacco use and older people, guardianship service providers, and adult guardianship. Contact the Center for information on publications, videos, training, and technical assistance.
Center for the Advancement of State Community Services Programs (CASCSP)

National Association of State Units on Aging (NASUA)
1225 I Street, NW, Suite 725
Washington, DC 20005
Phone: 202-898-2578
Fax: 202-898-2583
Email: info@nasua.org

Website: http://www.nasua.org
The Center, part of NASUA, provides information and support for community-based care for older people. The Center also helps State and Area Agencies on Aging design, develop, and manage these care systems and develop State policies. A list of publications and materials on long term and community-based care is available.

Center for the Study of Aging/International Association of Physical Activity, Aging and Sports (IAPAAS)
706 Madison Avenue
Albany, NY 12208-3604
Phone: 518-465-6927
Fax: 518-462-1339
Email: iapaas@acl.com
The Center is a free-standing, nonprofit organization promoting research, education, and training in the field of aging. IAPAAS is the Center's membership division. It organizes programs on health, fitness, prevention, and aging. Contact the Center for a list of publications and information about the quarterly newsletter, *Lifelong Health and Fitness*.

Centers for Disease Control and Prevention (CDC)
1600 Clifton Road
Atlanta, GA 30333
Phone: 1-800-311-3435 (toll-free)
404-639-3311
TTY: 1-800-255-0135 (toll-free)
Fax: 404-639-7392
Email: netinfo@cdc.gov
Website: http://www.cdc.gov
The CDC, part of the Federal Government, is the lead agency for protecting the health and safety of people at home or abroad. The CDC produces fact sheets that help people make informed decisions about their health and health care. Contact the CDC for public information, health statistics, funding opportunities, and prevention guidelines. Spanish language resources are available.

Children of Aging Parents (CAPS)
1609 Woodbourne Road, Suite 302A
Levittown, PA 19057
Phone: 1-800-227-7294 (toll-free)
215-945-6900
Fax: 215-945-8720
Website: http://www.caps4caregivers.org
CAPS is a nonprofit organization that provides support services to caregivers of older people. It serves as a clearinghouse for information on elder care resources and issues, including Instant Aging workshops to help communities understand the needs of older people. Send a self-addressed, stamped envelope to receive publications on aging or information about support groups.

Clearinghouse on Abuse and Neglect of the Elderly (CANE)
University of Delaware
College of Human Services, Education and Public Policy
Department of Consumer Studies
Newark, DE 19716
Phone: 302-831-3525
Fax: 302-831-6081
Website:
http://www.elderabusecenter.org/clearing/index.html
CANE, funded by the Administration on Aging, is a database of elder abuse materials and resources operated by the University of Delaware's National Center on Elder Abuse (NCEA). CANE staff will conduct customized information searches and provide resources and referrals to elder abuse support groups. *NCEA Exchange*, CANE's newsletter, is available free.

Community Transportation Association of America (CTAA)
1341 G Street, NW, 10th Floor
Washington, DC 20005
Phone: 202-628-1480
Fax: 202-737-9197
Website: http://www.ctaa.org

CTAA is a national association committed to removing barriers to isolation and improving mobility for all people. It offers educational programs and advocates making community transportation available, affordable, and accessible. CTAA provides information on transportation in medical emergencies and van conversions.

Continuing Care Accreditation Commission (CCAC)
2519 Connecticut Avenue, NW
Washington, DC 20008-1520
Phone: 202-508-9459
Fax: 202-220-0022
Email: afinnega@ccaconline.org
Website: http://www.ccaconline.org
CCAC helps consumers identify quality retirement options. CCAC also accredits aging services that meet or exceed industry-generated standards of excellence in three areas: governance and administration; financial resources and disclosure; and resident life, health, and wellness.

Corporation for National Service (CNS)
1201 New York Avenue, NW
Washington, DC 20525
Phone: 1-800-424-8867 (toll-free)
202-606-5000
TTY: 1-800-833-3722 (toll-free)
Fax: 202-565-2794
Email: acinfo@infosystec.com
Website: http://www.nationalservice.org
CNS oversees volunteer community enhancement programs including: the National Senior Services Corps (a network of Federally-supported programs helping older people get involved in community service); the Foster Grandparent Program (encouraging older people to work with children with special needs); and the Senior Companion Program (volunteers assisting older people with special needs in hospitals, social service agencies, or home health care agencies). Contact CNS for pamphlets, brochures, fact sheets, and program handbooks.

Council of Better Business Bureaus (CBBB)
4200 Wilson Boulevard, Suite 800
Arlington, VA 22203
Phone: 703-276-0100
Fax: 703-525-8277
Website: http://www.bbb.org
CBBB is a national organization promoting ethical practices between business and the public. Local BBBs can offer consumers help resolving complaints against companies. Publications include the *Tips On* series and booklets with advice on how to make wise buying decisions on a broad range of products and services.

The Dana Alliance for Brain Initiatives
745 Fifth Avenue, Suite 700
New York, NY 10151
Phone: 212-223-4040
Fax: 212-593-7623
Email: dabiinfo@danany.dana.org
Website: http://www.dana.org
The Dana Alliance promotes public education about brain research. The Alliance links the public, press, and policymakers with experts and resources in the field of neuroscience. It also hosts conferences on the brain and brain diseases. Contact the Dana Alliance for publications on brain research and diagnosis and treatment of brain disorders.

Delta Society
289 Perimeter Road East
Renton, WA 98055-1329
Phone: 425-226-7357
Fax: 425-235-1076
Email: info@deltasociety.org
Website: http://www.deltasociety.org
The Delta Society is a national, nonprofit organization whose mission is improving human health through service and therapy animals. Its program, Pet Partners, brings volunteers and their pets to nursing homes, hospitals, and schools. The Society website has information and resources about the human-animal-health connection.

Department of Justice (DOJ)
950 Pennsylvania Avenue, NW
Washington, DC 20530-0001
Phone: 202-514-2000
TTY: 202-514-0716
Email: ASKDOJ@usdoj.gov
Website: http://www.usdoj.gov/
DOJ, part of the Federal Government, works to protect older Americans in a variety of ways, including the Nursing Home Initiative and elder justice efforts to prosecute institutions whose wrongdoing results in harm or death for residents. DOJ prosecutes health care and consumer fraud and enforces civil rights addressing discrimination against older people. Publications and statistics on victimization of older people are available.

Department of Labor (DOL)
Office of Public Affairs
Room S1032
200 Constitution Avenue, NW
Washington, DC 20210
Phone: 202-693-4650
Fax: 202-693-4674
Website: http://www.dol.gov
DOL, part of the Federal Government, protects workers' rights. Contact DOL for information and assistance on pensions, employment, wages, discrimination, and occupational safety. The Senior Community Service Employment Program helps low-income older people through part-time employment and job training. The website includes links to information for employers, employees, and job seekers.

Department of Transportation (DOT)
National Highway Traffic Safety Administration (NHTSA) Information
400 Seventh Street, SW
Washington, DC 20590
Phone: 1-888-327-4236 (toll-free)
202-366-0123
TTY: 1-800-424-9153 (toll-free)

202-366-7800
Website: http://www.nhtsa.dot.gov/
The NHTSA is responsible for reducing deaths, injuries, and economic losses resulting from car accidents. It sets standards, investigates safety defects, and conducts research on driver behavior. Contact NHTSA for information on older drivers.

Department of Veterans Affairs (VA)
Office of Public Affairs
810 Vermont Avenue, NW
Washington, DC 20420
Phone: 1-800-827-1000 (toll-free)
TTY: 1-800-829-4833 (toll-free)
Website: http://www.va.gov
The VA, part of the Federal Government, provides benefits for eligible veterans and their families in outpatient clinics, medical centers, and nursing homes across the US. Contact the VA for information and publications on service locations and benefits, including comprehensive medical and dental care, other insurance benefits, vocational rehabilitation compensation, and pension.

DES Action
610 16th Street, Suite 301
Oakland, CA 94612
Phone: 1-800-DES-9288 (337-9288) (toll-free)
510-465-4011
Fax: 510-465-4815
Email: desaction@earthlink.net
Website: http://www.desaction.org
DES Action is a nonprofit organization providing information about the risks of exposure to diethylstilbestrol (DES), a hormone prescribed for pregnant women from the 1940s through 1971 that caused health problems in mothers and their children. Contact DES Action for referrals to specialists familiar with medical complications resulting from DES use. Free publications on the risks of DES are available.

Disabled American Veterans (DAV)
807 Maine Avenue, SW

Washington, DC 20024
Phone: 202-554-3501
TTY: 202-863-4414
Fax: 202-554-3581
Website: http://www.dav.org
DAV is a nonprofit organization representing disabled veterans and providing volunteer services and programs. DAV offers veterans job search training and help seeking their disability compensation and pension benefits. A list of free publications is available.

Elder Craftsmen (EC)
610 Lexington Avenue
New York, NY 10022
Phone: 212-319-8128
Fax: 212-319-8141
Email: eldercraftsmen@mindspring.com
Website: http://www.eldercraftsmen.org
EC offers programs and services that promote the skills and creativity of older people. Training programs are available for many types of crafts. Intergenerational programs, community service programs, and artist-in-residence are also offered.

Eldercare Initiative in Consumer Law (EICL)
National Consumer Law Center, Inc. (NCLC)
18 Tremont Street, Suite 400
Boston, MA 02108
Phone: 617-523-8010
Fax: 617-523-7398
Email: aoa@nclc.org
Website: http://www.consumerlaw.org
The Initiative provides assistance on legal issues of older people. The EICL conducts regional and national legal workshops focusing on aging issues, including threats to loss of shelter and financial exploitation. Contact the Initiative for publications and references.

Eldercare Locator
Phone: 1-800-677-1116 (toll-free)
Fax: 202-296-8134

Website: http://www.aoa.dhhs.gov
The Eldercare Locator is a nationwide, directory assistance service helping older people and caregivers locate local support and resources for older Americans. It is funded by the Administration on Aging.

Elderhostel
11 Avenue de Lafayette
Boston, MA 02111-1746
Phone: 1-877-426-8056 (toll-free)
617-426-7788
TTY: 1-877-426-2167 (toll-free)
Fax: 1-877-426-2166 (toll-free)
Email: registration@elderhostel.org
Website: http://www.elderhostel.org
Elderhostel is a nonprofit organization providing educational travel programs to people over age 55. Their catalog, published 10 times a year, lists thousands of national and international programs.

Elderweb
1305 Chadwick Drive
Normal, IL 61761
Phone: 309-451-3319
Fax: 866-422-8995
Email: ksb@elderweb.com
Website: http://www.elderweb.com
Elderweb is a research website for older people, professionals, and families seeking information on elder care and long term care. Visit Elderweb for news and information on legal, financial, medical, and housing issues for older people and provides links to other websites.

Environmental Protection Agency (EPA)
Public Information Center (PIC)
401 M Street, SW
Washington, DC 20460
Phone: 1-800-490-9198 (toll-free) (publications)
202-260-5922
Fax: 202-260-5153
Email: library-hq@epamail.epa.gov

Website: http://www.epa.gov
EPA, part of the Federal Government, is responsible for controlling environmental pollution. The PIC provides non-technical information about environmental issues such as clean air, clean water, pesticides, radon, and pollution. EPA's website has links to other health and environment-related websites. The toll-free number offers printed and audiovisual information on environmental issues.

Epilepsy Foundation
4351 Garden City Drive
Landover, MD 20785
Phone: 1-800-332-1000 (toll-free)
1-800-332-4050 (toll-free) (National Epilepsy Library)
301-459-3700
Fax: 301-577-2684
Email: postmaster@epilepsyfoundation.org
Website: http://www.epilepsyfoundation.org
The Foundation is a national volunteer health organization supporting research, education, advocacy, and services for people with seizure disorders. Contact the Foundation for a list of local chapters, referrals to local specialists, support groups, camps, travel assistance, respite care, and employment assistance. Videos and a catalog of publications are available.

Equal Employment Opportunity Commission (EEOC)
1801 L Street, NW
Washington, DC 20507
Phone: 1-800-669-3362 (toll-free) (publications)
202-663-4900 (headquarters)
TTY: 1-800-800-3302 (toll-free) (publications)
202-663-4494 (headquarters)
Website: http://www.eeoc.gov
The EEOC, part of the Federal Government, promotes equal opportunity in employment. It enforces the Age Discrimination in Employment Act (ADEA), conducts investigations, makes determinations, and effects reconciliations in age discrimination actions. Contact EEOC for information and referrals.

Federal Consumer Information Center (FCIC)
PO Box 100
Pueblo, CO 81009
Phone: 1-888-878-3256 (toll-free)
1-800-688-9889 (toll-free) (National Contact Center)
TTY: 1-800-326-2996 (toll-free)
1-800-326-2996 (toll-free) (National Contact Center)
Fax: 719-948-9724
Website: http://www.pueblo.gsa.gov/
FCIC, part of the Federal Government, distributes a wide range of consumer-oriented publications from many Federal agencies. The Consumer Information Catalog lists more than 200 publications on topics ranging from health and housing to food and nutrition; from money management to employment. The National Contact Center answers questions and provides referral information on Federal programs, benefits, and services.

Federal Trade Commission (FTC)
600 Pennsylvania Avenue, NW
Washington, DC 20580
Phone: 1-877-FTC-HELP (382-4357) (toll-free)
202-326-2222 (General Information Locator)
TTY: 202-326-2502
Email: webmaster@ftc.gov
Website: http://www.ftc.gov
FTC, part of the Federal Government, regulates trade and protects consumers from unfair and deceptive business practices. Its consumer protection programs include truth in advertising, packaging and labeling of products, product reliability, direct mail advertising, and nursing home business practices. Publications are available on refinancing a home, collecting a debt, buying a used car, and finding out credit history.

Food and Drug Administration (FDA)
HFE88
5600 Fishers Lane
Rockville, MD 20857
Phone: 1-888-INFO-FDA (463-6332) (toll-free)
1-888-723-3366 (toll-free) (Food Information Line)

1-800-822-7967 (toll-free) (Vaccine Adverse Event Reporting System)
1-800-838-7715 (toll-free) (Mammography Information Service)
Website: http://www.fda.gov
FDA, part of the Federal Government, regulates the safety and effectiveness of food products, additives, drugs, medical devices, and cosmetics. Contact FDA for information on safe drug use and side effects, vitamins, and laws regulating medicines and foods. FDA has information for older people on topics including cancer, health fraud, nutrition, buying medicines online, and food safety.

Food and Nutrition Information Center (FNIC)
Department of Agriculture
Agricultural Research Service/National Agriculture Library
10301 Baltimore Avenue, Room 304
Beltsville, MD 20705-2351
Phone: 301-504-5719
TTY: 301-504-6856
Fax: 301-504-6409
Email: fnic@nal.usda.gov
Website: http://www.nalusda.gov/fnic
FNIC, part of the Federal Government, provides information, publications, and audiovisual materials on nutrition. Resource guides on nutrition and older people, heart disease, diabetes, vegetarianism, food safety, and food labeling are available.

Foundation for Biomedical Research (FBR)
818 Connecticut Avenue, NW, Suite 200
Washington, DC 20006
Phone: 202-457-0654
Fax: 202-457-0659
Email: info@fbresearch.org
Website: http://www.fbresearch.org
FBR is a national organization advocating the ethical use of animals in scientific and medical research. Contact the Foundation for information and publications on how animal research helps scientists understand human health and aging.

John Douglas French Alzheimer's Foundation
11620 Wilshire Boulevard, Suite 270
Los Angeles, CA 90025
Phone: 1-800-477-2243 (toll-free)
310-445-4650
Fax: 310-479-0516
Website: http://www.jdfaf.org
The Foundation funds scientific research into the causes and cure for Alzheimer's disease. Contact the Foundation for the free publication *Caring for a Person with Memory Loss and Confusion*.

Generations Online
108 Ralston House
3615 Chestnut Street
Philadelphia, PA 19104
Phone: 215-222-6400
Fax: 215-222-6401
Website: http://www.generationsonline.com
Generations Online is a nonprofit website offering resources for older people unfamiliar with computers or the Internet. Generations Online provides self-training software for senior centers, libraries, retirement homes, and other locations for a one-time fee. The program is free for seniors. Its feature, Memories, links older people with school children for cultural, experiential, and personal exchanges on aging.

Generations Together (GT)
University Center for Social and Urban Research
University of Pittsburgh
121 University Place, Suite 300
Pittsburgh, PA 15260-5907
Phone: 412-648-7150
Fax: 412-648-7446
Email: sharris@pitt.edu
Website: http://www.pitt.edu/~gti/
GT promotes mutually beneficial interaction between young and old through community outreach, education, research, and dissemination of knowledge. GT develops, supports, and studies intergenerational programs and related issues. GT sponsors the annual International Intergenerational

Training Institute, which furthers collaboration between generations in workshops and resource development. Contact GT for a catalog of publications.

Gerontological Society of America (GSA)
1030 15th Street, NW, Suite 250
Washington, DC 20005-1503
Phone: 202-842-1275
Fax: 202-842-1150
Email: geron@geron.org
Website: http://www.geron.org
GSA is a professional organization providing information, advocacy, and support for research into the study of aging. GSA has a database of information on biological and social aspects of aging, links to aging information resources, and referrals to researchers and specialists in gerontology. GSA distributes publications on a variety of aging-related topics.

Glaucoma Research Foundation (GRF)
200 Pine Street, Suite 200
San Francisco, CA 94104
Phone: 1-800-826-6693 (toll-free)
415-986-3162
Fax: 415-986-3763
Email: info@glaucoma.org
Website: http://www.glaucoma.org
GRF is a national, nonprofit organization providing information and advocacy for people with glaucoma. Contact GRF for information on the causes, diagnosis, treatment, and prevention of glaucoma, referrals to specialists, and coping strategies for patients. Publications include the quarterly newsletter, *Gleams*, and a glaucoma patient guide.

Gray Panthers (GP)
733 15th Street, NW, Suite 437
Washington, DC 20005
Phone: 1-800-280-5362 (toll-free)
202-737-6637
Fax: 202-737-1160
Email: info@graypanthers.org
Website: http://www.graypanthers.org

Gray Panthers is a national advocacy organization of activists concentrating on social and economic issues. Local chapters organize intergenerational groups to address issues including universal health care, Medicare, preserving Social Security, affordable housing, and discrimination. Contact the national office for referrals to chapters, information on issues, links to resources for older people, and a list of publications.

Green Thumb, Inc. (GT)
2000 North 14th Street, Suite 800
Arlington, VA 22201
Phone: 703-522-7272
Fax: 703-522-0141
Website: http://www.greenthumb.org
GT is a national, nonprofit organization helping older, low-income workers train for and find work, particularly in rural areas. GT's Senior Community Service Employment Program, funded by the Department of Labor, provides training, work experience, educational opportunities, and placement in community service jobs. The Geezer.com website has information to help seniors supplement their income, launch new businesses, and market their handcrafted goods. Contact GT for a fact sheet and list of publications.

Health Care Financing Administration (HCFA)*
7500 Security Boulevard
Baltimore, MD 21244
Phone: 1-800-MEDICARE (633-4227) (toll-free) (Medicare hotline)
410-786-3000
Fax: 202-690-7675
Website: http://www.hcfa.gov
http://www.medicare.gov (Medicare information)
HCFA, part of the Federal Government, administers health insurance through Medicare and Medicaid. HCFA regulates hospitals, nursing homes, and home health agencies. Contact HCFA for *The Medicare Handbook* and other publications on related topics.

* Recent name change: The Centers for Medicare and Medicaid Services.

Health Insurance Association of America (HIAA)
1201 F Street, NW, 5th Floor
Washington, DC 20004
Phone: 202-824-1600
202-824-1849 (publications information)
Fax: 202-824-1722
Website: http://www.hiaa.org
HIAA is a trade association representing the interests of the privately-insured health care system. Contact HIAA for insurance information on health, long term care, dental, disability, and supplemental coverage. HIAA also provides information and publications on health care issues, including continuation of group health benefits, major medical, and Medicare supplements.

Hill-Burton Free Medical Care Program
Health Resources and Services Administration (HRSA)
Department of Health and Human Services
Division of Facilities Compliance and Recovery
5600 Fishers Lane, Room 10C-16
Rockville, MD 20857
Phone: 1-800-638-0742 (toll-free)
1-800-492-0359 (toll-free) (Maryland residents)
301-443-5656
Fax: 301-443-0619
Email: webmaster@hrsa.gov
Website: http://www.hrsa.gov/osp/dfcr
Hospitals and other health care facilities receive Federal funds for construction or modernization under the Hill-Burton Program. In return, these facilities provide a specific amount of free or below cost health care services to eligible people. Contact the program for a list of participating facilities as well as information on eligibility.

HIV/AIDS Treatment Information Service (ATIS)
PO Box 6303
Rockville, MD 20849-6303

Phone: 1-800-HIV-0440 (448-0440) (toll-free) (English, Spanish, Portuguese)
301-519-0459
TTY: 1-888-480-3739 (toll-free)
Fax: 301-519-6616
Email: atis@hivatis.org
Website: http://www.hivatis.org
ATIS, sponsored by the Federal Government, provides current treatment information on HIV and AIDS as well as answering HIV/AIDS-related questions. Referrals to national, State, and local organizations are provided. All information is free and confidential.

Huntington's Disease Society of America (HDSA)
158 West 29th Street, 7th Floor
New York, NY 10001-5300
Phone: 1-800-345-HDSA (4372) (toll-free)
212-242-1968, Ext.10
Fax: 212-239-3430
Email: hdsainfo@hdsa.org
Website: http://www.hdsa.org
The Society is a nonprofit organization providing information, services, and advocacy for people with Huntington's disease (HD) and their families. Contact HDSA for research information on causes, diagnosis, and treatment of HD as well as referrals to testing centers, specialists, self-help groups, and social services. Publications and audiovisual materials on HD are available.

Hysterectomy Educational Resources and Services Foundation (HERS)
422 Bryn Mawr Avenue
Bala Cynwyd, PA 19004
Phone: 610-667-7757
Fax: 610-667-8096
Email: HERSFdn@aol.com
Website: http://www.hersfoundation.com
HERS Foundation is a nonprofit organization providing information on hysterectomy (surgical removal of the uterus) and oophorectomy (removal of the ovaries). Contact HERS for telephone counseling and support services. A lending

library contains medical literature on topics such as fibroids, hyperplasia, and ovarian conditions. A list of publications is available on request.

Indian Health Service (IHS)
Parklawn Bldg., Room 6-35
5600 Fishers Lane
Rockville, MD 20857
Phone: 301-443-3593
Fax: 301-443-0507
Website: http://www.ihs.gov
The IHS, part of the Federal Government, operates a comprehensive health service program for American Indians and Alaska Natives. Services include hospital and community-based medical care, rehabilitation, and disease prevention. The IHS strives for maximum tribal involvement in all aspects of its services.

International Hearing Society (IHS)
16880 Middlebelt Road, Suite 4
Livonia, MI 48154
Phone: 1-800-521-5247 (toll-free) (Hearing Aid Helpline)
734-522-7200 (outside the US and Canada)
Fax: 734-522-0200
Website: http://www.hearingihs.org
IHS is a professional organization providing assistance to consumers in locating a hearing aid specialist, support, and repair services. The Hearing Aid Helpline offers information and publications on how hearing works, types of hearing loss, and design and use of hearing instruments.

International Tremor Foundation (ITF)
7046 West 105th Street
Overland Park, KS 66212-1803
Phone: 913-341-3880
Fax: 913-341-1296
Email: UPF_ITF@msn.com
Website: http://www.essentialtremor.org
ITF is an international, nonprofit organization providing support, information on medication use and surgical treatment, research, and other resources for people

diagnosed with essential tremor. Contact ITF for referrals to medical specialists, a list of support groups by State, and information on more than 20 tremor disorders. Members may write or call for background literature and answers to specific questions.

Japanese American Citizens League (JACL)
National Headquarters
1765 Sutter Street
San Francisco, CA 94115
Phone: 415-921-5225
Fax: 415-931-4671
Email: jacl@jacl.org
Website: http://www.jacl.org
JACL is a nonprofit educational organization fighting discrimination against Japanese Americans and their families by providing information, education, and advocacy. Contact JACL for assistance to retired people and information on programs on equal rights, racial violence, immigration, and fair employment. *Pacific Citizen*, a weekly newspaper, and other publications are available.

Kansas Geriatric Education Center (KS-GEC)
Center on Aging
University of Kansas Medical Center
3901 Rainbow Boulevard
Kansas City, KS 66160-7177
Phone: 913-588-1636
Fax: 913-588-3179
Email: hcallowa@kumc.edu
Website: http://coa.kumc.edu/gec
KS-GEC provides information and support for developing community-based, long term care for rural older people. The Center works closely with State and Area Agencies on Aging. Contact the Center for a list of publications.

Legal Counsel for the Elderly (LCE)
American Association of Retired Persons (AARP)
601 E Street, NW
Washington, DC 20049
Phone: 202-434-2120

TTY: 202-434-6562
Fax: 202-434-6464
Website: http://www.aarp.org

LCE, part of AARP, works to expand the availability of legal services to older people and to enhance the quality of those services. The National Volunteer Lawyers Project matches legal cases affecting large numbers of older people with volunteer law firms. The Senior Lawyers Project tests ways retired lawyers can provide free legal services to older people in need. The National Elderlaw Studies Program provides individual home study courses as well as a paralegal certificate from the Department of Agriculture Graduate School. Publications are available.

Legal Services for the Elderly (LSE)
130 West 42nd Street, 17th Floor
New York, NY 10036
Phone: 212-391-0120
Fax: 212-719-1939
Email: hn4923@handsnet.org

LSE is an advisory center for lawyers specializing in legal problems of older people. While LSE does not provide direct services to clients, staff lawyers offer advice and write memoranda and briefs to lawyers who serve older clients on issues including Medicaid, Medicare, Social Security, disability, voluntary and involuntary commitment, age discrimination, pensions, rent-increase exemptions for older people, and nursing home care. A list of publications is available.

Leukemia and Lymphoma Society, Inc. (LLS)
1311 Mamaroneck Avenue
White Plains, NY 10605
Phone: 1-800-955-4572 (toll-free)
914-949-5213
Fax: 914-949-6691
Email: infocenter@leukemia-lymphoma.org
Website: http://www.leukemia.org

LLS provides information, advocacy, and assistance for patients with leukemia and related cancers such as lymphoma, multiple myeloma, and Hodgkin's disease.

Contact LLS for information, referrals to specialists and local chapters offering financial assistance to patients with leukemia, and support groups. Publications on leukemia and related cancers are available.

Lighthouse National Center for Vision and Aging (LNCVA)
111 East 59th Street
New York, NY 10022
Phone: 1-800-829-0500 (toll-free)
212-821-9495
TTY: 212-821-9713
Fax: 212-821-9705
Email: info@lighthouse.org
Website: http://www.lighthouse.org
LNCVA provides advocacy, support, information, and resources on vision impairment and blindness. Contact the Lighthouse for referrals to specialists and resources on visual disability, vision rehabilitation, links to related services, as well as information on eye diseases such as macular degeneration, glaucoma, cataracts, and diabetic retinopathy. Publications and audiovisual materials are available on topics including vision, vision disorders, treatment options, and rehabilitation strategies.

Lupus Foundation of America (LFA)
1300 Piccard Drive, Suite 200
Rockville, MD 20850-4303
Phone: 1-800-558-0121 (toll-free) (information line)
301-670-9292
Fax: 301-670-9486
Email: lupusinfo@aol.com
Website: http://www.lupus.org
LFA is a nonprofit organization supporting research and distributing information about diagnosis and treatment of lupus erythematosus, a chronic autoimmune disease. Contact the LFA for referrals to specialists, information about treatment and research, a listing of local chapters and support groups, other resource organizations, and a list of publications.

Meals On Wheels Association of America (MOWAA)
1414 Prince Street, Suite 302
Alexandria, VA 22314
Phone: 703-548-5558
Fax: 703-548-8024
Website: http://www.mowaa.org
MOWAA is a national, nonprofit organization providing training and grants to programs that provide food to older people, and those who are frail, disabled, at-risk, or homebound.

MedicAlert Foundation
2323 Colorado Avenue
Turlock, CA 95382
Phone: 1-800-432-5378 (toll-free)
209-668-3333
Fax: 209-669-2495
Website: http://www.medicalert.org
MedicAlert is a nonprofit, membership organization providing identification and medical information in emergencies. Contact MedicAlert for information about its membership services and costs.

Medicare Rights Center (MRC)
1460 Broadway, 11th Floor
New York, NY 10036
Phone: 212-869-3850
Fax: 212-869-3532
Email: info@medicarerights.org
Website: http://www.medicarerights.org
MRC is a national, nonprofit service helping older adults and people with disabilities get good, affordable health care. Available educational materials include a train-the-trainer manual, booklets on Medicare basics, and Medicare home health.

National Academy of Elder Law Attorneys, Inc. (NAELA)
1604 North Country Club Road
Tucson, AZ 85716
Phone: 520-881-4005
Fax: 520-325-7925

Website: http://www.naela.org
NAELA is a nonprofit association assisting lawyers, bar associations, and others who work with older people and their families. Contact NAELA for information on lawyers specializing in issues pertinent to older people, resources to legal information, assistance, and education. A list of publications is available.

National Alliance for Hispanic Health
1501 16th Street, NW
Washington, DC 20036
Phone: 202-387-5000
Email: alliance@hispanichealth.org
Website: http://www.hispanichealth.org/
The Alliance is a network of health and human service providers fostering the health, well-being, and prosperity of Hispanics. Network members provide consumer information, help formulate culturally competent standards of care, support research into specific health concerns facing Hispanics, and promote appropriate use of technology. Spanish language resources are available.

National Alliance for the Mentally Ill (NAMI)
Colonial Place Three
2107 Wilson Boulevard, Suite 300
Arlington, VA 22201
Phone: 1-800-950-NAMI (950-6264) (toll-free) NAMI Helpline
703-524-7600
TTY: 703-516-7227
Fax: 703-524-9094
Website: http://www.nami.org
NAMI offers support groups, education, advocacy, and research to help people with mental illness. The Alliance seeks to educate all people about severe and persistent mental illnesses to eliminate stigma and promote access to services. Search the website for lists of local affiliates and state organizations.

National Institute of Arthritis and Musculoskeletal and Skin Diseases (NIAMS)
National Institutes of Health
1 AMS Circle
Bethesda, MD 20892-3675
Phone: 1-877-22-NIAMS (226-4267) (toll-free)
301-495-4484
TTY: 301-565-2966
Fax: 301-881-2731 (faxback service)
Email: NIAMSInfo@mail.nih.gov
Website: http://www.nih.gov/niams
NIAMS Information Clearinghouse is funded by NIAMS, part of NIH. The Clearinghouse provides information and resources on all forms of arthritis, musculoskeletal diseases such as fibromyalgia, as well as skin diseases. Contact the Clearinghouse for information on research and referrals to research programs and community resources. Publications are available on the causes, treatments, and prevention of arthritis, lupus, musculoskeletal disorders, and diseases of bones, joints, and skin.

National Asian Pacific Center on Aging (NAPCA)
1511 3rd Avenue, Suite 914
Seattle, WA 98101-1626
Phone: 206-624-1221
Fax: 206-624-1023
Email: info@napca.org
Website: http://www.napca.org
NAPCA is a nonprofit agency dedicated to serving aging Asian and Pacific Islanders. It offers employment programs, multilingual community forums and health care education. The Center works with elders, policy makers, program administrators, and community leaders. Publications include a newsletter and translated health care materials.

National Association for Continence (NAFC)
PO Box 8310
Spartanburg, SC 29305-8310
Phone: 1-800-252-3337 (toll-free) (ordering line)
Fax: 864-579-7902
Email: memberservices@nafc.org

Website: http://www.nafc.org
NAFC, formerly Help for Incontinent People, is a nonprofit organization providing advocacy, education, and support to people with incontinence and their families. Contact NAFC for referrals to specialists, resources, and information about the causes, prevention, diagnosis, treatments, and management alternatives for incontinence. Publications are available.

National Association for Health & Fitness (NAHF)
201 South Capitol Avenue, Suite 560
Indianapolis, IN 46225
Phone: 317-237-5630
Fax: 317-237-5632
Website: http://www.physicalfitness.org/
NAHF is a nonprofit organization promoting physical fitness, sports, and healthy lifestyles. The Association supports State Governor's Councils on Physical Fitness and Sports. NAHF supports employee health and fitness programs including Let's Get Physical, an interactive educational program based on the Surgeon General's 1996 report recommending moderate physical activity most days of the week.

National Association for Hispanic Elderly (Asociación Nacional Por Personas Mayores)
234 East Colorado Boulevard, Suite 300
Pasadena, CA 91101
Phone: 626-564-1988
Fax: 626-564-2659
The Association is a national, private, nonprofit organization providing a variety of services for older Hispanic people. Resources include a national Hispanic research center, research and consultation for organizations seeking to reach older Spanish-speaking people, and dissemination of written and audiovisual materials in English and Spanish. The Association administers Project AYUDA, a program providing employment counseling and placement services.

National Association for Home Care (NAHC)
228 7th Street, SE
Washington, DC 20003
Phone: 202-547-7424
Fax: 202-547-3540
Email: webmaster@nahc.org
Website: http://www.nahc.org
NAHC promotes hospice and home care, sets standards of care, and conducts research on aging, health, and health care policy. Association publications include *How to Choose a Home Care Provider* and other free consumer guides on home care and hospice care.

National Association for Human Development (NAHD)
1424 16th Street, NW, Suite 102
Washington, DC 20036
Phone: 202-328-2191
Fax: 202-265-6682
Email: nahdcasa@worldnet.att.net
NAHD is a nonprofit organization providing information and materials for national, State, and local groups helping people maintain their physical, mental, and social well-being. Contact NAHD program specialists for slides, videos, booklets, posters, and training manuals on health and physical fitness. Program materials focusing on older people include topics such as wellness, physical fitness, preventive medicine, self-care, and retirement planning.

National Association for Practical Nurse Education and Services (NAPNES)
1400 Spring Street, Suite 330
Silver Spring, MD 20910
Phone: 301-588-2491
Fax: 301-588-2839
Email: napnes@bellatlantic.net
NAPNES is a professional organization of licensed practical nurses, other nurses, physicians, nursing home administrators, and the general public specializing in direct long term care of older people. NAPNES offers long term care certification to practical/vocational nurses. Contact

NAPNES for information on practical nursing and referrals to member nurses and resource organizations.

National Association of Activity Professionals (NAAP)
PO Box 5530
Sevierville, TN 37864
Phone: 865-429-0717
Fax: 865-453-9914
Email: THENAAP@aol.com
Website: http://www.thenaap.com
NAAP is a professional organization providing activity education, advocacy, industry standards, and programming for long term-care facilities, retirement living communities, and adult day care centers. Contact NAAP for referrals to specialists and information on therapeutic and restorative activities, regulation and policy updates, and program models. Publications are available.

National Association of Area Agencies on Aging (N4A)
927 15th Street, NW, 6th Floor
Washington, DC 20005
Phone: 1-800-677-1116 (toll-free) (Eldercare Locator)
202-296-8130
Fax: 202-296-8134
Website: http://www.n4a.org
N4A is the umbrella organization for the AoA-funded Area Agencies on Aging. It also represents the interests of Title VI Native American aging programs. The Association administers the AoA-sponsored Eldercare Locator, a toll-free number linking older adults and their family members with local aging resources. N4A publishes the *National Directory for Eldercare Information and Referral.*

National Association of Community Health Centers (NACHC)
1330 New Hampshire Avenue, NW, Suite 122
Washington, DC 20036
Phone: 202-659-8008
Fax: 202-659-8519
Email: dhawkins@nachc.org
Website: http://www.nachc.com

NACHC is a national association representing community health centers nationwide. Contact NACHC for referrals to local health centers and information on the Association's programs as well as health care regulation and policy updates.

National Association of Nutrition and Aging Service Programs (NANASP)
1101 Vermont Avenue, NW, Suite 1001
Washington, DC 20005
Phone: 202-682-6899
Fax: 202-682-3984
Website: http://www.nanasp.org
NANASP, a membership organization, supports a broad range of nutrition and related services for community-dwelling older people by training nutrition providers and advocating for older people. Publications include a *Legislative Action Manual* and *The Washington Bulletin*.

National Association of Professional Geriatric Care Managers (NAPGCM)
1604 North Country Club Road
Tucson, AZ 85716-3102
Phone: 520-881-8008
Fax: 520-325-7925
Email: info@caremanager.org
Website: http://www.caremanager.org
NAPGCM is a nonprofit organization representing the interests of elder care practitioners and advocating for older peoples' independence, autonomy, and quality of health care. Contact NAPGCM for resources, referrals to local Association chapters, and information on counseling and treatment programs. Publications and referrals to professional care managers are available through the website.

National Association of Social Workers (NASW)
750 First Street, NE, Suite 700
Washington, DC 20002-4241
Phone: 1-800-638-8799 (toll-free)
202-408-8600

Fax: 202-336-8310
Email: info@naswdc.org
Website: http://www.naswdc.org
NASW is a membership organization promoting, advocating, developing, and protecting social workers and the practice of social work. Contact NASW for referrals to counseling resources and specialists, information about social work, and information from the members section focusing on aging issues and health care.

National Association of State Units on Aging (NASUA)
1225 I Street, NW, Suite 725
Washington, DC 20005
Phone: 202-898-2578
Fax: 202-898-2583
Email: info@nasua.org
Website: http://www.nasua.org
NASUA is a public-interest organization providing information, assistance, and advocacy on behalf of older people. Contact NASUA for information on rights of older people, health care and social services regulations, and referrals to lawyers specializing in elder law and aging issues. Publications are available on topics such as the Older Americans Act, long term care, older worker issues, elder abuse, and nutrition programs. The Association cooperates in administering the Eldercare Locator, AoA's toll-free information service.

National Association of the Deaf (NAD)
814 Thayer Avenue
Silver Spring, MD 20910-4500
Phone: 301-587-1788
TTY: 301-587-1789
Fax: 301-587-1791
Email: NADinfo@nad.org
Website: http://www.nad.org
NAD is a private, nonprofit organization representing the interests and rights of people who are deaf or hearing impaired. It advocates for greater access to education, employment, health care, and social services. Contact NAD for information on legal assistance, public policy on

deafness and disabilities, and referrals to products that assist deaf and hearing impaired people. Publications are available.

National Association on HIV Over Fifty (NAHOF)
Southwest Boulevard Family Health Care Services, Inc.
340 Southwest Boulevard
Kansas City, KS 66103
Phone: 816-421-5263
Fax: 913-722-2542
Email: janepfowler@mindspring.com
Website: http://www.hivoverfifty.org
NAHOF is a membership organization promoting the availability of a full range of educational, prevention, service, and health care programs for people over age 50 and affected by HIV. NAHOF provides a forum to exchange information and share concerns about HIV and older adults.

National Bar Association (NBA)
1225 11th Street, NW
Washington, DC 20001
Phone: 202-842-3900
Fax: 202-289-6170
Website: http://www.nationalbar.org
NBA uses its national membership, statewide minority bar programs, minority law students, minority bar group alliances, and private attorneys, to form links with community groups providing legal assistance to low-income, minority older people. Publications include *Saving The Home* and *Defending Against Fraud and Scams*, a resource book on second mortgages.

National Cancer Institute (NCI)
National Institutes of Health
Public Inquiries Office
Building 31, Room 10A03
31 Center Drive MSC 2580
Bethesda, MD 20892-2580
Phone: 1-800-4-CANCER (422-6237) (toll-free) (Cancer Information Service-CIS)
TTY: 1-800-332-8615 (toll-free)

301-435-3848
Email: webmaster@cancer.gov
Website: http://www.nci.nih.gov
NCI, part of NIH, is the lead agency for cancer research and statistics, treatments, clinical trials, patient education, and public information on all types of cancer, risk factors, and prevention. NCI's toll-free CIS provides immediate, science-based answers to the public's specific questions about cancer. The CIS provides referrals to cancer specialists and other related resources, including where to find survivor groups. Many free publications are available.

National Caucus and Center on Black Aged, Inc. (NCBA)
1424 K Street, NW, Suite 500
Washington, DC 20005
Phone: 202-637-8400
Fax: 202-347-0895
Email: ncba@aol.com
Website: http://www.ncba-blackaged.org
NCBA is a national, nonprofit organization providing health and social service information, advocacy, and assistance to African Americans and low-income older people. Contact NCBA for information on its local chapters and programs including senior employment and training, housing, health promotion, and advocacy. Publications include a support-service reference guide, job placement guides, and a *Profile of Black Elderly*.

National Center for Complementary and Alternative Medicine Clearinghouse (NCCAM)
National Institutes of Health (NIH)
PO Box 8218
Silver Spring, MD 20907-8218
Phone: 1-888-644-6226 (toll-free)
301-231-7357
TTY: 1-888-644-6226 (toll-free)
Fax: 1-888-644-6226 (toll-free) (Fax-on-demand)
Fax: 301-495-4957
Email: nccam-info@nccam.nih.gov
Website: http://www.nccam.nih.gov

The Clearinghouse, funded by NCCAM, provides information on alternative medical therapies not commonly used or previously accepted in conventional Western medicine. Contact the Clearinghouse for information on holistic healing traditions, including acupuncture, herbs, homeopathy, therapeutic massage, and traditional oriental medicine. NCCAM does not recommend specific therapies. Publications are available by fax-on-demand and on the website.

National Center for Health Statistics (NCHS)
Centers for Disease Control and Prevention (CDC)
6525 Belcrest Road
Hyattsville, MD 20782-2003
Phone: 301-458-4636
Website: http://www.cdc.gov/nchs/
NCHS, part of the Federal Government, is the agency that monitors and compiles information on the Nation's health. NCHS statistical programs on aging collect information on the health of older people, their lifestyles, exposure to unhealthy influences, diagnosis and age of onset for illnesses or disabilities, and patterns of health care service use. Contact NCHS for reports on trends in health and aging.

National Center on Elder Abuse (NCEA)
1225 I Street, NW, Suite 725
Washington, DC 20005
Phone: 202-898-2586
Fax: 202-898-2583
Email: NCEA@nasua.org
Website: http://www.elderabusecenter.org/
NCEA is operated jointly by the National Association of State Units on Aging, the National Committee for the Prevention of Elder Abuse, and the University of Delaware to disseminate information about abuse and neglect of older people. NCEA operates the Clearinghouse on Abuse and Neglect of the Elderly and can provide referrals to agencies and specialists. Publications are available on prevention of abuse, neglect, and State regulations.

National Center on Minority Health and Health Disparities (NCMHD)
National Institutes of Health (NIH)
6707 Democracy Boulevard
MSC 5465
Bethesda, MD 20892-5465
Phone: 301-402-1366
Fax: 301-496-4035
NCMHD, part of NIH, conducts and supports research, training, dissemination of information, and other programs with respect to minority health conditions and other populations with health disparities.

National Center on Poverty Law, Inc. (NCPL)
205 West Monroe Street
Chicago, IL 60606
Phone: 312-263-3830
Fax: 312-263-3846
Website: http://www.povertylaw.org
NCPL is a professional organization advocating for low-income people and providing assistance, resources, and information on poverty law. Contact NCPL for referrals to poverty law specialists, program information on welfare, work force, housing, and community development. Publications are available on topics such as grandparents' visitation, access to home health care for older people, protecting older homeowners from refinancing scams, and the needs of multigenerational low-income families.

National Citizen's Coalition for Nursing Home Reform (NCCNHR)
1424 16th Street, NW, Suite 202
Washington, DC 20036-2211
Phone: 202-332-2275
Fax: 202-332-2949
Email: nccnhr@nccnhr.org
Website: http://www.nccnhr.org
NCCNHR provides information on nursing home reform, promotes quality standards, and works to empower residents. Contact NCCNHR for information on community-based, consumer/citizen action, and long term care

ombudsmen groups. Publications on nursing homes and long term care are available.

National Coalition for Adult Immunization (NCAI)
4733 Bethesda Avenue, Suite 750
Bethesda, MD 20814
Phone: 301-656-0003
Fax: 301-907-0878
Email: ncai@nfid.org
Website: http://www.nfid.org/ncai
NCAI is a network of organizations formed to achieve better health through immunizations and support for science-based recommendations. NCAI helps coordinate National Adult Immunization Awareness Week, an annual observance in the fall. Check the website for a chart outlining the NCAI-recommended adult immunization schedule. Spanish language resources are available.

National Committee to Preserve Social Security and Medicare (NCPSSM)
10 G Street, NE, Suite 600
Washington, DC 20004-4215
Phone: 1-800-966-1935 (toll-free)
202-216-0420
Fax: 202-216-0451
Website: http://www.ncpssm.org
NCPSSM, an advocacy and education membership organization, works to protect and enhance Federal programs vital to seniors' health and economic well-being. Contact NCPSSM for details on membership as well as information on seniors' rights, Medicare, Social Security, long term care, and disability issues. Free informational brochures are available.

National Consumer's League (NCL)
1701 K Street, NW, Suite 1200
Washington, DC 20006
Phone: 1-800-876-7060 (toll-free) (National Fraud Information Center- NFIC)
202-835-3323
Fax: 202-835-0747

Email: info@nclnet.org
Website: http://www.natlconsumersleague.org (National Consumer's League)
http://www.fraud.org (National Fraud Information Center)
NCL is a private, nonprofit advocacy group representing consumers on marketplace and workplace issues, providing government, businesses, and other organizations with consumer's perspectives on social issues. Contact the NCL for information on topics such as privacy, consumer credit, food safety, and drug safety. NFIC supports victims of telemarketing and Internet fraud, and informs law enforcement of fraud cases. Publications are available.

National Council Against Health Fraud (NCAHF)
PO Box 1276
Loma Linda, CA 92354
Phone: 201-723-2955 (consumer health information)
Website: http://www.ncahf.org
NCAHF is a nonprofit agency that provides a website listing reliable sources of health information on the Internet. Contact the Council for information on health fraud, misinformation, and quackery, or to report fraud and investigate health claims by companies or organizations. NCAHF provides information on legitimate health groups, sponsors discussion groups that evaluate new health organizations, and suggests alternative medical techniques. A free weekly email newsletter is available online.

National Council of La Raza (NCLR)
1111 19th Street, NW, Suite 1000
Washington, DC 20036
Phone: 202-785-1670
Fax: 202-776-1794
Website: http://www.nclr.org
NCLR is a private, nonprofit organization established to reduce poverty and discrimination, and improve opportunities for Hispanics. NCLR health programs develop culturally-relevant, bilingual health education and promotional materials. The Hispanic Health Project works to lower the incidence of a variety of preventable conditions.

National Council on Aging, Inc. (NCOA)
409 3rd Street, SW, Suite 200
Washington, DC 20024
Phone: 202-479-1200
Fax: 202-479-0735
Email: info@ncoa.org
Website: http://www.ncoa.org
NCOA is a private, nonprofit organization providing information, training, technical assistance, advocacy, and leadership in all aspects of aging services and issues. Contact NCOA for information on training programs and in-home services for older people. NCOA publications are available on topics such as lifelong learning, senior center services, adult day care, long term care, financial issues, senior housing, rural issues, intergenerational programs, and volunteers in aging.

National Council on Alcoholism and Drug Dependence (NCADD)
20 Exchange Place, Suite 2902
New York, NY 10005
Phone: 1-800-NCA-CALL (622-2255) (toll-free)
212-269-7797
Fax: 212-269-7510
Email: national@ncadd.org
Website: http://www.ncadd.org
NCADD is a nonprofit organization providing advocacy, assistance, and information on alcoholism and drug addiction. Contact NCADD for information on causes, diagnosis, and treatments; referrals to specialists; lists of community resource centers; and NCADD-affiliated organizations nationwide. Fact sheets, brochures, and videotapes also are available.

National Council on Patient Information and Education (NCPIE)
4915 Saint Elmo Avenue, Suite 505
Bethesda, MD 20814-6053
Phone: 301-656-8565
Fax: 301-656-4464
Email: ncpie@erols.com

Website: http://www.talkaboutrx.org
NCPIE is a nonprofit coalition providing advocacy, information, and services to educate and empower consumers to make sound decisions about use of prescription and over-the-counter medicines. Contact NCPIE to discuss drug safety or facts about specific drugs. NCPIE's website and publications provide information on medications, side effects, and manufacturers' recalls.

National Diabetes Information Clearinghouse (NDIC)
National Institute of Diabetes and Digestive and Kidney Diseases (NIDDK)
National Institutes of Health (NIH)
1 Information Way
Bethesda, MD 20892-3560
Phone: 1-800-860-8747 (toll-free)
301-654-3327
Fax: 301-907-8906
Email: ndic@info.niddk.nih.gov
Website: http://www.niddk.nih.gov
NDIC, funded by NIDDK, part of NIH, provides referrals to diabetes specialists and organizations, and searches from its database of patient and professional education materials. Call for publications on topics such as alternative therapies, controlling diabetes, complications of diabetes, and diabetes in Asian, Hispanic, and other ethnic groups. Spanish-language publications are available.

National Digestive Diseases Information Clearinghouse (NDDIC)
National Institute of Diabetes and Digestive and Kidney Diseases (NIDDK)
National Institutes of Health (NIH)
2 Information Way
Bethesda, MD 20892-3570
Phone: 1-800-891-5389 (toll-free)
301-654-3810
Fax: 301-907-8906
Email: nddic@info.niddk.nih.gov
Website: http://www.niddk.nih.gov

NDDIC, funded by NIDDK, part of NIH, provides referrals to digestive diseases organizations and support groups, as well as searches from its database of patient and professional education materials. Fact sheets are available on gastroesophageal reflux disease, hemorrhoids, constipation, ulcers, and irritable bowel syndrome.

National Eye Health Education Program (NEHEP)
National Eye Institute (NEI)
National Institutes of Health (NIH)
2020 Vision Place
Bethesda, MD 20892-3655
Phone: 301-496-5248
Fax: 301-402-1065
Email: 2020@nei.nih.gov
Website: http://www.nei.nih.gov
NEHEP, funded by the NEI, part of NIH, is a partnership of professional, civic, and voluntary organizations and Federal agencies. NEHEP provides referrals to vision professionals and other health resources. The Program offers free materials to educate the public about how to protect eye health and prevent vision loss, and distributes information on such topics as preventing diabetic eye disease, glaucoma, and low vision.

National Family Caregivers Association (NFCA)
10400 Connecticut Avenue, #500
Kensington, MD 20895-3944
Phone: 1-800-896-3650 (toll-free)
Fax: 301-942-2302
Email: info@nfcacares.org
Website: http://www.nfcacares.org
NFCA is a grass roots organization providing advocacy, support, and information for family members who care for chronically ill, older, or disabled relatives. There is no charge for family members to be on the mailing list and to receive the newsletter, *Take Care!* Contact NFCA for help finding resources.

National Gerontological Nursing Association (NGNA)
7794 Grow Drive
Pensacola, FL 32514
Phone: 1-800-723-0560 (toll-free)
Fax: 850-484-8762
Email: ngna@puetzamc.com
Website: http://www.ngna.org
NGNA, an organization of nurses specializing in care of older adults, informs the public on health issues affecting older people, supports education for nurses and other health care practitioners, and provides a forum to discuss topics such as nutrition in long term care facilities and elder law for nurses. NGNA offers information on gerontological nursing and conducts nursing research related to older people.

National Health Information Center (NHIC)
Office of Disease Prevention and Health Promotion (ODPHP)
Department of Health and Human Services
PO Box 1133
Washington, DC 20013-1133
Phone: 1-800-336-4797 (toll-free)
301-565-4167
Fax: 301-984-4256
Faxback: 301-468-1204
Email: nhicinfo@health.org
Website: http://www.health.gov/NHIC
NHIC, a service of the Federal Government, links consumers and health professionals with resources and information. The Center provides health information, contacts for Federally-supported health information centers, lists of national health observances, and toll-free numbers sponsored by the Federal Government.

National Heart, Lung, and Blood Institute (NHLBI) Information Center
PO Box 30105
Bethesda, MD 20824-0105
Phone: 1-800-575-WELL (9355) (toll-free) (recorded information)
301-592-8573

Fax: 301-592-8563
Email: NHLBIinfo@rover.nhlbi.nih.gov
Website: http://www.nhlbi.nih.gov
The Information Center, funded by NHLBI, part of NIH, provides referrals to resource organizations and information on elevated cholesterol, high blood pressure, heart disease, exercise, risk of and recovery from stroke, chronic cough, asthma, cystic fibrosis, and sleep disorders. Publications include two newsletters, *HeartMemo* and *AsthmaMemo*.

National Hispanic Council on Aging (NHCoA)
2713 Ontario Road, NW
Washington, DC 20009
Phone: 202-265-1288
Fax: 202-745-2522
Email: nhcoa@worldnet.att.net
Website: http://www.nhcoa.org
NHCoA is a national organization providing advocacy, education, and information for older Hispanic people. Contact the Council for facts and resources on health, employment, housing, strengthening families, and building communities, as well as referrals to local Council chapters. Publications in English and Spanish are available.

National Hospice and Palliative Care Organization (NHPCO)
1700 Diagonal Road, Suite 300
Alexandria, VA 22314
Phone: 1-800-658-8898 (toll-free) (Hospice Helpline and Locator)
703-837-1500
Email: info@nhpco.org
Website: http://www.nhpco.org
NHPCO is a nonprofit, membership organization working to enhance the quality of life for individuals who are terminally ill and advocating for people in the final stage of life. Contact NHPCO for information, resources, and referrals to local hospice services. Publications, fact sheets, and website resources are available on topics including how to find and evaluate hospice services.

National Hospice Foundation (NHF)
1700 Diagonal Road, Suite 300
Alexandria, VA 22314
Phone: 1-800-338-8619 (toll-free)
703-516-4928
Fax: 703-525-5762
Email: info@nhpco.org
Website: http://www.hospiceinfo.org
NHF, a nonprofit, charitable organization affiliated with the National Hospice and Palliative Care Organization, provides support and information about hospice care options. NHF publications include *Hospice Care: A Consumer's Guide to Selecting a Hospice Program*, *Communicating Your End-of-Life Wishes*, and *Hospice Care and the Medicare Hospice Benefit*.

National Human Genome Research Institute (NHGRI)
National Institutes of Health (NIH)
Office of Policy and Public Affairs
Building 31; Room 4B09
Bethesda, MD 20892
Phone: 301-402-0911
Website: http://www.nhgri.nih.gov
NHGRI, part of NIH, coordinates the Human Genome Project, an international research effort to characterize the genomes of human and selected model organisms through complete mapping and sequencing of their DNA.

National Indian Council on Aging (NICOA)
10501 Montgomery Boulevard, NE, Suite 210
Albuquerque, NM 87111-3846
Phone: 505-292-2001
Fax: 505-292-1922
Email: dave@nicoa.org
Website: http://www.nicoa.org
NICOA provides services, advocacy, and information on aging issues for older American Indian and Alaska Native people. Contact NICOA for information about its resources and support groups serving the national Indian community, and NICOA's clearinghouse for issues affecting older Indian

people. Publications are available, including the newsletter *Elder Voices*.

National Information and Referral Support Center (NIRSC)
1225 I Street, NW, Suite 725
Washington, DC 20005-3914
Phone: 202-898-2578
Fax: 202-898-2583
Email: staff@nasua.org
Website: http://www.nasua.org
NIRSC provides technical assistance, consultation, and training to State and Area Agencies on Aging and to local information and referral providers funded under the Older Americans Act. Contact the Center for referrals, resources, and information on how to locate services for older people. A list of Center publications is available.

National Institute of Allergy and Infectious Diseases (NIAID)
National Institutes of Health (NIH)
Bethesda, MD 20892-2520
Phone: 301-496-5717
Fax: 301-402-0120
Email: niaidoc@nih.gov
Website: http://www.niaid.nih.gov
NIAID, part of NIH, conducts and supports research on the prevention, diagnosis, and treatment of HIV/AIDS and other infectious and allergic diseases. Contact NIAID for information on allergies, as well as viral and bacterial illnesses. The Institute provides referrals to specialists, support groups, and other resources; publications and fact sheets are available, some in Spanish.

National Institute of Child Health and Human Development (NICHD) Information Clearinghouse
PO Box 3006
Rockville, MD 20847
Phone: 1-800-370-2943
Fax: 301-984-1473
Email: NICHDClearinghouse@mail.nih.gov

Website: http://www.nichd.nih.gov
The Clearinghouse, funded by NICHD, part of NIH, is a resource for publications and health issues related to NICHD research. The Institute conducts and supports research on neurobiologic, developmental, and behavioral processes that determine and maintain the health of children, adults, families, and populations. Spanish language resources are available.

National Institute of Dental and Craniofacial Research (NIDCR)
National Institutes of Health (NIH)
Bethesda, MD 20892-2290
Phone: 301-496-4261
301-402-7364 (National Oral Health Information Clearinghouse - NOHIC)
TTY: 301-656-7581
Fax: 301-469-9988
Email: nidcrinfo@mail.nih.gov
nohic@nidcr.nih.gov
Website: http://www.nidcr.nih.gov/
http://www.nohic.nidcr.nih.gov
NIDCR, part of NIH, conducts and supports research on the causes, treatment, and prevention of diseases of the teeth, gums, and facial bones. Contact NOHIC for facts about oral health in people with disabling conditions and referrals to additional resources. Contact NIDCR for information on available publications, audiovisual materials, and fact sheets.

National Institute of Environmental Health Sciences (NIEHS)
National Institutes of Health (NIH)
PO Box 12233
Research Triangle Park, NC 27709
Phone: 919-541-3345
Website: http://www.niehs.nih.gov/home.htm
NIEHS, part of NIH, conducts and supports research on potential environmental contributors to human illnesses and dysfunction, including asthma, Alzheimer's, bronchitis, cancer, lead poisoning, Parkinson's and other chronic

diseases. NIEHS also studies variable human susceptibilities to these environmental factors. The National Toxicology Program, headquartered at NIEHS, tests natural and man-made chemicals for safety.

National Institute of General Medical Sciences (NIGMS)
National Institutes of Health (NIH)
Office of Communications and Public Liaison
Bethesda, MD 20892-6200
Phone: 301-496-7301
Fax: 301-402-0224
Email: pub_info@nigms.nih.gov
Website: http://www.nigms.nih.gov
NIGMS, part of NIH, conducts and supports research in medical fields such as genetics, cellular and molecular biology, and pharmacology. Publications include *Medicines for You* (also available in Spanish), and *Inside the Cell*.

National Institute of Mental Health (NIMH)
National Institutes of Health (NIH)
Bethesda, MD 20892-9663
Phone: 1-800-421-4211 (toll-free)
301-443-4513
TTY: 301-443-8431
Fax: 301-443-4279
Email: nimhinfo@nih.gov
Website: http://www.nimh.nih.gov
NIMH, part of NIH, conducts and supports mental health research including mental disorders of aging. Contact NIMH for information on mental health and aging, Alzheimer's disease, anxiety disorders, depression, and suicide.

National Institute of Neurological Disorders and Stroke (NINDS)
National Institutes of Health (NIH)
Office of Communications and Public Liaison
Bethesda, MD 20892-2540
Phone: 1-800-352-9424 (toll-free) (information service)
301-496-5751
Fax: 301-402-2186
Website: http://www.ninds.nih.gov

NINDS, part of NIH, conducts and supports research on stroke and neurological disorders. NINDS provides information on its research targets, including stroke, head and spinal injuries, tumors of the central nervous system, epilepsy, multiple sclerosis, Huntington's disease, Parkinson's disease, and Alzheimer's disease. A directory of voluntary health agencies is available.

National Institute of Nursing Research (NINR)
Office of Science Policy and Public Liaison
National Institutes of Health (NIH)
31 Center Drive
Building 31, Room 5B10
Bethesda, MD 20892-2178
Phone: 301-496-0207
Fax: 301-480-8845
Website: http://www.nih.gov/ninr
NINR, part of NIH, conducts and supports basic and clinical research to establish a scientific basis for the care of individuals across the life span. Studies addressed by nurse researchers inlcude the management of chronic diseases, health disparities, improving palliative end-of-life care, and telehealth technology.

National Institute on Aging (NIA)
National Institutes of Health (NIH)
Office of Communications and Public Liaison
Bethesda, MD 20892-2292
Phone: 1-800-222-2225 (toll-free) (NIA Information Center - NIAIC)
1-800-438-4380 (toll-free) (Alzheimer's Disease Education and Referral Center-ADEAR)
301-496-1752
TTY: 1-800-222-4225 (toll-free) (NIAIC)
Fax: 301-589-3014 (NIAIC)
301-495-3334 (ADEAR)
Email: niainfo@jbs1.com (NIAIC)
adear@alzheimers.org (ADEAR)
Website: http://www.nih.gov/nia
http://www.alzheimers.org

NIA, part of NIH, conducts and supports biomedical, social, and behavioral research on aging processes, disease, and the special problems and needs of older people. NIA develops and disseminates publications on topics such as the biology of aging, exercise, doctor/patient communication, and menopause. The Institute produces the Age Pages - a series of fact sheets for consumers on a wide range of subjects including nutrition, medications, forgetfulness, sleep, driving, and long term care. Information, publications, referrals, resource lists, and database searches on Alzheimer's disease are available through the Institute-funded ADEAR Center.

National Institute on Alcohol Abuse and Alcoholism (NIAAA)
National Institutes of Health (NIH)
Bethesda, MD 20892-7003
Phone: 301-443-3860
Fax: 301-443-6077
Email: niaaaweb-r@exchange.nih.gov
Website: http://www.niaaa.nih.gov
NIAAA, part of NIH, conducts and supports research on alcoholism and alcohol abuse. Contact the NIAAA for information on genetic and behavioral aspects of alcoholism, physiologic effects of alcohol abuse, and diagnosis, treatment, and prevention of alcohol-related problems.

National Institute on Deafness and Other Communication Disorders (NIDCD)
National Institutes of Health (NIH)
Office of Communication and Public Liaison
Bethesda, MD 20892-2320
Phone: 1-800-241-1044 (toll-free) (NIDCD Information Clearinghouse)
301-496-7243
TTY: 1-800-241-1055 (toll-free) (NIDCD Information Clearinghouse)
301-402-0252
Fax: 301-402-0018
Email: nidcd@nidcd.nih.gov
Website: http://www.nidcd.nih.gov

NIDCD, part of NIH, conducts and supports research on normal mechanisms as well as diseases and disorders of hearing, balance, smell, taste, voice, speech, and language. NIDCD develops and disseminates health information to the public based on scientific discovery.

National Institute on Drug Abuse (NIDA)
National Institutes of Health (NIH)
Public Information and Liaison Branch
Bethesda, MD 20892-9561
Phone: 1-800-729-6686 (toll-free) (National Clearinghouse for Alcohol and Drug Information–NCADI)
301-443-1124
TTY: 1-800-487-4889 (toll-free)
Fax: 1-888-644-6432 (toll-free) (NIDA Infofax)
1-888-889-6432 (toll-free) (TTY NIDA Infofax)
301-443-7397
Email: info@nida.nih.gov
Website: http://www.nida.nih.gov
NIDA, part of NIH, conducts and supports research on the physiology of specific drug addictions, effects of abused substances, and current and potential treatments. Contact NIDA for scientific information, and patient and public education materials on drug abuse, its causes, consequences, prevention, and treatment. Spanish language resources are available.

National Interfaith Coalition on Aging (NICA)
National Council on Aging (NCOA)
409 3rd Street, SW, Suite 200
Washington, DC 20024
Phone: 1-800-424-9046 (toll-free)
202-479-1200
Fax: 202-479-0735
Website: http://www.ncoa.org
The Coalition, a constituent unit of NCOA, consists of individuals and organizations of various faiths concerned with issues of religion, spirituality, and aging. NICA provides networking opportunities and educational programs.

National Kidney and Urological Diseases Information Clearinghouse (NKUDIC)

National Institute of Diabetes and Digestive and Kidney Diseases (NIDDK)
3 Information Way
Bethesda, MD 20892-3580
Phone: 1-800-891-5390 (toll-free)
301-654-4415
Fax: 301-907-8906
Email: nkudic@info.niddk.nih.gov
Website: http://www.niddk.nih.gov
NKUDIC, funded by NIDDK, provides referrals to specialists, resource organizations, and support groups. Publications and information on subjects such as kidney stones, prostate gland problems, urinary incontinence, and urinary tract infections are available.

National Kidney Foundation (NKF)
30 East 33rd Street
New York, NY 10016
Phone: 1-800-622-9010 (toll-free)
212-889-2210
Fax: 212-779-0068
Website: http://www.kidney.org
NKF is a nonprofit organization providing information on the diagnosis, treatment, and prevention of kidney and urinary tract diseases. The Foundation supports research and organ donation programs. Contact the NKF for a list of local chapters that provide services, including blood and drug banks, screening programs, transportation assistance, publications, and referrals to specialists.

National Legal Support for Elderly People with Mental Disabilities Project
Judge David L. Bazelon Center for Mental Health Law
1101 15th Street, NW, Suite 1212
Washington, DC 20005-5002
Phone: 202-467-5730
TTY: 202-467-4232
Fax: 202-223-0409
Email: hn1660@handsnet.org
Website: http://www.bazelon.org

The Project focuses on legal issues of older people, training legal aid lawyers, organizing workshops, and providing information on legal issues facing older people with mental disabilities. Contact the Project for publications on disability rights for older people.

National Library of Medicine (NLM)
National Institutes of Health (NIH)
Bethesda, MD 20894
Phone: 1-888-FIND-NLM (346-3656) (toll-free)
301-496-6308
Fax: 301-496-4450
Email: custserv@nlm.nih.gov
Website: http://www.nlm.nih.gov (MEDLINE)
http://www.nlm.nih.gov/medlineplus (MEDLINEplus)
http://www.clinicaltrials.gov (Clinical Trials database)
NLM, part of NIH, is the world's largest medical library. The collection can be consulted in the reading room or requested on interlibrary loan. NLM offers nationwide access to information through a National Network of Libraries of Medicine. The database, MEDLINE, is available via the worldwide web. MEDLINEplus links the public to many sources of consumer health information.

National Library Service for the Blind and Physically Handicapped (NLSBPH)
Library of Congress
Reference Section
1291 Taylor Street, NW
Washington, DC 20542
Phone: 1-800-424-8567 (toll-free)
202-707-5100
Fax: 202-707-0712
Email: nls@loc.gov
Website: http://www.lcweb.loc.gov/nls/
NLSBPH, funded by the Library of Congress, is a network of regional and local libraries that provide free library services to blind and physically disabled people. Contact NLSBPH about programs such as postage-free delivery and return-mailing of audio-books and books and magazines in Braille. Specially designed Talking Books and cassette players also

are lent to the public free. NLSBPH provides information on blindness and physical disabilities.

National Long term Care Ombudsman Resource Center (NLTCORC)
National Citizens' Coalition for Nursing Home Reform (NCCNHR)
1424 16th Street, NW, Suite 202
Washington, DC 20036
Phone: 202-332-2275
Fax: 202-332-2949
Email: ombudcenter@nccnhr.org
NLTCORC is operated by the NCCNHR in collaboration with the National Association of State Units on Aging. The Center supports groups under Federal mandate to identify and resolve residents' problems at long term care facilities. Contact the Center for information and publications on nursing home reform and adult care.

National Long term Care Resource Center (NLTCRC)
Division of Health Services, Research and Policy
University of Minnesota School of Public Health
Mayo Mailcode 197, Room D527
420 Delaware Street, SE
Minneapolis, MN 55455
Phone: 612-624-5171
Fax: 612-624-5434
Website: http://www.hsr.umn.edu
The Center assists State and Area Agencies on Aging and other community-based service agencies to monitor, develop, and refine community long term care systems through legal reform. NLTCRC provides information on long term health care, rehabilitation and acute care reform, ethics, and quality of life issues in nursing homes. A list of publications is available.

National Medical Association (NMA)
1012 10th Street, NW
Washington, DC 2001
Phone: 1-888-662-7497 (toll-free) (Automated Physician Referral)

202-347-1895
Fax: 202-842-3293
Email: rwilliams@nmanet.org
Website: http://www.nmanet.org
NMA promotes the interests of doctors and patients of African descent. NMA offers a physician referral service and the brochure *Looking for Dr. Right: Guide to Choosing a Physician* Using 1-888-NMAPHYSicians.

National Mental Health Association (NMHA)
1021 Prince Street
Alexandria, VA 22314-2971
Phone: 1-800-969-NMHA (6642) (toll-free) (National Mental Health Information Center)
703-684-7722
Fax: 703-684-5968
Email: infoctr@nmha.org
Website: http://www.nmha.org
The NMHA Information Center provides referrals to mental health specialists, as well as publications such as *Coping with Growing Older, Answers to Your Questions About Clinical Depression*.

National Multiple Sclerosis Society (NMSS)
733 3rd Avenue, 6th Floor
New York, NY 10017-3288
Phone: 1-800-FIGHT-MS (344-4867) (toll-free)
212-986-3240
Fax: 212-986-7981
Email: nat@nmss.org
Website: http://www.nmss.org
The Society is a nonprofit organization providing support and information on the diagnosis and treatment of multiple sclerosis (MS). Contact NMSS for referrals to specialists and local chapter offices. A list of free publications and films on MS is available from local chapters.

National Organization for Rare Disorders (NORD)
PO Box 8923
New Fairfield, CT 06812-8923
Phone: 1-800-999-6673 (toll-free)

203-746-6518
TTY: 203-746-6927
Fax: 203-746-6481
Email: orphan@rarediseases.org
Website: http://www.rarediseases.org
NORD is a federation of voluntary health organizations and individuals, dedicated to helping people with rare diseases and assisting the organizations that serve them. NORD is committed to the identification, treatment, and cure of rare disorders through education, advocacy, research, and service.

National Organization for Victim Assistance (NOVA)
1757 Park Road, NW
Washington, DC 20010
Phone: 202-232-6682 (includes crisis hotline service)
Fax: 202-462-2255
Email: nova@try-nova.org
Website: http://www.try-nova.org
NOVA is a nonprofit organization dedicated to improving services to survivors of violent crimes or disasters. NOVA offers a toll-free, 24-hour crisis counseling hotline that refers victims to support services throughout the country. NOVA provides a list of publications on subjects, including older crime victims, victim assistance, and victim rights.

National Osteoporosis Foundation (NOF)
1232 22nd Street, NW
Washington, DC 20037-1292
Phone: 202-223-2226
Fax: 202-223-2237
Website: http://www.nof.org
NOF is a nonprofit, voluntary health organization dedicated to promoting lifelong bone health to reduce the widespread prevalence of osteoporosis and related fractures. NOF works to find a cure for osteoporosis through research, education, and advocacy. The Foundation provides general information on osteoporosis; its quarterly newsletter and booklets are available through membership.

National Policy and Resource Center on Nutrition and Aging
Department of Dietetics and Nutrition
Florida International University (FIU)
University Park, OE200
Miami, FL 33199
Phone: 305-348-1517
Fax: 305-348-1518
Email: nutreldr@fiu.edu
Website: http://www.fiu.edu/~nutreldr

The FIU Center, funded primarily by the Administration on Aging, works to reduce malnutrition and promotes good nutritional practices among older adults nationwide. The Center provides information dissemination, training and technical assistance, and policy analysis.

National Policy and Resource Center on Women and Aging (NPRCWA)
Heller Graduate School
Brandeis University, Mail Stop 035
PO Box 9110
Waltham, MA 02254-9110
Phone: 1-800-929-1995 (toll-free)
781-736-3866
Fax: 781-736-3865
Email: natwomctr@binah.cc.brandeis.edu
Website: http://www.brandeis.edu/heller/national/

NPRCWA focuses on older women's issues and provides policy analysis, research, and assistance to the network of Administration on Aging-funded State and Area Agencies on Aging. The Center provides information and publications on women's health, caregiving, income security, and housing as well as prevention of crime and violence toward older women.

National Prevention Information Network (NPIN)
Centers for Disease Control and Prevention (CDC)
Public Health Service
PO Box 6003
Rockville, MD 20849-6003
Phone: 1-800-458-5231 (toll-free)

301-562-1098
TTY: 1-800-243-7012 (toll-free)
Fax: 1-888-282-7681 (toll-free)
301-562-1050
Email: info@cdcnpin.org
Website: http://www.cdcnpin.org
NPIN, sponsored by the CDC, is a national reference, referral, and distribution service for information on HIV/AIDS, other sexually transmitted diseases, and tuberculosis. NPIN's services are designed to facilitate information sharing about prevention, treatment, and support services. NPIN does not provide medical advice.

National Psoriasis Foundation (NPF)
6600 SW 92nd Avenue, Suite 300
Portland, OR 97223-7195
Phone: 1-800-723-9166 (toll-free)
503-244-7404
Fax: 503-245-0626
Email: getinfo@npfusa.org
Website: http://www.psoriasis.org
NPF is a nonprofit organization providing free information on psoriasis and psoriatic arthritis research and treatment. NPF provides directories of specialists and products, opportunities to volunteer for research projects, links to support groups, and educational newsletters and booklets.

National Rehabilitation Information Center (NARIC)
1010 Wayne Avenue, Suite 800
Silver Spring, MD 20910-5633
Phone: 1-800-346-2742 (toll-free)
301-562-2400
Fax: 301-562-2401
Email: naricinfo@kra.com
Website: http://www.naric.com
NARIC, funded by the Department of Education, provides information on rehabilitation of people with physical or mental disabilities. Contact NARIC for database searches on all types of physical and mental disabilities, as well as referrals to local and national facilities and organizations. All of NARIC's database information is available online, free.

National Resource and Information Center (NRIC) Women's Bureau (WB)

Department of Labor
200 Constitution Avenue, NW, Room S-3111
Washington, DC 20210
Phone: 1-800-827-5335 (toll-free)
1-800-347-3741 (toll-free)
TTY: 1-800-326-2577 (toll-free)

NRIC, funded by the WB, provides information on issues of concern to working women, their families, and employers. Contact NRIC for facts on programs such as the Fair Pay Clearinghouse, which provides updates on efforts to identify and eliminate sexism, ageism, racism, and other forms of workplace discrimination. Single copies of publications, including *Work and Elder Care* and *Hiring Someone to Work in Your Home*, are available free.

National Resource Center: Diversity and Long term Care (NRCDLTC)

The Heller School Schneider Institute for Health Policy
Brandeis University
PO Box 9110
Waltham, MA 02454-9110
Phone: 1-800-456-9966 (toll-free)
781-736-3930
Fax: 781-736-3965
Website: http://www.sihp.brandeis.edu

NRCDLTC, a partnership between Brandeis University and San Diego State University, provides information on methods, resources, systems, and services for caring for older people. The Center provides referrals to health policy resources and information on issues of diversity in aging, including disabilities, race, ethnicity, gender, generations, and chronic diseases. A list of publications is available on request.

National Resource Center on Native American Aging (NRCNAA)

PO Box 9037
Grand Forks, ND 58202-9037
Phone: 1-800-896-7628 (toll-free)

701-777-3437
Fax: 701-777-2389
Website: http://www.und.edu/dept/nrcnaa
The Resource Center, funded by the Administration on Aging, provides support, advocacy, and information for older Native Americans, including American Indians, Alaska Natives, and Native Hawaiians. Contact the Center for legal information and references, geriatric leadership training, cultural awareness, and a variety of publications.

National Resource Center on Supportive Housing & Home Modifications
USC Andrus Gerontology Center
3715 McClintock Avenue
Los Angeles, CA 90089-0191
Phone: 213-740-1364
Fax: 213-740-7069
Website: http://www.homemods.org
The Center is funded in association with The Archstone Foundation and The California Endowment. Contact the Center for information on government-assisted housing, assisted living policies, home modifications for older people, training and education courses, and technical assistance. Publications and fact sheets are available.

National Rural Health Association (NRHA)
One West Armour Boulevard, Suite 203
Kansas City, MO 64111
Phone: 816-756-3140
Fax: 816-756-3144
Website: http://www.nrharural.org
NRHA is a nonprofit, professional organization targeting health care problems unique to rural areas and serving as a liaison between rural health care providers and older people. Contact NRHA for information on health care delivery to rural providers and for its quarterly *Journal of Rural Health*.

National Self-Help Clearinghouse (NSHC)
365 Fifth Avenue, Suite 3300
New York, NY 10016-4309
Phone: 212-817-1822

Fax: 212-817-2990
Email: info@selfhelpweb.org
Website: http://www.selfhelpweb.org
NSHC collects and distributes information about support and self-help groups nationwide. Contact NSHC for publications or referrals to self-help groups, helping networks, and support systems.

National Senior Citizens Education and Research Center (NSCERC)
8403 Colesville Road, Suite 1200
Silver Spring, MD 20910
Phone: 301-578-8900
Fax: 301-578-8947
Website: http://www.nscerc.org
NSCERC is a nonprofit organization providing employment opportunities, conducting research programs and workshops, and publishing its research findings.

National Senior Citizens Law Center (NSCLC)
1101 14th Street, NW, Suite 400
Washington, DC 20005
Phone: 202-289-6976
Fax: 202-289-7224
Email: nsclc@nsclc.org
Website: http://www.nsclc.org
NSCLC offers assistance to Legal Aid Offices and private lawyers working on behalf of low-income older and disabled people. The Center does not accept individual clients but acts as a clearinghouse of information on legal problems such as age discrimination, Social Security, pension plans, Medicaid, Medicare, nursing homes, and protective services.

National Senior Games Association (NSGA)
3032 Old Forge Drive
Baton Rouge, LA 70808
Phone: 225-925-5678
Fax: 225-216-7552
Website: http://www.nsga.com

NSGA is a nonprofit organization promoting healthy lifestyles for older people through education, fitness, and sports. Its website announces Association events and activities and offers videotapes of group activities.

National Sleep Foundation (NSF)
1522 K Street, NW, Suite 500
Washington, DC 20005
Phone: 202-347-3471
Fax: 202-347-3472
Email: nsf@sleepfoundation.org
Website: http://www.sleepfoundation.org
NSF is a nonprofit organization providing services and information about sleep disorders. Contact the Foundation for a list of accredited sleep centers and local specialists. A variety of NSF publications on sleep, sleep disorders, and related topics are available.

National STD and AIDS Hotlines
Centers for Disease Control and Prevention (CDC)
Public Health Service
1600 Clifton Road
Atlanta, GA 30333
Phone: 1-800-342-AIDS (2437) (toll-free) (English)
1-800-227-8922 (toll-free) (English)
1-800-344-SIDA (7432) (toll-free) (Spanish)
TTY: 1-880-243-7889 (toll-free)
Email: hivnet@ashastd.org
Website: http://www.ashastd.org
The Hotlines offer information, referrals, and free publications about prevention, risks, and treatment of sexually transmitted diseases.

National Stroke Association (NSA)
9707 East Easter Lane
Englewood, CO 80112-3747
Phone: 1-800-STROKES (787-6537) (toll-free)
303-754-0930
Fax: 303-649-1328
Website: http://www.stroke.org

The Association provides information about stroke prevention, acute treatment, recovery, and rehabilitation to the public. NSA offers referrals to support groups, care centers, and local resources for stroke survivors, caregivers, and family members.

National Urban League
120 Wall Street, 8th Floor
New York, NY 10005
Phone: 212-558-5300
Fax: 212-344-5332
Website: http://www.nul.org
The Urban League is a nonprofit, community service organization helping older African Americans through advocacy and service programs which include health awareness, nutrition, housing, and intergenerational activities. Contact the League for information about its Seniors in Community Service Program, which provides training and part-time employment to low-income, older people. The Health Promotion Project helps local groups plan and carry out disease prevention activities in communities nationwide. Newsletters and bulletins are available.

National Women's Health Information Center (NWHIC)
Phone: 1-800-994-WOMAN (96626) (toll-free)
TTY: 1-888-220-5446 (toll-free)
Email: 4woman@soza.com
Website: http://www.4woman.gov
NWHIC, part of the Federal Government, is a health and referral center for women. Spanish language resources are available.

National Women's Health Network (NWHN)
514 10th Street, NW, Suite 400
Washington, DC 20004
Phone: 202-347-1140
Fax: 202-347-1168
Website: http://www.womenshealthnetwork.org
NWHN works to ensure that women have access to quality, affordable health care, serving as a clearinghouse of

information on women's health issues. The Network also lobbies for increased governmental support for women's health care. Contact NWHN for information and publications on women's health issues.

Native Elder Health Care Resource Center (NEHCRC)
University of Colorado Health Sciences Center
Campus Box A011-13
4455 East 12 Avenue
Denver, CO 80220
Phone: 303-315-9228
Fax: 303-315-9579
Email: dawn.wright@uchsc.edu
Website: http://www.uchsc.edu/sm/nehcrc
NEHCRC promotes the health of older Native people, including Alaska Natives and Native Hawaiians by increasing cultural competence among health care professionals. The Center focuses on four target areas: determining health status, improving medical standards, increasing access to care, and mobilizing community resources. Contact NEHCRC for information on its programs and publications.

NIH Osteoporosis and Related Bone Diseases National Resource Center (NIH-ORBD- NRC)
1232 22nd Street, NW
Washington, DC 20037-1292
Phone: 1-800-624-BONE (2663) (toll-free)
202-223-0344
TTY: 202-466-4315
Fax: 202-293-2356
Email: orbdnrc@nof.org
Website: http://www.osteo.org
The Resource Center provides patients, health professionals, and the public with resources and information on osteoporosis, Paget's disease of the bone, osteogenesis imperfecta, and other metabolic bone diseases. The Center is supported by the National Institute of Arthritis and Musculoskeletal and Skin Diseases and six other Institutes and Offices.

North American Menopause Society (NAMS)
PO Box 94527
Cleveland, OH 44101
Phone: 440-442-7550
Fax: 440-442-2660
Email: info@menopause.org
Website: http://www.menopause.org
NAMS is a nonprofit multidisciplinary organization promoting women's health during midlife and beyond through an understanding of menopause. The Society supports research and serves as a resource for women and health care professionals. Spanish language resources are available.

Office on Smoking and Health (OSH)
Centers for Disease Control and Prevention
Mail Stop K-50
4770 Buford Highway, NE
Atlanta, GA 30341-3741
Phone: 1-800-CDC-1311 (232-1311) (toll-free)
770-488-5705
Fax: 770-488-5939
Email: tobaccoinfo@cdc.gov
Website: http://www.cdc.gov/tobacco
OSH, part of the Federal Government, develops and distributes the annual *Surgeon General's Report on Smoking and Health*. Contact OSH for information on tobacco and details about the smoking and health database which is available on CD-ROM. Print publications on smoking also are available.

Older Women's League (OWL)
666 11th Street, NW, Suite 700
Washington, DC 20001
Phone: 1-800-TAKE-OWL (825-3695) (toll-free)
1-800-863-1539 (toll-free) (PowerLine)
202-783-6686
202-783-6689 (PowerLine)
Fax: 202-638-2356
Email: owlinfo@owl-national.org
Website: http://www.owl-national.org

OWL is a national organization advocating for the special concerns of older women. OWL helped develop the Campaign for Women's Health and the Women's Pension Policy Consortium. Contact OWL's 24-hour PowerLine for information about legal and political activity related to health care, access to housing, economic security, individual rights, and violence against women and older people. OWL newsletters are available.

Opticians Association of America (OAA)
7023 Little River Turnpike
Annandale, VA 22003
Phone: 703-916-8856
Fax: 703-916-7966
Email: oaa@oaa.org
Website: http://www.oaa.org
OAA represents the optometric industry and provides information on eye health and industry regulation. OAA sets industry standards for prescription eyeglasses, contact lenses, and low-vision aids and can give referrals to qualified opticians. Contact the OAA for publications on optometry news and information.

Organization of Chinese Americans (OCA)
1001 Connecticut Avenue, NW, Suite 601
Washington, DC 20036
Phone: 202-223-5500
Fax: 202-296-0540
Email: oc@ocanatl.org
Website: http://www.ocanatl.org
OCA advocates for the rights of Chinese Americans. Contact OCA for referrals to legal specialists and legislative information on age discrimination, education, and employment opportunities for Chinese Americans, as well as access to health care and Social Security. OCA also publishes a national directory of Asian and Pacific American organizations.

Paget Foundation for Paget's Disease of Bone and Related Disorders (PF)
120 Wall Street, Suite 1602

New York, NY 10005-4001
Phone: 212-509-5335
Fax: 212-509-8492
Email: PagetFdn@aol.com
Website: http://www.paget.org
PF provides information and programs for consumers and medical professionals about Paget's disease of bone and other bone disorders including primary hyperparathyroidism, fibrous dysplasia, osteoporosis, breast cancer metastatic to bone, and prostate cancer metastatic to bone.

Parkinson's Disease Foundation (PDF)
833 West Washington Boulevard
Chicago, IL 60607
Phone: 1-800-457-6676 (toll-free)
312-733-1893
Fax: 312-664-2344
PDF is a nonprofit organization providing research funding, information, and supportive services to people with Parkinson's Disease. Contact the Foundation for referrals to specialists. Publications are available.

Partnership for Caring, Inc. (PFC)
America's Voices for the Dying
1620 Eye Street, NW, Suite 202
Washington, DC 20006
Phone: 1-800-989-9455 (toll-free)
Fax: 202-296-8352
Website: http://www.partnershipforcaring.org/
PFC is a national, nonprofit organization providing advocacy, resources, and information on the reform and enhancement of care for the dying. Contact the Partnership for referrals to resources and support groups, legal assistance, information on end-of-life issues, and the Consumers' End-Of-Life Bill of Rights. Links to member organizations, publication, and fact sheets are available.

Pension and Welfare Benefits Administration (PWBA)
Department of Labor
200 Constitution Avenue, NW, Room N5625
Washington, DC 20210

Phone: 202-219-8776 (Technical Assistance and Inquiries)
1-800-998-7542 (publications)
Fax: 202-219-8141
Website: http://www.dol.gov/dol/pwba
PWBA, part of the Federal Government, protects the integrity of private pension, health, and other employee benefits plans. The Administration assists workers in obtaining inappropriately denied benefits. Contact PWBA for assistance with technical questions and publications on topics such as pension and health care benefits, 401(k) and cash balance plans, planning for retirement, simplified employee pensions, and retiree health benefits. Most publications are also found on the website.

Pension Rights Center (PRC)
1140 19th Street, NW, Suite 602
Washington, DC 20036
Phone: 202-296-3776
Fax: 202-833-2472
Email: pnsnrights@aol.com
PRC's Legal Outreach Program advocates for the pension rights of workers, retirees, and their families. Contact the PRC for referrals to pension attorneys or for publications on pension law, divorce, Federal retirement plans, self-help guides on pension problems, or pension plan handbooks. Spanish language resources are also available.

President's Council on Physical Fitness and Sports (PCPFS)
Hubert H. Humphrey Building, Room 738-H
200 Independence Avenue, SW
Washington, DC 20201
Phone: 202-690-9000
Fax: 202-690-5211
Website: http://www.fitness.gov
PCPFS is an advisory body to the President and Secretary of the Department of Health and Human Services. The Council promotes opportunities in physical activity, fitness, and sports for all Americans. Contact PCPFS for information on physical activity/fitness, nutrition, health, and Council

programs. Publications on physical education and health are available on the website.

Prevent Blindness America (PBA)
500 East Remington Road
Schaumburg, IL 60173
Phone: 1-800-331-2020 (toll-free)
847-843-2020
Fax: 847-843-8458
Email: info@preventblindness.org
Website: http://www.preventblindness.org
PBA sponsors community services and public education about eye care, safety, and the diagnosis, treatment, and prevention of eye diseases. Local chapters offer community services, including vision screenings and self-help groups for those with glaucoma. Contact PBA for information and a list of publications.

Project Aliento
National Association for Hispanic Elderly (Asociación Nacional Pro Personas Mayores)
1452 West Temple Street, Suite 100
Los Angeles, CA 90026
Phone: 213-487-1922
Fax: 213-202-5905
Project Aliento works to make the Administration on Aging-funded network of State and Area Agencies on Aging accessible to older Hispanic people and their families. Contact Project Aliento for information, publications, and videos about community care and in-home support issues, as well as links to the formal aging network. Publications are available in English and Spanish.

Pulmonary Fibrosis Foundation (PFF)
1075 Santa Fe Drive
Denver, Colorado 80204
Phone: 720-932-7850
Fax: 303-825-5078
Email: breathe@pulmonaryfibrosis.org
Website: http://www.pulmonaryfibrosis.org

PFF is a private, nonprofit organization providing assistance, resources, and information on pulmonary fibrosis and its related illnesses. Contact PFF for information on the diagnosis and treatment of PF and idiopathic pulmonary fibrosis, as well as referrals to specialists, resources, and support groups. Publications are available.

Restless Legs Syndrome Foundation
819 Second Street, SW
Rochester, MN 55902
Phone: 507-287-6465
Fax: 507-287-6312
Email: RLSFoundation@rls.org
Website: http://www.rls.org/foundation
The Foundation is a nonprofit agency that provides information about restless legs syndrome. It develops support groups and seeks to find better treatments and a definitive cure.

Robert Wood Johnson Foundation (RWJF)
Route 1 College Road
Princeton, NJ 08543
Phone: 609-452-8701
Fax: 609-987-8845
Email: mail@rwjf.org
Website: http://www.rwjf.org
The RWJ Foundation is a private, philanthropic organization that supports basic health services and pursues improved services for people with chronic illnesses, prevention of substance abuse, and control of health care costs. Publications about the Foundation's programs on health care issues are available.

Self Help for Hard of Hearing People, Inc. (SHHH)
7910 Woodmont Avenue, Suite 1200
Bethesda, MD 20814
Phone: 301-657-2248
Fax: 301-913-9413
Email: national@shhh.org
Website: http://www.shhh.org

SHHH provides information and services for people who are hard of hearing, including assistance on education, legal issues, and self-help. Local SHHH chapters can provide information on community references and referrals to specialists. Contact SHHH for information on coping with hearing problems, hearing aids, and educational workshops for older people with hearing loss. A list of publications and materials is available.

Senior Job Bank
PO Box 30064
Savannah, GA 31410
Email: info@seniorjobbank.org
Website: http://www.seniorjobbank.org
Senior Job Bank is an online resource that provides free job information and resources for members. Contact the Job Bank to find listings for occasional, part-time, flexible, temporary, or full-time jobs for older people.

SeniorNet (SN)
121 Second Street, 7th Floor
San Francisco, CA 94105
Phone: 1-800-747-6848 (toll-free)
415-495-4990
Fax: 415-495-3999
Email: press@seniornet.org
Website: http://www.seniornet.org
SeniorNet is a nonprofit, educational organization that provides information and services to help older people become computer literate. Locally funded SN teaching sites offer introductory computer classes on various topics, providing older people with discounts on computer hardware, software, and publications. Members can access SN from any online computer and order publications on buying and using computers.

Simon Foundation for Continence
PO Box 835
Wilmette, IL 60091
Phone: 1-800-237-4666 (toll-free)
847-864-3913

Fax: 847-864-9758
Website: http://www.simonfoundation.org
The Simon Foundation is a nonprofit, educational organization providing information on urinary and bowel incontinence. It offers support to people with incontinence and publications on its diagnosis and treatment. A guide booklet and videotapes are available.

The Skin Cancer Foundation
245 Fifth Avenue
New York, NY 10016
Phone: 1-800-SKIN-490 (754-6490) (toll-free)
212-725-5176
Fax: 212-725-5751
Website: http://www.skincancer.org
The Skin Cancer Foundation is a nonprofit organization providing information on the detection and treatment of skin cancer. The Foundation's brochures, newsletters, posters, and a new membership program give medical information and practical guidance on skin cancer. Send a self-addressed, stamped envelope for a list of publications.

Social Security Administration (SSA)
Office of Public Inquiries
6401 Security Boulevard
Baltimore, MD 21235
Phone: 1-800-772-1213 (toll-free)
Fax: 410-965-0695
Website: http://www.ssa.gov
SSA, part of the Federal Government, is the agency responsible for Social Security retirement programs, survivor benefits, disability insurance, and Supplemental Security Income. Contact SSA for information and assistance with Social Security benefits as well as eligibility and disability issues. A directory is available listing the SSA offices in each state.

Society for Neuroscience
11 Dupont Circle, NW, Suite 500
Washington, DC 20036
Phone: 202-462-6688

Fax: 202-462-1547
Email: info@sfn.org
Website: http://www.sfn.org
The Society is an organization of scientists and physicians interested in the brain, spinal cord, and peripheral nervous system. Contact the Society for the fact sheet series called *Brain Briefings*, short newsletters explaining how basic neuroscience research leads to clinical applications.

SPRY Foundation
10 G Street, NE, Suite 600
Washington, DC 20002
Phone: 202-216-0401
Fax: 202-216-0779
Email: spryfoundation@nepssm.org
Website: http://www.spry.org
SPRY—Setting Priorities for Retirement Years—is a nonprofit foundation that develops research and education programs to help older adults plan for a healthy and financially secure future. The website links consumers to national health resources.

Substance Abuse and Mental Health Services Administration (SAMSHA)
Department of Health and Human Services
5600 Fishers Lane
Rockville, MD 20857
Phone: 1-800-729-6686 (toll-free) (National Clearinghouse for Alcohol and Drug Information-NCADI)
TTY: 1-800-487-4889 (toll-free)
Fax: 301-468-7394
Email: info@samhsa.gov
Website: http://www.samhsa.gov
SAMHSA, part of the Federal Government, is responsible for improving the quality and availability of prevention, treatment, and rehabilitation services in order to reduce the illness, death, disability, and cost resulting from substance abuse and mental illness. Spanish language resources are available from NCADI.

United Seniors Health Council (USHC)
409 3rd Street, NW, Suite 200
Washington, DC 20024
Phone: 1-800-637-2604 (toll-free) (orders only)
202-479-6973
Fax: 202-479-6660
Email: info@unitedseniorshealth.org
Website: www.unitedseniorshealth.org/
USHC is a nonprofit organization dedicated to helping older consumers, caregivers, and professionals. The Council produces publications on topics such as financial planning, managed care, and long term care insurance. The Council pioneered a Health Insurance Counseling Program, which helps consumers understand their many insurance options. Its Eldergames program is a comprehensive series of materials designed to stimulate the imagination and memories of older people.

United Way of America
701 North Fairfax Street
Alexandria, VA 22314-2045
Phone: 1-800-892-2757 (toll-free)
703-836-7100
Fax: 703-683-7813
Website: http://www.unitedway.org
United Way is a philanthropic organization providing support for community programs. Contact the United Way to find local chapters linking people with resources such as dental and health services for low-income people or to volunteer for service programs in the community.

Vestibular Disorders Association (VEDA)
PO Box 4467
Portland, OR 97208-4467
Phone: 1-800-837-8428 (toll-free)
503-229-7705
Fax: 503-229-8064
Email: veda@vestibular.org
Website: http://www.vestibular.org
VEDA is a nonprofit organization providing information and support for people with disorders such as Meniere's

disease, BPPV, and labyrinthitis. The Association provides lists of clinics and vestibular specialists and offers information on disorders of the inner ear and management and diagnosis of dizzy spells. Publications are available on recent advances, rehabilitation, and support therapy.

Visiting Nurse Associations of America (VNAA)
11 Beacon Street, Suite 910
Boston, MA 02108
Phone: 1-888-866-8773 (toll-free)
617-523-4042
Fax: 617-227-4843
Email: vnaa@vnaa.org
Website: http://www.vnaa.org
VNAA is an association of nonprofit, community-based home health care providers. Visiting nurses offer quality in-home medical care including physical, speech, and occupational therapy; social services; and nutritional counseling. Local agencies operate adult day-care centers, wellness clinics, hospices, and meals-on-wheels programs. A fact sheet and caregiver's handbook are available.

Volunteers of America
1660 Duke Street
Alexandria, VA 22314
Phone: 1-800-899-0089 (toll-free)
703-341-5000
Fax: 703-341-7000
Website: http://www.VolunteersofAmerica.org
Volunteers of America is a national, nonprofit, spiritually-based organization providing local human service programs and opportunities for individual community involvement. Specific programs include housing, assisted living, meals-on-wheels, transportation and health care services.

Well Spouse Foundation (WSF)
30 East 40th Street
New York, NY 10016
Phone: 1-800-838-0879 (toll-free)
212-685-8815
Fax: 212-685-8676

Email: wellspouse@aol.com
Website: http://www.wellspouse.org
WSF is a not-for-profit association of spousal caregivers. It offers support to the wives, husbands, and partners of chronically ill or disabled people. The Foundation has lists of support groups nationwide and sponsors recreational respite opportunities.

Young Men's Christian Association (YMCA)
101 North Wacker Drive, 14th Floor
Chicago, IL 60606
Phone: 1-800-USA-YMCA (872-9622) (toll-free)
312-977-0031
Fax: 312-977-9063
Website: http://www.ymca.net
YMCA is a membership organization providing physical fitness and health programs. Local YMCAs nationwide design Active Older Adult programs to meet the needs of older members, provide volunteer opportunities for senior citizens, and offer intergenerational programs.

Young Women's Christian Association (YWCA)
350 Fifth Avenue, Suite 301
New York, NY 10118
Phone: 212-273-7800
Fax: 212-465-2281
Website: http://www.ywca.org
YWCA is a membership organization providing health, fitness, and community services for women. Educational workshops, recreational activities, and counseling services are available. ENCORE programs for women after breast cancer surgery combine group discussion with exercise to promote recovery. Informational brochures are available.

Information Tips
Did You Know?
MEDLINEplus is a goldmine of up-to-date, quality health care information from the world's largest library, the National Library of medicine. The service provides extensive information about specific disease and conditions. Visit the website at http://www.nlm.nih.gov/medlineplus/.

Did You Know?
CHID (Combined Health Information Database), is a cooperative effort among several Federal Government agencies. Use it to find consumer information and educational resources on a wide variety of health-related topics. Check out CHID online at http://www.chid.nih.gov/.

Did You Know?
The Department of Energy's website has facts about Internet hoaxes. Visit the website for the latest information on hoaxes-how to recognize them and what to do about them. Go to http://hoaxbusters.ciac.org/.

Did You Know?
The website FirstGov.gov (located at http://www.FirstGov.gov) is designed to provide you with easy, one step access to all online Federal Government resources. You can use it to browse a wealth of information-everything from researching resources at the Library of Congress to tracking a NASA mission.

Did You Know?
You can search a database of clinical trials on Alzheimer's disease and dementia as well as learn how to participate in clinical trials by searching http://www.alzheimers.org/trials/.

Did You Know?
Your local library is always a good place to start looking for information. Before you go, make a list of the topics you are interested in-that will help the librarian direct you to the most helpful resources.

Did You Know?
Not all consumer health information on the web is of equal quality. To decide if a website is accurate and reliable, you might ask:
- Is the original source for the information clear? Is there a review date?

- Is the medical information reviewed by an advisory board? Are their names and affiliations clearly noted?
- Is your confidentiality assured? If you have to register, do you know how your personal information will be used?
- Does it sound too good to be true? Scientific studies rarely use words like "breakthrough", "secret ingredient", or "miracle cure."
- Is the information promotional? Are advertisements separated from content?

Did You Know?
Lots of health information on the web is available from websites that have paid advertising and/or shopping options. One way to make sure you aren't being sold "a bill of goods" is to check whether the editorial content of a website is separated from advertisements or shopping zones.

Did You Know?
There is no single correct way to search for information on the Internet. The only meaningful measure of success is if you get the results you desire. It's a good idea to try to use multiple search services to increase the likelihood of your results being complete.

AoA/NIA Appendix A: State Agencies on Aging

ALABAMA
Alabama Department of Senior Services
RSA Plaza, Suite 470
770 Washington Avenue
Montgomery, AL 36130-1851
(334) 242-5743
FAX: (334) 242-5594
http://www.adss.state.al.us/

ALASKA
Alaska Commission on Aging
Division of Senior Services
Department of Administration
PO Box 110209
Juneau, AK 99811-0209
(907) 465-3250
FAX: (907) 465-4716
http://www.alaskaaging.org/

ARIZONA
Aging and Adult Administration
Department of Economic Security
1789 West Jefferson Street - #950A
Phoenix, AZ 85007
(602) 542-4446
FAX: (602) 542-6575
http://www.de.state.az.us/links/aaa/default.asp

ARKANSAS
Division Aging and Adult Services
Arkansas Department of Human Services
PO Box 1437, Slot 14121417 Donaghey Plaza South
Little Rock, AR 72203-1437
(501) 682-2441
FAX: (501) 682-8155
http://www.state.ar.us/dhs/aging/

CALIFORNIA
California Department of Aging
1600 K Street
Sacramento, CA 95814
(916) 322-5290
FAX: (916) 324-1903
http://www.aging.state.ca.us/

COLORADO
Aging and Adult Services
Colorado Department of Human Services
1575 Sherman Street, Ground Floor
Denver, CO 80203
(303) 866-2800
FAX: (303) 866-2696
http://www.cdhs.state.co.us/oss/aas/index1.html

CONNECTICUT
Division of Elderly Services
25 Sigourney Street, 10th Floor
Hartford, CT 06106-5033
(860) 424-5298
FAX: (860) 424-4966
http://www.dss.state.ct.us/

DELAWARE
Delaware Division of Services for Aging and Adults with Physical Disabilities
Department of Health and Social Services
1901 North DuPont Highway
New Castle, DE 19720
(302) 577-4791
FAX: (302) 577-4793
http://www.dsaapd.com/index.htm

DISTRICT OF COLUMBIA
District of Columbia Office on Aging
One Judiciary Square - 9th Floor
441 Fourth Street, NW
Washington, DC 20001
(202) 724-5622

FAX: (202) 724-4979
http://www.ci.washington.dc.us/aging/aghome.htm

FLORIDA
Department of Elder Affairs
Building B - Suite 152
4040 Esplanade Way
Tallahassee, FL 32399-7000
(850) 414-2000
FAX: (850) 414-2004
http://elderaffairs.state.fl.us/

GEORGIA
Division of Aging Services
Department of Human Resources
2 Peachtree Street NE 36th Floor
Atlanta, GA 30303 - 3176
(404) 657-5258
FAX: (404) 657-5285
http://www.state.ga.us/Departments/DHR/aging.html

GUAM
Division of Senior Citizens
Department of Public Health & Social Services
PO Box 2816
Agana, Guam 96910
011-671-475-0263
FAX: 671-477-2930

HAWAII
Hawaii Executive Office on Aging
250 South Hotel Street, Suite 109
Honolulu, HI 96813-2831
(808) 586-0100
FAX (808) 586-0185
http://www.hawaii.gov/health/eoa/

IDAHO
Idaho Commission on Aging
PO Box 83720
Boise, ID 83720-0007

(208) 334-3833
FAX: (208) 334-3033
http://www.idahoaging.com/

ILLINOIS
Illinois Department on Aging
421 East Capitol Avenue, Suite 100
Springfield, IL 62701-1789
(217) 785-2870
Chicago Office: (312) 814-2916
FAX: (217) 785-4477
http://www.state.il.us/aging/

INDIANA
Bureau of Aging and In-Home Services
Division of Disability, Aging and Rehabilitative Services
Family and Social Services Administration
402 W. Washington Street, #W454
PO Box 7083
Indianapolis, IN 46207-7083
(317) 232-7020
FAX: (317) 232-7867
http://www.state.in.us/fssa/elderly/index.html

IOWA
Iowa Department of Elder Affairs
Clemens Building, 3rd Floor
200 Tenth Street
Des Moines, IA 50309-3609
(515) 242-3333
FAX: (515) 242-3300
http://www.state.ia.us/elderaffairs/

KANSAS
Department on Aging
New England Building
503 S. Kansas Avenue
Topeka, KS 66603-3404
(785) 296-4986
FAX: 785-296-0256
http://www.k4s.org/kdoa

KENTUCKY
Office of Aging Services
Cabinet for Families and Children
Commonwealth of Kentucky
275 East Main Street
Frankfort, KY 40621
(502) 564-6930
FAX: (502) 564-4595
http://chs.state.ky.us/aging/

LOUISIANA
Governor's Office of Elderly Affairs
PO Box 80374
Baton Rouge, LA 70898-0374
(225) 342-7100
FAX: (225) 342-7133
http://www.gov.state.la.us/depts/elderly.htm

MAINE
Bureau of Elder and Adult Services
Department of Human Services
35 Anthony Avenue
State House - Station #11
Augusta, ME 04333
(207) 624-5335
FAX: (207) 624-5361
http://www.state.me.us/dhs/beas

MARYLAND
Maryland Department of Aging
State Office Building, Room 1007
301 West Preston Street
Baltimore, MD 21201-2374
(410) 767-1100
FAX: (410) 333-7943http://www.mdoa.state.md.us

MASSACHUSETTS
Massachusetts Executive Office of Elder Affairs
One Ashburton Place, 5th Floor
Boston, MA 02108
(617) 727-7750

FAX: (617) 727-9368
http://www.state.ma.us/elder/

MICHIGAN
Michigan Office of Services to the Aging
611 W. Ottawa, N. Ottawa Tower, 3rd Floor
PO Box 30676
Lansing, MI 48909
(517) 373-8230
FAX: (517) 373-4092
http://www.mdch.state.mi.us/mass/masshome.html

MINNESOTA
Minnesota Board on Aging
444 Lafayette Road
St. Paul, MN 55155-3843
(651) 296-2770
TTY: (800) 627-3529
FAX: (651) 297-7855
http://www.mnaging.org/

MISSISSIPPI
Division of Aging and Adult Services
750 N. State Street
Jackson, MS 39202
(601) 359-4925
FAX: (601) 359-4370
http://www.mdhs.state.ms.us/aas.html

MISSOURI
Division on Aging
Department of Social Services
PO Box 1337615 Howerton Court
Jefferson City, MO 65102-1337
(573) 751-3082
FAX: (573) 751-8687
http://www.dss.state.mo.us/da/da.htm

MONTANA
Senior and Long Term Care Division
Department of Public Health & Human Services

PO Box 4210
111 Sanders, Room 211
Helena, MT 59620
(406) 444-4077
FAX: (406) 444-7743
http://www.dphhs.state.mt.us/sltc

NEBRASKA
Division on Aging
Department of Health and Human Services
PO Box 95044
1343 M Street
Lincoln, NE 68509-5044
(402) 471-2307
FAX: (402) 471-4619
http://www.hhs.state.ne.us/ags/agsindex.htm

NEVADA
Nevada Division for Aging Services
Department of Human Resources
State Mail Room Complex
3416 Goni Road, Building D-132
Carson City, NV 89706
(775) 687-4210
Fax: (775) 687-4264
www.nvaging.net/

NEW HAMPSHIRE
Division of Elderly and Adult Services
State Office Park South
129 Pleasant Street, Brown Building #1
Concord, NH 03301
(603) 271-4680FAX: (603) 271-4643
http://www.dhhs.state.nh.us/

NEW JERSEY
New Jersey Division of Senior Affairs
Department of Health and Senior Services
PO Box 807
Trenton, New Jersey 08625-0807
(609) 943-3436

1-800-792-8820
FAX: (609) 588-3317
http://www.state.nj.us./health/senior/sraffair.htm

NEW MEXICO
State Agency on Aging
La Villa Rivera Building
228 East Palace Avenue Ground Floor
Santa Fe, NM 87501
(505) 827-7640
FAX: (505) 827-7649
http://www.nmaging.state.nm.us/

NEW YORK
New York State Office for The Aging
2 Empire State Plaza
Albany, NY 12223-1251
1-800-342-9871
(518) 474-5731
FAX: (518) 474-0608
http://aging.state.ny.us/nysofa/

NORTH CAROLINA
Division of Aging
Department of Health and Human Services
2101 Mail Service Center
Raleigh, NC 27699-2101
(919) 733-3983
FAX: (919) 733-0443
http://www.state.nc.us/DHR/DOA/home.htm

NORTH DAKOTA
Aging Services Division
Department of Human Services
600 South 2nd Street, Suite 1C
Bismarck, ND 58504
(701) 328-8910
(800) 451-8693
TDD (701) 328-8968
FAX: (701) 328-8989

http://lnotes.state.nd.us/dhs/dhsweb.nsf/ServicePages/AgingServices

NORTHERN MARIANA ISLANDS
CNMI Office on Aging
PO Box 2178
Commonwealth of the Northern Mariana Islands
Saipan, MP 96950
(670) 233-1320/1321
FAX: (670) 233-1327/0369

OHIO
Ohio Department of Aging
50 West Broad Street - 9th Floor
Columbus, OH 43215-5928
(614) 466-5500
FAX: (614) 466-5741
http://www.state.oh.us/age/

OKLAHOMA
Aging Services Division
Department of Human Services
PO Box 25352
312 N.E. 28th Street
Oklahoma City, OK 73125
(405) 521-2281
FAX: (405) 521-2086
http://www.okdhs.org/aging

OREGON
Senior and Disabled Services Division
500 Summer Street, NE, 3rd Floor
Salem, OR 97301-1073(503) 945-5811
FAX: (503) 373-7823
http://www.sdsd.hr.state.or.us/

PENNSYLVANIA
Pennsylvania Department of Aging
Commonwealth of Pennsylvania
Forum Place
555 Walnut Street, 5th floor

Harrisburg, PA 17101-1919
(717) 783-1550
FAX: (717) 772-3382
http://www.aging.state.pa.us/

PUERTO RICO
Governor's Office of Elderly Affairs
Commonwealth of Puerto Rico
Call Box 50063
Old San Juan Station, PR 00902
(787) 721-5710, (787) 721-4560, (787) 721-6121
FAX: (787) 721-6510

RHODE ISLAND
Department of Elderly Affairs
160 Pine Street
Providence, RI 02903-3708
(401) 222-2858
FAX: (401) 222-2130
http://www.state.ri.us/manual/data/queries/stdept_.idc?id=23

SOUTH CAROLINA
Office of Senior and Long Term Care Services
Department of Health and Human Services
PO Box 8206
Columbia, SC 29202-8206
(803) 898-2501
FAX: (803) 898-4515
http://www.dhhs.state.sc.us/

SOUTH DAKOTA
Office of Adult Services and Aging
Richard F. Kneip Building
700 Governors Drive
Pierre, SD 57501-2291
(605) 773-3656
FAX: (605) 773-6834
http://www.state.sd.us/social/ASA/index.htm

TENNESSEE
Commission on Aging
Andrew Jackson Building, 9th floor
500 Deaderick Street
Nashville, Tennessee 37243-0860
(615) 741-2056
FAX: (615) 741-3309
http://www.state.tn.us/comaging/

TEXAS
Texas Department on Aging
4900 North Lamar, 4th Floor
Austin, TX 78751-2316
(512) 424-6840
FAX: (512) 424-6890
http://www.texas.gov/agency/340.html

UTAH
Division of Aging & Adult Services
Box 45500
120 North 200 West
Salt Lake City, UT 84145-0500
(801) 538-3910
FAX: (801) 538-4395
http://www.hsdaas.state.ut.us/SrvAge.htm

VERMONT
Vermont Department of Aging and Disabilities
Waterbury Complex
103 South Main Street
Waterbury, VT 05671-2301
(802) 241-2400
FAX: (802) 241-2325
http://www.dad.state.vt.us/

VIRGINIA
Virginia Department for the Aging
1600 Forest Avenue, Suite 102
Richmond, VA 23229
(804) 662-9333
FAX: (804) 662-9354
http://www.aging.state.va.us/

VIRGIN ISLANDS
Virgin Islands Department of Human Services
Knud Hansen Complex, Building A
1303 Hospital Ground
Charlotte Amalie, VI 00802
(340) 774-0930
FAX: (340) 774-3466

WASHINGTON
Aging and Adult Services Administration
Department of Social & Health Services
PO Box 45050
Olympia, WA 98504-5050
(360) 725-2310
In-state only: 1-800- 422-3263
FAX: (360) 438-8633
http://www.aasa.dshs.wa.gov/

WEST VIRGINIA
West Virginia Bureau of Senior Services
Holly Grove - Building 10
1900 Kanawha Boulevard East
Charleston, WV 25305
(304) 558-3317
FAX: (304) 558-5699
http://www.state.wv.us/seniorservices/

WISCONSIN
Bureau of Aging and Long Term Care Resources
Department of Health and Family Services
1 West Wilson Street, Room 450
Madison, WI 53707-7850
(608) 266-2536FAX: (608) 267-3203
http://www.dhfs.state.wi.us/Aging/

WYOMING
Division on Aging
Wyoming Department of Health
6101 Yellowstone Road, Suite 259B
Cheyenne, WY 82002-0710
(307) 777-7986
FAX: (307) 777-5340
http://wdhfs.state.wy.us/aging/

AoA/NIA Appendix B: State Long Term Care Ombudsman Programs

ALABAMA
State Long term Care Ombudsman
Commission on Aging
RSA Plaza, Suite 470
770 Washington Avenue
Montgomery, AL 36130
(334) 242-5743
FAX: (334) 242-3862

ALASKA
State Long term Care Ombudsman
Older Alaskans Commission
3601 C Street, Suite 260
Anchorage, AK 99503-5209
(907) 334-4480
FAX: (907) 334-4486

ARKANSAS
State Long term Care Ombudsman
Arkansas Division of Aging and Adult Services
PO Box 1437, Slot 1412
Little Rock, AR 72201-1437
(501) 682-2441
FAX: (501) 682-8155

ARIZONA
State Long term Care Ombudsman
Aging and Adult Administration
Department of Economic Security
1789 West Jefferson - 950A
Phoenix, AZ 85007
(602) 542-4446
FAX: (602) 542-6575

CALIFORNIA
State Long term Care Ombudsman

Department of Aging
1600 K Street
Sacramento, CA 95814
(916) 324-3968
FAX: (916) 323-7299

COLORADO
State Long term Ombudsman
The Legal Center
455 Sherman Street, Suite 130
Denver, CO 80203
(303) 722-0300 ext. 217
FAX: (303) 722-0720

CONNECTICUT
State Long term Care Ombudsman
Department on Aging
25 Sigourney Street - 10th Floor
Hartford, CT 06106-5033
(860) 424-5200 ext. 5221
FAX: (860) 424-4966

DELAWARE
State Long term Care Ombudsman
Delaware Services for Aging and Adults
1901 North Dupont Highway
Main Administration Bldg. Annex
New Castle, DE 19702
(302) 577-4791
FAX: (302) 577-4793

DISTRICT OF COLUMBIA
Long term Care Ombudman
AARP - Legal Counsel for the Elderly
601 E Street, NW, 4th Floor, Building A
Washington, DC 20049
(202) 434-2140
Fax: (202) 434-6595

FLORIDA
State Long term Care Ombudsman

Florida State Long term Care Ombudsman Council
Holland Building, Rm. 270
600 South Calhoun Street
Tallahassee, FL 32301
1-888-831-0404
FAX: (850) 488-5657

GEORGIA
State Long term Care Ombudsman
Division of Aging Services2 Peachtree Street NW, 36th Floor
Suite 36-385
Atlanta, GA 30303-3176
(888) 454-5826
FAX: (404) 463-8384

HAWAII
State Long term Care Care Ombudsman
EXECUTIVE OFFICE ON AGING
Office of the Governor
250 South Hotel Street, Suite 107
Honolulu, HI 96813-2831
(808) 586-0100
FAX: (808) 586-0185

IDAHO
State Long term Care Ombudsman
Idaho Commission on Aging
PO Box 83720
3380 American Terrace, Suite 1
Boise, ID 83720-0007
(877) 471-2777
FAX: (208) 334-3033

ILLINOIS
State Long term Care Ombudsman
ILLINOIS DEPARTMENT ON AGING
421 East Capitol Avenue Suite 100
Springfield, IL 62701-1789
(217) 785-3143
FAX: (217) 524-9644

INDIANA
State Long term Care Ombudsman
Indiana Division of Aging & Rehabilitation Services
PO Box 7083-W454
402 W. Washington Street
Indianapolis, IN 46207-7083
1-800-545-7763
FAX: (317) 232-7867

IOWA
State Long term Care Ombudsman
Iowa Department of Elder Affairs
Clemens Building
200 10th Street, 3rd FloorDes Moines, IA 50309-3609
(515) 242-3327
FAX: (515) 242-3300

KANSAS
State Long term Care Ombudsman
Office of the State Long term Care Ombudsman
610 SW 10th Street, 2nd Floor
Topeka, KS 66612-1616
(785) 296-3017
Fax: (785) 296-3916

KENTUCKY
State Long term Care Ombudsman
Division of Family/Children Services
275 E Main St - 5th Fl W
Frankfort, KY 40621
(800) 372-2991
Fax: (502)-564-4595

LOUISIANA
State Long term Care Ombudsman
Governor's Office of Elderly Affairs
412 N. 4th Street - 3rd Floor
PO Box 80374
Baton Rouge, LA 70802
(225) 342-7100

Fax: (225) 342-7144

MAINE
Maine State Long term Care Ombudsman Program
1 Weston Court
PO Box 128
Augusta, ME 04332
(207) 621-1079
FAX: (207) 621-0509

MARYLAND
State Long Term Care Ombudsman
Office on Aging
State Office Building, Room 1007
301 West Preston Street
Baltimore, MD 21201
(410) 767-1074
FAX: (410) 333-7943

MASSACHUSETTS
State Long term Care Ombudsman
Executive Office of Elder Affairs
1 Ashburton Place, 5th floor
Boston, MA 02108-1518
(617) 727-7750
Fax: (617) 727-9368

MICHIGAN
State Long term Care Ombudsman
Citizens for Better Care
4750 Woodward Avenue, Suite 410
Detroit, MI 48201-1308
(313) 832-6387
Fax: (313) 832-7407

MINNESOTA
State Long term Care Ombudsman
Office of Ombudsman for Older Minnesotans
121 East Seventh Place, Suite 410
St. Paul, MN 55101
1-800-657-3591

FAX: (651) 297-5654

MISSISSIPPI
State Long term Care Ombudsman
Division of Aging & Adult Services
750 North State Street
Jackson, MS 39202
(601) 359-4929
FAX: (601) 359-4970

MISSOURI
State Long term Care Ombudsman
Division on Aging
Department of Social Services
PO Box 1337
615 Howerton Court
Jefferson City, MO 65102-1337
(800) 309-3282
FAX: (573) 751-8687

MONTANA
State Long term Care Ombudsman
Office on AgingDepartment of Health and Human Services
Senior & Long term Care Division
PO Box 4210
111 Sanders
Helena, MT 59604-4210
1-800-551-3191
FAX: (406) 444-7743

NEBRASKA
State Long term Care Ombudsman
Department on Aging
PO Box 95044
301 Centennial Mall-South
Lincoln, NE 68509-5044
(402) 471-2307
FAX: (402) 471-4619

NEVADA
State Long term Care Ombudsman

Nevada Division for Aging Services
445 Apple Street #104
Reno, NV 89502
Work: (775) 688-2964
FAX: (775) 688-2969

NEW HAMPSHIRE
State Long term Care Ombudsman
Division of Elderly & Adult Services
129 Pleasant Street
Concord, NH 03301-3857
(603) 271-4375
FAX: (603) 271-4771

NEW JERSEY
State Long term Care Ombudsman for Institutionalized Elderly
PO Box 807
Trenton, NJ 08625-0807
(609) 943-4026
FAX: (609) 588-3365

NEW MEXICO
State Long term Care Ombudsman
State Agency on Aging
1410 San Pedro Ne
Albuquerque, NM 87110(505) 255-0971
FAX: (505) 255-5602

NEW YORK
State Long term Care Ombudsman
Office for the Aging
2 Empire State Plaza
Agency Bldg. #2
Albany, NY 12223-0001
(518) 474-0108
FAX: (518) 474-7761

NORTH CAROLINA
State Long term Care Ombudsman
Division of Aging

693 Palmer Drive
Caller Box# 29531
Raleigh, NC 27626-0531
(919) 733-8395
FAX: (919) 715-0868

NORTH DAKOTA
State Long term Care Ombudsman
Aging Services Division, DHHS
600 South 2nd Street, Suite 1C
Bismarck, ND 58504
1-800-451-8693
FAX: (701) 328-8989

OHIO
State Long term Care Ombudsman
Department of Aging
50 West Broad Street - 9th Floor
Columbus, OH 43215-5928
(614) 644-7922
FAX: (614) 644-5201

OKLAHOMA
State Long term Care Ombudsman
Aging Services Division, DHS
312 NE 28th Street - Suite 109
Oklahoma City, OK 73105
(405) 521- 6734
FAX: (405) 521-2086

OREGON
State Long term Care Ombudsman
Office of the Long Term Care Ombudsman
3855 Wolverine NE, Suite 6
Salem, OR 97305 - 1251
(503) 378-6533
FAX: (503) 373-0852

PENNSYLVANIA
State Long term Care Ombudsman
Department of Aging

555 Walnut Street, 5th Floor
PO Box 1089
Harrisburg, PA 17101
(717) 783-7247
FAX: (717) 783-3382

PUERTO RICO
State Long term Care Ombudsman
Governor's Office for Elder Affairs
Call Box 50063, Old San Juan Station
San Juan, Puerto Rico 00902
(787) 725-1515
FAX: (787) 721-6510

RHODE ISLAND
State Long term Care Ombudsman
Alliance for Better Long term Care
422 Post Road, Suite 204
Warwick, RI 02888
(401) 785-3340
Fax: (401) 785-3340

SOUTH CAROLINA
State Long term Care Ombudsman
Division on Aging
1801 Main Street
PO Box 8206
Columbia, SC 29202-8206
(803) 868-9095
FAX: (803) 898-4513

SOUTH DAKOTA
State Long term Care Ombudsman
Office of Adult Services and Aging 700 Governors Drive
Pierre, SD 57501-2291
(605) 773-3656
FAX: (605) 773-6834

TENNESSEE
State Long term Care Ombudsman
Commission on Aging

Andrew Jackson Building, 9th Floor
500 Deaderick Street
Nashville, TN 37243-0860
(615) 741-2056
FAX: (615) 741-3309

TEXAS
State Long term Care Ombudsman
Department on Aging
4900 North Lamar Boulevard, 4th Floor
PO Box 12786
Austin, TX 78751-2316
512-424-6875
FAX: (512) 424-6890

UTAH
State Long term Care Ombusman
Division of Aging and Adult Services
Dept. Of Social Services
120 North 200 West, Room 401
Salt Lake City, Utah 84103
(801) 538-3924
FAX: (801) 538-4395

VERMONT
State Long term Care Ombudsman
Vermont Legal Aid, Inc.
PO Box 1367
Burlington, VT 05402
(802) 863-5620
FAX: (802) 863-STET

VIRGINIA
State Long term Care Ombudsman
Virginia Association of Area Agencies on Aging
530 East Main Street, Suite 428
Richmond, Virginia 23219(800) 552-3402
FAX: (804) 644-5640

WASHINGTON
State Long term Care Ombudsman

South King County Multi-Services Center
1200 South 336th Street
PO Box 23699
Federal Way, WA 98093
(253) 838-6810
FAX: (253) 874-7831

WEST VIRGINIA
State Long term Care Ombudsman
Commission on Aging
1900 Kanawha Boulevard East
Charleston, WV 25309
(304) 558-3317
FAX: (304) 558-0004

WISCONSIN
State Long term Care Ombudsman
Board on Aging and Long term Care
214 North Hamilton Street
Madison, WI 53703-2118
1-800-815-0015
FAX: (608) 261-6570

WYOMING
State Long term Care Ombudsman
Wyoming Senior Citizens, Inc.
756 Gilchrist, PO Box 94
Wheatland, WY 82201
(307) 322-5553
FAX: (307) 322-3283

AUTHORS

The authors are Lillian S. Kachmar, Esq. and John F. Steele. In their more than 20 years of marriage, they have provided caregiving services to a number of elderly relatives. After years of informally counseling others with caregiving issues, and being urged time and again to write a book about this difficult topic, they finally reduced their experiences and expertise to writing.

Lillian graduated from The University of Villanova School of Law in 1978, and has practiced extensively in the health care field, representing hospitals, nursing homes and home health care agencies. John operates the family business, and Lillian currently acts as General Counsel to a regional home health care provider. They reside outside of Philadelphia, PA with their daughter, three dogs, three cats and three fish.